MW01195170

Blood in the Water

Blood in the Water

Feeding Frenzies and the Mass Tort Phenomenon

Walter Champion
Carlos A. Velasquez

LEXINGTON BOOKS
Lanham • Boulder • New York • London

Published by Lexington Books
An imprint of The Rowman & Littlefield Publishing Group, Inc.
4501 Forbes Boulevard, Suite 200, Lanham, Maryland 20706
www.rowman.com

6 Tinworth Street, London SE11 5AL, United Kingdom

British Library Cataloguing in Publication Information Available

Library of Congress Control Number: 2021933120
ISBN 978-1-7936-5212-6 (cloth)
ISBN 978-1-7936-5213-3 (electronic)

To Ralph Nader. —W. T. C.
To my family, Professor Champion, and my clients. —C. A. V.

Contents

Foreword

This is the book on class actions and mass tort litigation that I wish I had many years ago in my practice as a personal injury attorney and partner in the Abraham Law Centre in Lafayette, LA.

Class actions, after all, are the great equalizers in courtrooms. They allow the less privileged, including minorities, an opportunity to fight injustices levied by powerful corporations that otherwise could use their money to bury individual claims.

In *Blood in the Water: Feeding Frenzies and the Mass Tort Phenomenon*, two uniquely qualified authors present the histories and key elements of pivotal cases in mass tort litigation in America. Walter T. Champion is a long-tenured professor of law at the Thurgood Marshall School of Law at Texas Southern University in Houston, an adjunct professor at South Texas College of Law-Houston, and the author of some 500 articles and many treatises and casebooks on sports law, gaming law, entertainment law, and other subjects. Carlos A. Velasquez is a highly successful personal injury attorney. He is principal partner at Velasquez Dolan, PA, in Plantation, FL, with special expertise in wrongful death and aviation disaster litigation. Together, the two have worked to create a comprehensive guide to class actions and mass tort litigation.

Exhaustively researched with extensive citations and footnotes, *Blood in the Water* explores the history of many of the most important cases and issues in mass tort litigation: design defects in General Motors' rear-engine Chevrolet Corvair and in Ford's notorious exploding Pinto; Big Pharma and some of its dangerous drugs, including Merrell's Bendectin, Merck's Vioxx, and Purdue Pharma's opioids; Agent Orange herbicide; asbestos (the longest ongoing mass tort litigation in history); tobacco (the largest ever master settlement, at over $206 billion); gun manufacturers and mass shootings; airline crashes; and many others.

The authors provide carefully reasoned analysis of the role of the FDA and other regulators, so-called "tort reform" efforts, and other issues facing personal injury litigators. They even delve into today's headlines and breaking news stories, such as the Monsanto and Bayer Roundup litigation, the #MeToo movement and Colin Kaepernick's symbolic First Amendment protests.

Throughout this invaluable book, the authors take pains to present a balanced approach to mass tort litigation. They explain modern American class action practice from its emergence in the 1960s through the changes in mass tort litigation in the twenty-first century. The authors rightly take "greedy corporations" and "shoddy manufacturing" to task for the blood in the water due to self-inflicted wounds, but they also flag the mistakes of regulators, insurance companies, doctors and, yes, attorneys in tort litigation involving silica, breast implants, Fen-Phen diet drugs, and other products.

Blood in the Water could become the definitive treatise on mass torts for students in law schools and a comprehensive guide for personal injury lawyers everywhere. Yet, its appeal extends beyond the law school classroom and the law firm library. Journalists and reporters will find a wealth of information and referenced leads in this book, as will university educators in fields other than law. Even individual consumers will find *Blood in the Water* a fascinating read.

Walter Champion and Carlos Velasquez deserve congratulations and thanks for shining new light on these important cases and issues in American mass tort history.

David Abraham
Lafayette, LA

Preface

Nanny, a former Vietnam M.A.S.H. nurse, Peace Corps volunteer, and a Denny's waitress, told me that Roundup is just a toned-down version of Agent Orange. She should know; she doused off orange dust from wounded soldiers. Her first husband, a Marine Corps enlisted man, died at 39 from the effects of this known carcinogen.

"Now is the winter of our discontent" (Shakespeare, *Richard III*, Act 1, Sc. 1). It is an ill wind that blows no one any good. Examples of disaster springing from the bowels of rampant corporate greed abound. Oftentimes, internal memoranda prove their culpability. They truly are disasters waiting to happen, as was the Amazing Exploding Pinto and Big Pharma's direct-to-consumer advertising shell game, not to mention the looming pandemic.

The personal injury bar must protect the hapless consumer; there is nobody else. Boundless greed is not self-correcting. Hopefully, this little book will remind us of the disadvantages that accompany unbridled capitalism.

Walter T. Champion
Houston, TX, May 2020
Carlos A. Velasquez
Plantation, FL, May 2020

Acknowledgments

This book is a family affair. Professor Champion taught Carlos A. Velasquez many years ago. Carlos is the senior partner of Velasquez Dolan, PA, Plantation, FL, and an acknowledged expert in wrongful death and aviation disaster litigation (cvelasquez@vdlawyers.com). Champion is no slouch himself. He is the author of *Sports Law in a Nutshell*, *Gaming Law in a Nutshell*, *Sports Ethics for Sports Management Professionals*, *Fundamentals of Sports Law*, *Intellectual Property Law in the Sports and Entertainment Industries*, and casebooks in Sports Law, Baseball and the Law, Recreational Injuries, Amateur Sports, Entertainment Law, and Music Industry Contracts (wchampionjr@gmail.com).

The authors also thank JoAnn Kvintus, for formatting; Charles Henry Champion, for the cover art (hatit@live.com); Charles's significant other, Karen Pugh, for copy editing; and Christopher Velasquez (Carlos's son) and his wife, Paola Garcia, for research and writing.

Introduction

Mass tort plaintiffs are the blood in the water igniting a feeding frenzy among attorneys to sign the most clients. But plaintiffs' blood is the result of greedy corporations producing shoddy merchandise. Potential mass torts can include negligently-designed or -manufactured vehicles and aircraft, dangerous pharmaceuticals, sexual abuse, natural and man-made disasters, dangerous products that contain deadly chemicals, surgical procedures, and even football concussions.

These potential mass torts are aided and abetted by greedy manufacturers, enabling professional organizations, and complicit practitioners. A case in point is the direct-to-consumer advertising of giant pharmaceutical companies (Big Pharma) pitching their products to unsuspecting would-be patients. There should be a buffer between snake oil salesmen and the unsuspecting public. The medical establishment is the perfect candidate for diagnosis and treatment as opposed to Big Pharma's constant huckstering of dubiously beneficial, dangerous drugs.

The Federal Drug Administration (FDA) allows these marketing ploys on the basis that it is protected by the First Amendment freedom of speech. It is a system that is guaranteed to produce dangerous, shoddily manufactured drugs. The plaintiff's bar is the only establishment that polices Big Pharma's nefarious practices and forces it to at least reimburse those citizens that corporations have maimed and killed.

The feeding frenzy mentality began with the Corvair design defect litigation made famous by Ralph Nader's book, *Unsafe at Any Speed*. Individual personal injury litigation is the predecessor of mass torts. Trial lawyers adapted their single accident litigation strategy to conform to mass torts with multiple plaintiffs and many deaths.

After World War II, corporations competed with other corporations to lure the unsuspecting consumer by slick marketing techniques. The corporations made mistakes and put greed before safety. The Ford Pinto is the classic case where, for a few dollars, literally, Ford designed and manufactured an automobile where the bumper was positioned in such a way that it would puncture the gas tank on rear-end collisions.

The personal injury bar reacted to the large number of deaths by developing protocol for dealing with thousands of victims. This is an expensive proposition. Eventually, multi-district litigation (MDL) was created to assist in organizing nascent "feeding frenzies."

From the Corvair's design defect, corporations cut costs and/or performed minimal R&D (research and development) before sending drugs, automobiles, airplanes, etc., to the unsuspecting public. With every disaster, it was the personal injury bar that sounded the alarm. As one witness said, "we'd still be driving Pintos without lawyers."

Most lawsuits in mass torts are based on negligence. As Justice Cardozo said, "negligence in the air so to speak will not do." Negligence consists of a duty, breach of duty, proximate cause, and damages. Defendants argue that only "junk science" connects the injury to their negligence. But the truth is that corporations choose profits over the consumer's safety. The personal injury bar is the only available watch dog to police the excesses of corporate greed.

Legally, each mass tort possesses nuances that must be remembered for future torts. For example, Agent Orange was created by the U.S. government and certain American chemical companies as a defoliant to use in the jungles during the Vietnam War. The corporations knew that Agent Orange was a deadly herbicide that causes cancer and its toxicity was well known before use in Vietnam. During five years of use, some 112 million gallons were sprayed over 10 percent of South Vietnam's land area. This herbicide entered the food system, affected the DNA, and caused birth defects to both the Vietnamese and American servicemen.

This was a great tragedy with a long-term impact, but the question of liability remains because of the many possible manufacturers who often indiscriminately mixed their product. It is the duty of the attorney to ascertain probable cause as to who was specifically responsible. The judicial and legal community devised a multi-district litigation scheme to deal with the number of potential plaintiffs and the complexity of multiple tortfeasors.

"Blood in the water" may be allegorical, but it is real enough. The Corvair was an accident waiting to happen, and the Pinto was a bomb waiting to happen. Mass tort lawsuits were initiated to right an unsupervised wrong. It is a palliative cure but won only through months of expensive discovery.

Alleged "tort reform" is a slick marketing tool focusing all the blame for the rising cost of insurance on lawyers. It is at best mean-spirited, but unfortunately, it puts a damper on all personal injury lawsuits, including mass torts. The lawyers were the only protection for defenseless victims, but now they are mislabeled as greedy opportunists.

In the blink of a marketing eye, people forgot that Abraham Lincoln, Mahatma Gandhi, and Nelson Mandela were lawyers. The legal profession has always been the first line of defense against aggression, oppression, dangerous products, deadly chemicals, and racial and sexual bias and intolerance. But the tire hit the road in the McDonald's hot coffee case, where a little old lady (literally) was badly scalded when coffee was spilled on her lap. That was the moment that corporate marketing was waiting for, although the coffee was super-heated, the lid was defective, and the victim only asked for compensation for her extensive medical expenses.

Mass tort litigation is the only available method to police the "profits over customers' safety" regime. There are many new rallying cries, where Big Business introduces products that they know are dangerous. Monsanto's Roundup has been linked to cancer, but it is wildly popular and lucrative. It is a known risk to public health. The people who suffer from obscure cancers are those who cannot defend themselves, like minimum wage high school groundskeepers. Bullies always target those who are least able to protect themselves. Although it was reduced to $87 million, a California jury awarded a groundskeeper $2 billion after he was diagnosed as suffering from non-Hodgkin's lymphoma. Lawsuits have been filed against Bayer and Monsanto for selling Roundup without disclosing that the weed killer has been linked to cancer. The World Health Organization in 2015 reported that Roundup's main ingredient glyphosate was a human carcinogen.

The personal injury bar issues a clarion call to force corporations to "Do the Right Thing" and listen to their better angels. The constant is that the legal profession is the last beacon of self-restraint available to solve problems, redress wrongs, and assess damages.

Lawyers are also called upon to address public health crises affecting the various states that are forced to minister to the needs of their dying citizens. Tobacco litigation and now opioid litigation are attempts by states' attorney generals to make the guilty corporations responsible for the billions of dollars that the states paid to remediate the effects of these deadly public health epidemics. In the tobacco litigation, most state attorneys farmed out the lawsuits to personal injury lawyers, who were eventually handsomely remunerated for their services. But these litigations were financed by the law firms on a contingency basis, so all the risks and expense were initially attributed solely to them.

The opioid litigation is a monster that appears to be the only defense against the rampages of Big Pharma's greed that is literally destroying America. Opioids were once prescribed only for intense pain, like the birthing process. But, through direct-to-consumer advertising and the not-so-benign indifference of the health care industry, fueled by Big Pharma's insatiable greed, opioids are now available for any pain or inconvenience. The spread of opioids both legally and illegally has gutted states' health care providers. It appears that the opioid litigation is mostly filed by state and local attorney generals and district attorneys. More than 13,400 lawsuits have been filed and the number is climbing.

In one such lawsuit filed by the Attorney General of Pennsylvania, they alleged that Purdue Pharma created the market for chronic use of opioids in Pennsylvania through a relentless campaign of deception without any scientific evidence supporting long-term opioid use while ignoring illegal or suspicious prescriptions. In short, the attorney general is making Purdue Pharma financially responsible for the "Opioid Epidemic that is killing Pennsylvanians" on the basis that defendant knew that opioids are dangerous and potentially deadly narcotics that are highly addictive. Opioids can cause patients to stop breathing and suffocate: this danger has been known for over 100 years. An Oklahoma judge on August 26, 2019, ordered Johnson & Johnson to pay $572 million to remedy the opioid drug abuse crisis in Oklahoma.

Attorneys who seek representation of mass airplane disaster plaintiffs, usually for wrongful death, are first typically accused of barratry, which can be described as vexatious litigation as a part of alleged tort reforms. But who else will stand up for the victims? An aircraft manufacturer, for example, that is allowed to self-regulate the safety parameters of the aircraft it builds, and the FAA, whose self-professed role is "the safety of civil aviation," that delegates that responsibility to the manufacturer, is tantamount not only to allowing the fox to guard the hen house but also not providing the hens with an illuminated, readily-identifiable pathway to the emergency escape route. What but disaster could result?

Although the Corvair was the first feeding frenzy, the Pinto the most notorious, asbestos the most lucrative, but it is the recall of Merck's popular pain medication Vioxx which self-defined the feeding frenzy standard since Merck engineered and controlled the ensuing litigation. The resulting controlled feeding frenzy became just another acceptable debit of doing business as a multi-national, multi-billion-dollar corporate giant, along with direct-to-consumer marketing and lobbying for tort reform.

Because of the duplicity and wealth of big corporations, attorneys were coerced to affect a gambler's persona. Trial lawyers must dedicate themselves to locate and market the next big feeding frenzy. Then, there is the competition to secure the most and the best clients. But, unlike corporate America, attorneys must maintain a high ethical standard, or suffer severe consequences. Big Pharma, on the other hand, has long ago replaced ethics with greed under the banner of maximizing stockholder returns.

A constant throughout all these lawsuits is that big corporations, sometimes with the active duplicity of the government, attempt to avoid liability for the damages they created through design defect, faulty warnings, and/or shoddy manufacturing. Mass torts accentuate the problem and the aspirational solution. If corporations cannot or will not police themselves, then it is the duty of the plaintiff's bar to keep these corporations honest. The corporations know better, but they are willing to risk catastrophic mass torts if it aids the bottom line of immense profitability.

Chapter 1

The Feeding Frenzy Mentality

"The shark was not an accident. He had come from deep down in the water as the dark cloud blood had settled and dispersed in the mile-deep sea." (Ernest Hemingway, *The Old Man and the Sea*, 100 [New York: 1952]). The mass tort phenomenon is fueled by the feeding frenzy of personal injury litigation. The plaintiffs' attorneys react to the "blood" in the water. However, much of the "blood" is produced by shoddy manufacturers and greedy corporations. Attorneys, like sharks, smell a feeding frenzy and sue in class action suits for millions of dollars in damages.[1] It can be honestly said that most of the blood is self-inflicted by the corporations themselves. For example, Merck's voluntary withdrawal of Vioxx after hiding negative test results led to a "feeding frenzy" as attorneys sought clients allegedly harmed by the drug.[2]

Added to this equation is tort reform which severely limits the legal profession's ability to police tort disasters. For example, Big Pharma just reduces research and adds the cost of litigation to the drug's price. Big Pharma's direct-to-consumer advertising creates a demand for unnecessary prescription drugs regardless of deadly results. Trial lawyers counter with advertisements soliciting clients that warn of the drug's harmful side effects. Both advertising campaigns reduce the quality of civilization.

Big Pharma's lobbyists are now calling the kettle black by blaming the legal ads for patients suffering harm or even death after dropping their prescribed medical treatment. The Titanic was a mass tort with many fatalities. Another large-scale disaster was the Hindenburg explosion of May 6, 1937, where 35 passengers and crew died. From single disasters, the personal injury bar segued into ongoing, repetitive tragedies that create a multitude of potential plaintiffs. Ralph Nader's 1965 book *Unsafe at Any Speed* exposed the Chevrolet Corvair (1960–1964) as a fraudulently designed vehicle that sacrificed safety for style. The Chevrolet Corvair was the only American-designed, mass-produced passenger car to use a rear-mounted air-cooled engine. Unfortunately, designed defects contributed to a loss of road grip, and oversteering creating a dynamically unstable condition where the car spins out of control. The rear engine swing axle combination distributes a greater inertial mass over the rear wheels with a corresponding higher center of gravity during rebound camber conditions which causes the Corvair to dangerously oversteer while cornering. The Corvair was an inherently unsafe car that jump-started the first feeding frenzy. Public response to Nader's book played a role in the National Traffic and Motor Vehicle Safety Act in 1966.

Mass torts are the by-products of industrialization by way of a systemized process of production and sale on an unprecedented scale, which creates a potential for error. After the problem is discovered the lawyers then must recruit clients, which can be expensive. Although John Grisham's *The King of Torts* (2003) is a fictional account of a feeding frenzy, it accurately describes the mindset of personal injury lawyers who troll for mass injury clients. In the *King of Torts*, the wonder drug Tarvan cures addiction; but the drug company desperately needed human trials, so they attracted junkies/guinea pigs with ersatz clinics in "places far outside the jurisdiction of the FDA" (p. 86). They were "nothing but human laboratories." Tarvan was very effective, but 8 percent of the patients after about 100 days developed "an irresistible impulse to draw blood" which resulted in at least 80 dead people (p. 88). Grisham's protagonist, Clay Carter, once a humble public defender, became obsessed with greed and transformed into the manipulative and immoral "The King of Torts."

Mass torts are more about the lawyers' "strategies [of] . . . gathering the cases and settling them . . ." (p. 165). Class action lawsuits for dangerous drugs began with Bendectin, a drug used for pregnant women to combat nausea, but tragically caused birth defects in children.

The current legal advertisements for asbestosis and mesothelioma proclaim that "asbestos is known to cause cancer and yet it is still legal." Asbestos litigation is America's longest running mass tort. Litigation is controlled by multi-district litigation (MDL) which acknowledges the criminal culpability of the asbestos industry. Asbestos litigation is an honorable feeding frenzy whose goal is to right a heinous wrong. Asbestos is *not* based on junk science. However, that cannot be said with absolute certainty for silicosis litigation which was allegedly manufactured by "mad-dog" lawyers who modified their asbestosis litigation kits by recruiting serial plaintiffs. The nascent silicosis crisis was debunked by Judge Jack in a massive opinion, titled *in re Silica.*

Products Liability Litigation—Vioxx, or Rofecoxib, was Merck's non-steroidal anti-inflammatory drug that was marketed to cure acute pain conditions. It gained widespread acceptance and was used to treat patients with arthritis and other conditions that cause acute or chronic pain. Over 80 million people worldwide were prescribed Rofecoxib at some time. On September 30, 2004, Merck *voluntarily* withdrew Vioxx because of concerns about an increased risk of heart attack and stroke associated with long-term high-dosage usage; between 88,000 and 140,000 cases of serious heart disease were reported. Merck had sales revenue of $2.5 billion and reserved $970 million for acceptable legal expenses.

Merck's strategy was to admit no liability unless there was a sustained history of usage for at least 18 months. Merck's attorneys drew a line in the sand and did not concede cases and settlements; thus, the plaintiff's bar was unable to create momentum. Merck's case-by-case approach guaranteed that the Vioxx litigation would be slowed down to a snail's pace, thereby negating the possibility of "stampede justice."

The tortfeasors will also strategically settle or feign bankruptcy if the evidence is overwhelming. For example, several automakers agreed to pay more than $550 million to resolve claims stemming from rupture-prone Tanaka Corp. airbags. There was enough scientific evidence to convince the automakers that Tanaka's negligence caused a long-running safety crisis linked to many deaths and injuries.

Lawsuits based on negligence might be subject to tort reform and thus have their final award reduced—this is known by defendants like Big Pharma or car manufacturers who look at potential litigation as an expected line-item debit. However, new class action lawsuits are now based on other theories of recovery, such as Title IX, sexual harassment, civil rights, and sexual assaults as represented by the Baylor University football sexual assault scandal and the hideous Larry Nassar's sexual attacks against young female gymnasts.

The medical establishment is likewise guilty in spreading blood in the water. Elisabeth Rosenthal in *An American Sickness: How Healthcare Became Big Business and How You Can Take It Back* (Penguin Press, 2017) asserts that "[i]n the past quarter century, the American medical system has stopped focusing on health or even science. Instead, it attends single-mindedly to its own profits" (p. 1). In short, the current market for healthcare is fatally flawed. Doctor Rosenthal excoriates Big Pharma's argument that it must inflate prices to recoup alleged research costs.

Doctor Rosenthal also blames outrageous billing practices and the healthcare system's inherent greed. Class action lawsuits of this sort might avoid "tort reform" since they are based on the violation of specific federal and state statutes, for example, the Generic Drug Enforcement Act of 1992, state Deceptive Trade Practices Acts, state and federal safety statutes, state and federal discrimination statutes, Title IX, the Civil Rights Act of 1964, the Uniform Commercial Code, and the Health Insurance Portability and Accountability Act of 1996.

There are new feeding frenzies such as lawsuits based on the allegation that Johnson & Johnson's baby powder causes cancer. For example, a Virginia jury on May 4, 2017, awarded a 62-year-old woman $110.5 million. Three juries in St. Louis awarded $197 million; all the cases are under appeal. The

Virginia plaintiff was diagnosed with ovarian cancer that spread to her liver; she blames her illness on her use of Johnson & Johnson's talcum-containing products for more than 40 years.[3] Of course, Johnson & Johnson disputes the plaintiff's evidence as junk science.

There is evidence that Johnson & Johnson knew for decades that their talc-based products might contain deadly asbestos fibers. These recently unsealed documents show that Johnson & Johnson was alerted to asbestos contamination risks in the early 1970s and trained employees to reassure the public that their baby powder products were never contaminated with the known carcinogenic asbestos. In a 2012 study, the FDA averred that it found no traces of asbestos in dozens of talc-containing cosmetic products. But, the FDA acknowledges that the results were inconclusive since only four of the nine requested talc suppliers submitted samples.[4] Regardless, by late September 2017, thousands of women have filed suit claiming that Johnson & Johnson's popular, over-the-counter baby powder causes ovarian cancer. However, unlike most mass torts, the plaintiffs are filing uncoordinated individual law suits.[5] Both sides are essentially determining the strengths and weaknesses of the ongoing litigation, partly because the science is inconclusive.

Talcum powders contain talc, which includes moisture-absorbing particles of oxygen, magnesium, and silicon. Asbestos, a known carcinogen that sometimes appears in natural talc, was stripped from all commercially used talc in the 1970s, according to the American Cancer Society.[6] "Plaintiffs cite studies that show talc in baby powder can be absorbed by the reproductive system and cause inflammation in the ovaries when applied for feminine hygiene purposes."[7] The National Cancer Institute scoffs at this idea and asserts that the weight of scientific evidence does not support the conclusion that perineal talc exposure increases the risk of ovarian cancer.[8]

Johnson & Johnson is no stranger to massive legal challenges stemming from both its blood thinner Xarelto and its pelvic mesh products. As of late September 2017, nearly 900 out of the 4,800 baby powder cases have been consolidated into multi-district litigation (MDLs) and are bundled in federal district court in New Jersey, where Johnson & Johnson is based.[9]

However, a $417 million award in California and a $72 million award in Alabama were tossed out by appellate judges in October 2017. Johnson & Johnson responded that although "[o]varian cancer is a devastating disease—. . . it is not caused by the cosmetic-grade talc we have used in Johnson & Johnson's baby powder for decades. The science is clear, and we will continue to defend the safety of Johnson & Johnson's baby powder as we prepare for additional trials in the U.S. . . ."[10]

In *Fox v. Johnson & Johnson,* judgment, 2016 WL 799325 (Mo. Cir.) (Trial Order) (Oct. 17, 2017), a jury found compensatory damages of 10 million dollars and punitive damages of 22 million dollars in a case where the estate of Jacqueline Fox brought a product liability suit against Johnson & Johnson as the manufacturer of talc powder alleging strict liability based on the powder increasing the consumer's risk of ovarian cancer.

In an order signed on June 21, 2016, the *Fox* court (2016 WL 8416860) (Mo. Cir., Trial Order, June 21, 2016) denied the defendant's request to decrease damages. However, in *Fox v. Johnson & Johnson*, 2017 WL 4629383 (Mo. Ct. App. Oct. 17, 2017), the Missouri Court of Appeals dismissed the case on the basis that there was a lack of personal jurisdiction over the late Ms. Fox and the other 64 individual plaintiffs:

> Two of the 65 individual plaintiffs are Missouri residents. Tiffany Hogans is a St. Louis City resident who bought and used the defendant's products in St. Louis City and later developed ovarian cancer. Marianne Westerman is a St. Louis County resident who bought and used the Defendant's products in St. Louis County and later developed ovarian cancer. Sixty-three other plaintiffs, including Jacqueline Fox, bought and used Defendant's products in other states and later developed ovarian cancer; these non-resident plaintiffs joined their claims to the Missouri resident plaintiffs' claims in this action pursuant to Missouri Rule 52.05 (*1).

> The plaintiffs asserted theories of strict liability for failure to warn, negligence, breach of express and implied warranty, civil conspiracy, concert of action, and negligent representation, alleging that Defendants marketed and sold their talc products knowing that the products increased consumers' risk of ovarian cancer. (*Id.*)

Professor Jane Eggen of Widener Law School asserts that the talc powder cases will be harder to prove than the traditional asbestos cases since the plaintiff must prove actual exposure to asbestos in the talc. However, not all talc products contain asbestos since not all the talc mines contain asbestos. So, the plaintiff must prove that the talc product was contaminated with asbestos. But, historic asbestos litigation against insulation makers might help prove causation, since new plaintiffs have epidemiological studies showing causation between asbestos fiber inhalation and mesothelioma.[11]

PALSGRAF AND FORESEEABILITY

The seminal case of *Palsgraf v. Long Island R. Co.*[12] states the issue of foreseeability in terms of duty. *Palsgraf* is "the most distinguished and debated of all tort cases. . . . It involved what many called. . .the unforeseeable plaintiff."[13] *Palsgraf* is a law professor's dream of an examination question. A passenger was running to catch one of the defendant's trains. The defendant's servants, trying to assist him to board it, dislodged a package from his arms, and it fell upon the rails. The package contained fireworks, which exploded with some violence. The concussion overturned some scales, many feet away on the platform, and they fell upon the plaintiff injuring her.[14]

Judge Cardozo, speaking for a majority of four, held that there was no liability because there was no negligence toward the plaintiff.[15] "Negligence . . . was a matter of relation between the parties which must be founded upon the foreseeability of harm to the person in fact injured."[16]

Negligence is any conduct that falls below the reasonable man standard. Negligence is measured against the particular facts and circumstances in each case. The burden is on the plaintiff to show that a negligent act or omission occurred on the part of the defendant and that it was the proximate cause of the injury. That is, there must be an established duty of care, a breach of that duty, a proximate cause between a defendant's action and the injury, and damages that result from that breach.[17] The *Palsgraf* standard of the foreseeability of harm resonates in mass tort lawsuits.[18] Class action status is difficult to attain, since there are various ways that the negligent product can be sold and used. Cases against corporate malfeasance are often individually litigated with the expectation that there will eventually be a mass payout. Each successive successful verdict establishes a target amount that plaintiffs can expect to be paid when the company agrees to settle.[19] The trouble with litigating talc-based baby powder cases is the Palsgrafian question of causation, since there are varying sources of talc. The latest talc cases against Johnson & Johnson "will be both easier and harder to litigate than both traditional asbestos suits involving insulation materials, and the ovarian cases the company is already fighting."[20]

The current suits against Johnson & Johnson are "[u]nlike failure-to-warn lawsuits against asbestos insulation manufacturers, who intentionally added the toxic mineral to products, claims against talc companies gives plaintiffs a new angle—negligence in the failure to detect a contaminant and falsely ensuring a product's safety."[21] But, since asbestos in talc is a contaminant, there are other claims in addition to failure to warn, such as negligence in the failure to detect the contaminant and/or the warranty-like failure to assure unsuspecting consumers that the talc products were pure.[22]

Lawsuits based on mass torts and other class actions are an integral part of our everyday consciousness. We are bombarded by Big Pharma's nefarious and mean-spirited direct-to-consumer advertising and corresponding whining lawyer ads that solicit confused clients. It is an ongoing dance of self-fulfilling prophecies based on the avarice of all parties including the often-gullible victims. The focus of class action personal injury lawsuits and their accompanying feeding frenzies have segued from Pinto design defects to Big Pharma's greed-based calculations and finally to mass social injustices based on race, ethnicity, and sex.

The spark that first ignited the feeding frenzy mentality was the Corvair litigation crisis that was created by a lawyer who saw that class action products liability was the only way to hold General Motors accountable for the tragic deaths that occurred due to the Corvair's design defects.

NOTES

1. There is a great deal of scholarship on the mass tort phenomenon (this list is by no means exclusive), see "Books" and "Articles" after this "Notes" section.

2. Walter T. Champion, *A Tale of Two Cities: A Commentary on the Media's Response to Personal Injury "Feeding Frenzies" as a Result of the Vioxx and Silicosis Litigation,* 31 Whittier L. Rev. 47, 47 (2009).

3. *Woman Awarded $110M in Suit Over Talc Powder,* Houston Chronicle at A13 (May 6, 2017).

4. Matt Manney, *Asbestos Talcum Powder Lawsuits,* Asbestos.com (Oct. 3, 2017).

5. Tiffany Hsu, *4800 File Suits Claiming Cancer from Baby Powder,* New York Times at B1 (Sept. 29, 2017).

6. *Id.*

7. *Id.*

8. *Id.*

9. *Id.*

10. *Judge Rejects $417 Million Baby Powder Award,* Houston Chronicle at B2 (Oct. 21, 2017).

11. *Johnson & Johnson's Newest Talc Problem: Asbestos,* Bloomberg BNA at p. 5 (Sept. 14, 2017) at http://www.bna.com/johnson-johnsons-newest-n579820879581.com.

12. *Palsgraf v. Long Island R. Co.,* 248 N.Y. 339, 162 N.E. 99 (1928). See also Brenna Gaytan, *The Palsgraf "Duty" Debate Resolved: Rodriguez v. Del Sol Moves to a Foreseeability Free Duty Analysis,* 45 N.M.L. Rev. 753, 753–54 (Sum. 2015); William L. Prosser, *The Law of Torts,* 254–55 (West 4th ed. 1971); and William Prosser, *Palsgraf Revisited,* 52 Mich. L. Rev. 1, 8–12 (1953).

13. Prosser, *The Law of Torts,* 254.

14. *Id.* at 254–55 (footnotes omitted).

15. *Palsgraf,* 162 N.E. at 100–101.

16. Prosser, *The Law of Torts,* 255.

17. See generally Walter T. Champion, *Sports Law in a Nutshell,* 145 (West 5th ed., 2017).

18. See *Comstock v. General Motors Corp.,* 99 N.W. 2d 627, 635 (Mich. 1959).

19. See generally Hsu, *4800 File Suits,* New York Times at B1.

20. *J & J's Newest Talc Problem?* Bloomberg BNA at p. 3 (Sept. 14, 2017).

21. Mauney, *Asbestos Talcum Powder Lawsuits,* Asbestos.com (Oct. 03, 2017).

22. *J & J's Newest Talc Problem?* Bloomberg BNA at p. 4.

BOOKS

Jack Weinstein. *Individual Justice in Mass Tort Litigation* (Evanston: Northwestern University Press, 1995).

Frederick Dunbar, Denise Martin, & Phoebus Dhrymes. *Estimating Future Claims: Case Studies from Mass Tort and Product Liability* (Wayne, PA: Andrews Professional Books, 1996).

Paul Niemeyer & Anthony Scirica, eds. *Report on Mass Tort Litigation* (Diane Pub., 1999).

Richard A. Nagareda. *Mass Torts in a World of Settlement* (Chicago: University of Chicago Press, 2007).

Linda Mullenix. *Mass Tort Litigation: Cases and Materials, 2nd ed.* (Thomson West, 2008).

ARTICLES

Kenneth Abraham. *Individual Action and Collective Responsibility: The Dilemma of Mass Reform.* 73 Va. L. Rev. 845 (1987).

John C. Coffee. *The Regulation of Entrepreneurial Litigation: Balancing Fairness and Efficiency in the Large Class Action.* 95 Chicago L. Rev. 1343 (1987).

Susan Olson. *Federal Multidistrict Litigation: Its Impact on Litigants.* 13 Justice Sys. J. 341 (1988–1989).

Francis McGovern. *Resolving Mature Mass Tort Litigation.* 69 B.U.L. Rev. 659 (1989).

Deborah Hensler & Mark Peterson. *Understanding Mass Personal Injury Litigation: A Socio-Legal Analysis.* 59 Brooklyn L. Rev. 961 (1993).

Kevin Walsh. *Corporate Spinoffs and Mass Torts Liability.* 1995 Colum. Bus. L. Rev. 675.

Geoffrey Hazard. *The Settlement Black Box.* 75 B.U.L. 1257 (1995).

Roger Cramton. *Individualized Justice Mass Torts, Settlement Class Actions: An Introduction.* 80 Cornell L. Rev. 811 (1995).

Heidi Feldman. *Science and Technology in Mass Exposure Litigation.* 74 Tex. L. Rev. 1 (1995).

Michael Perino. *Class Action Chaos: A Theory of the Case and an Analysis of Opt-Out Rights in Mass Tort Class Actions.* 46 Emory L.J. 85 (1997).

George Priest. *Procedural Versus Substantive Controls of Mass Tort Class Actions.* 26 J. Legal Studies 521 (1997).

Nancy Moore. *The Case against Changing the Aggregate Settlement Rule in Mass Tort Lawsuits.* 41 S. Tex. L. Rev. 149 (1999).

Donald Gifford. *Public Nuisance as a Mass Product Liability Tort.* 71 U. Cin. L. Rev. 741 (2003).

David Rosenberg. *Mandatory Litigation Class Action: The Only Option for Mass Tort Cases.* 115 Harv. L. Rev. 831 (2002).

Anthony Sebok. *Pretext Transparency and Motive in Mass Restitution Litigation.* 57 Vand. L. Rev. 2177 (2004).

Randy Kozel and David Rosenberg. *Solving the Nuisance-Value Settlement Problem: Mandatory Summary Judgment.* 90 Va. L. Rev. 1849 (2004).

Chapter 2

Car Foes

Unsafe at Any Speed

Chevrolet's new compact model in 1960, the Corvair, is the epitome of design over function. Ralph Nader, in his book *Unsafe at Any Speed: The Designed-In Dangers of the American Automobile*, saw the Corvair as an accident waiting to happen. The legal reaction to the Corvair's design defects created the first feeding frenzy.[1] Chevrolet's rapacious corporate mentality of profit over safety reaffirms the need to discuss class actions as a purging mechanism for corporate greed, racism, and the culture of rape.

RALPH NADER GENERALLY

Ralph Nader, a.k.a. "Citizen Nader," in November 1965 was a young Harvard Law School graduate who wrote *Unsafe at Any Speed* exposing General Motors and the American auto industry for its "designed in dangers." Ralph Nader began a movement that used class action lawsuits as a means to effectuate change.[2] "The Corvair, it turned out, had some particularly dangerous designed in features that made the car prone to spins and rollovers under certain circumstances."[3] This epochal book and its author were featured at one U.S. Senate hearing in early 1966; additionally, it was discovered that General Motors hired private investigators to trail him so as to discredit Nader as a congressional witness.[4] Nader and his book helped spark changes in Washington's political culture, investigative journalism, and the consumer protection movement.[5] Even in law school, he envisioned a system that would hold corporations responsible for safety defects. Nader first criticized the auto industry publicly in an April 1959 article in *The Nation* magazine titled, "The Safe Car You Can't Buy." In that piece, he wrote "It is clear Detroit today is designing automobiles for style, cost, performance, and calculated obsolescence, but not . . . for safety." This is true, even though annually there

17

were 5 million reported accidents, including nearly 40,000 fatalities, 110,000 permanent disabilities, and 1.5 million injuries. People were dying and being injured unnecessarily. Nader believed that engineering and design could prevent many deaths and injuries, and he would pursue that argument with great fervor and determination in the years ahead.[6]

By 1964, he was a part-time consultant to the Labor Department and "compiled a report titled, *Context, Condition and Recommended Direction of Federal Activity in Highway Safety;* a report that was meant primarily for background purposes and received little attention."[7]

Senator Abraham Ribicoff began a year-long series of hearings on the federal government's role in traffic safety. Ribicoff was chairman of the Senate Government Operations Committee's Subcommittee on Executive Reorganization. Nader was invited to serve as a paid advisor to help the subcommittee prepare for its hearing.[8] Nader left the Department of Labor to work on his book, which asks, "Why were thousands of Americans being killed and injured in car accidents when technology already existed that could make cars safer?"[9]

UNSAFE AT ANY SPEED

The hardback edition of *Unsafe at Any Speed* by Grossman Publishers was 305 pages and had a photo of a mangled auto wreck on its cover. The back cover opined that it was "The Complete Story That Has Never Been Told Before About Why the American Automobile Is Unnecessarily Dangerous." The November 30, 1965, *New York Times* article on the book's release indicated that it criticized the auto industry, tire manufacturers, the National Safety Council, and the American Automobile Association for ignoring auto safety problems. The *Times* article says that Nader asserts that "auto safety takes a back seat to styling, comfort, speed, power and the desire of automakers to cut cost." Nader also charged that the President's Committee for Traffic Safety was "little more than a private-interest group running a public agency that speaks with the authority of the President." The following day, the *New York Times* ran an article in which the auto industry reacted to Nader's book and denied that they ignored safety. In his State of the Union address, President Lyndon B. Johnson called for the enactment of a National Highway Safety Act.[10]

The book became THE hot topic of reform debate and action when GM was caught spying on Nader as a pre-Watergate exercise in paranoia.[11] The public reaction was immediate and intense. When details of GM's investigation of Nader became public, Senator Ribicoff and others on Capitol Hill were outraged. Ribicoff, for one, announced that his subcommittee would hold hearings into the incident and that he expected "a public explanation of the alleged harassment of a Senate Committee witness. . . ." Ribicoff and Senator Gaylord Nelson from Wisconsin called for a Justice Department investigation into the harassment. "No citizen of this country should be forced to endure the kind of clumsy harassment to which Mr. Nader has apparently been subjected since the publication of his book," said Ribicoff. If great corporations can engage in this kind of intimidation, it is an assault upon freedom in America.[12]

"Routine" corporate spying turned a somewhat obscure book for policy "wonks" into a legal and political crusade. "In the six years since the first publication of *Unsafe at Any Speed*, over three hundred and thirty thousand Americans have died on the highways and about twenty-five million more have been injured. Yet, it can be said that in this same period America has begun to wake up to the realistic remedies needed to deal with this relentless carnage."[13]

Pre-Corvair Auto Design Defects

Comstock v. GMC—The 1959 Michigan Supreme Court case of *Comstock v. General Motors Corp.*[14] established the line of reasoning that was used to great effect by trial lawyers in lawsuits based on the Corvair's design defects. This case is about defective brakes, failure to warn, and proximate cause. *Comstock* was specifically referred to by Ralph Nader in *Unsafe at Any Speed* in Chapter 2, "Disaster deferred: studies in automotive time bombs."[15]

> Robert Comstock, a veteran garage mechanic at the Lawless Buick Company in Ferndale, Michigan, found out what a brakeless Roadmaster felt like. On the morning of January 18, 1954, he was putting a license plate on another car inside the garage when a Roadmaster driven by Clifford Wentworth, the assistant service manager, ran into his leg and crushed it. Wentworth had taken the car from its owner, Leon Friend, a few minutes earlier. Friend was complaining that the day before he had experienced a sudden and total loss of braking power. . . .[16]

Wentworth admitted that the 1953 Buicks would habitually suffer brake loss in "[a] matter of weeks . . . loss of fluid and failure of the brakes. The 'O' ring seals would fail and fluid would be sucked into the engine and burned with the gasoline.'[17] Wentworth was even told by General Motors that they were worried about the Buicks' brake loss, and was advised to fix the brakes if a Buick was brought in for repair, "but I couldn't get the parts . . . so it dragged on and on."[18] Buick failed miserably to alert car owners since "Buick does not under any circumstances send letters directly to owners."[19]

Justice Edwards, in *Comstock*, overruled the trial judge sending the case back for a new trial:

> The braking system is obviously one of the most crucial safety features of the modern automobile. The greatly increased speed and weight of a modern automobile are factors that must be considered in relation to the care that would be reasonable for a manufacturer to use in designing, fabricating, assembling, and inspecting a power brake. A modern automobile equipped with brakes that fail without notice is as dangerous as a loaded gun. In legal terms, an automobile with defective brakes is clearly a dangerous instrumentality.[20]

Although Buick was warned by its dealers, it did not warn the ultimate user, whichit could have easily done. Instead, Buick put this dangerous instrument in the hands of the consumer, without warning. This case imposes a duty on the defendant to take all reasonable means to convey effective safety to all those who had purchased the 1953 Buicks with power brakes, once the latent defect was discovered.[21] Buick was in no mood for another trial, so it settled for $75,000 as compensation for a leg.[22] Buick deliberately withheld "lifesaving facts that would have prompted, in other fields of public safety, an investigation by authorities."[23] Public agencies, however, neglected *Comstock* lessons, but "it has become a keystone case for attorneys representing the car manufacturers."[24]

The Corvair's Design Defect

A one-handed Rose Pierini was injured in her 1961 Corvair when "something went wrong with my steering,"[25] "Mrs. Pierini's experience with a Corvair going unexpectedly and suddenly out of control was not unique."[26]

> By October 1965, more than one hundred suits alleging instability in the Corvair had been filed around the country. In none of the three suits, whatever their resolution may be on appeal, did General Motors reveal the technical data and test results that would have placed before the public the full facts about the. . . Corvair's peculiar friskiness. . . . The Corvair was different.[27]

> Automotive engineers will say, in defending their performance, that every car is a compromise with economic and stylistic factors. This statement if true, is also meaningless. For the significant question is, who authorizes what compromises of engineering safety?[28]

A smoking gun was an internal memo from the Ford Motor Co. on June 17, 1960, on the handling of the Chevrolet Corvair.

A question arose in the Advanced Product Planning meeting of May 31, 1960, as to whether the poor handling and stability characteristics of the Chevrolet Corvair had adversely affected its sales. In comparative tests of the Corvair and the Ford Falcon, the Corvair has a low limit of maximum permissible speed in a turn once exceeded, the vehicle became totally uncontrollable.[29]

The question is whether Chevrolet knew or should have known about the Corvair's instability and handling problems. The problem with the Corvair's design was that it was rear-engine and rear-wheel drive. The car's relative heavy rear weight exerts a spin-out force like that on the end ice-skater in a crack-the-whip line.[30] "The Corvair originally was intended to have a front-rear weight distribution of 40% to 60%. But the rear suspension came in heavier than planned, and some engine parts intended to be aluminum was made from cast iron. Thus, the car's actual front-rear weight distribution was 38–62. The difference seemed small, but it wasn't."[31]

In a typical Corvair-design case, the plaintiff contends that because of the defective design, he either received injuries that he would not have received, or alternatively, that his injuries would not have been as severe.[32] The Court held in *Larson v. General Motors Corp.*, "[t]he sole function of an automobile is to provide a means of safe transportation or as safe transportation as is reasonably possible under the present state of the art."[33] In *Larson*, the negligent design in the steering assembly enhanced the risk and was the cause of the accident.[34]

However, in *Cardullo v. General Motors Corp.*,[35] the plaintiff unsuccessfully argued that an allegedly defective ball joint caused the right front wheel, backing plate, hub, and steering knuckle to come off in the 1966 Corvair. The question presented is whether GMC acted as a reasonable and prudent automobile manufacturer equipping the 1966 Corvair with a single-cylinder braking system.[36] Plaintiff lost because it failed to present expert evidence as to the state of art with respect to the design of braking systems for automobiles at the time that this 1966 Corvair was designed and manufactured and to establish that in using the single-cylinder braking system, defendant failed to use reasonable care to adopt a safe design, which plaintiffs failed to do.[37]

Senate Showdown

The congressional auto safety hearings with the Senate Commerce Committee concerned "Corvair litigation, a larger than usual increase in highway fatalities, the General Motors snooping episode, secret defect recall campaigns, and a coalescing of a small number of auto engineering safety advocates inside and outside the government in Washington." The result was that "a major unregulated industry was brought under the law—the National Traffic and Motor Vehicle Safety Act of 1966—signed by President Johnson on September 9, 1966. A companion statute, the Highway Safety Act of 1966, was enacted simultaneously to help improve state safety efforts."[38]

"On March 22, 1966, the hearing was set in a large U.S. Senate committee room. Television cameras were set up and a throng of print reporters had come out for the hearing. An overflow audience also packed the hearing room to standing room only."[39] GM head James Roche explained to the committee that GM had started its investigation of Nader before his book came out and before he was scheduled to appear in Congress. GM wanted to know if Nader had any connection with the damage claims being filed against GM regarding the Corvair.[40]

> Senator Robert Kennedy, in questioning Roche, agreed that GM was justified in the face of charges about the Corvair to make an investigation to protect its name and its stockholders. But Kennedy also questioned whether GM's earlier statement of March 9, which had acknowledged the investigation as a routine matter, wasn't misleading or false in denying the harassment of Nader.[41]

In the making of the Corvair, there was a breakdown in the flow of both authority and initiative. "Initiative would have meant an appeal by the Corvair design engineers to top management to overrule the cost-cutters and stylists whose incursions had placed unsafe constraints on engineering choice."[42] Nader's *Unsafe at Any Speed* opened the doors for class action product liability lawsuits.[43] The exposé of the Corvair design defect initiated a sea change in the way lawyers looked at potential litigation.

NOTES

1. See Ralph Nader, *Unsafe at Any Speed* (New York: Grossman Pub., 1965) and *Since Unsafe at Any Speed, 2nd edition* (New York: Grossman Pub., 1972); Jack Doyle, *GM & Ralph Nader 1965–1971,* www.PopHistoryDig.com at www.pophistory.com/topic's/tag/Corvair-safety (Mar. 31, 2013) (last updated, May 21, 2016); and Paul Ingrassia, *How the Corvair's Rise and Fall Changed America Forever,* TheGreatDebate.com at http://blogs.reuters.com/great-debate/2012/05/09/How-the-Corvairs-Rise-and-FallChanged-America-Forever/ (May 9, 2012).

2. For a partial bibliography on Ralph Nader see Doyle, *GM & Ralph Nader,* PopHistoryDig.com at 11–15.

3. Doyle, *Ralph Nader and GM*, PopHistoryDig.com at 11.

4. *Id.*

5. *Id.*

6. *Id.* at 2.

7. *Id.*

8. *Id.* at 2–3.

9. *Id.* at 3.

10. *Id.*

11. *Id.* at 4, 5.

12. *Id.* at 5.

13. *Id.*; *Comstock v. General Motors Corp.*, 99 N.W.2d 627 (Mich. 1959).

14. Nader, *Unsafe at Any Speed*, 43–51 (1965).

15. *Id.* at 43.

16. *Id.* at 44.

17. *Id.* 45–46.

18. *Id.* at 49.

19. *Comstock v. GMC*, 99 N.W.2d 627, 632 (footnotes omitted).

20. *Id.* at 633–34.

21. Nader, *Unsafe at Any Speed,* 51.

22. *Id.*

23. *Id.*

24. *Id.* at 5.

25. *Id.*

26. *Id.* at 9–10.

27. *Id.* at 27.

28. *Id.* at 346–97 (App. F).

29. Ingrassia, *How the Corvair's Rise and Fall Changed America.*

30. *Id.*

31. *Larson v. GMC*, 391 F.2d 495 (8th Cir. 1968).

32. *Id.* at 502.

33. *Id.*

34. *Cardullo v. GMC*, 378 F. Supp. 890 (E.D. Pa. 1974).

35. *Id.* at 893.

36. *Id.*

37. Nader, *Since Unsafe at Any Speed,* xvii (1972).

38. Doyle, *Ralph Nader and GM*, www.PophistoryDig.com at 5.

39. *Id.*

40. *Id.* at 6.

41. *Id.* at 8.

42. Ingrassia, *How the Corvair's Rise and Fall Changed America Forever* at www.TheGreatDebate.com.

43. Nader, *Unsafe at Any Speed,* 40 (1965).

Chapter 3

Car Woes

Pinto Combustibles

It is a truism that if it weren't for lawyers, we would still be driving Ford Pintos, if there were any left. The Ford Pinto's structural design allowed its fuel tank filler neck to break off and the fuel tank to be punctured in rear-end collisions, causing deadly fires.[1] In 1978, *all* 1971–1976 Pintos were recalled and had safety shielding and reinforcements installed to protect the fuel tank. It is the preeminent example of a faulty and precipitously dangerous cost-benefit analysis. The cost of fixing this firetrap was as low as $1.00 for a piece of plastic to protect its mounting bolts from ever contacting the fuel tank.[2]

After the Corvair litigation, the now-energized plaintiff's bar was given the gift of the exploding Pinto, which ignited the class design defect feeding frenzy. The Ford Pinto was the second generation of American subcompacts; planning began in 1967. A design decision was made to place the fuel tank behind the rear axle rather than above the axle on the basis that the usual positioning of the gas tank would greatly reduce trunk space. But, as a hatchback, the behind-the-axle location rendered it much more vulnerable to rear collision since now there were only nine inches of "crush space"—the bumper was essentially ornamental. The Pinto's rear structure was without the reinforcement of horizontal cross-members and longitudinal side members, or the "hot sections." Additionally, several bolts protruded from the differential housing threatening the gas tank; also, the fuel filler pipe was defectively designed so that there was a greater chance of gas tank disconnection from rear-end collisions which would result in gas spillage.[3]

The exploding Pintos and their considerable jury awards created front-page headlines with the subplot that Ford discounted human lives to save dollars.

As early as 1972, reports of explosions in low-speed collisions involving Pintos struck from the rear started to come into the National Highway Safety and

Transportation Administration. Accident investigations . . . revealed that victims . . . burned to death when the cars exploded into flames. Some had been trapped inside the cars due to the body buckling and door becoming jammed shut.[4]

In December 1970, months after the Pinto had been in production, Ford began conducting rear-end collision tests on the car. "Initially, 11 carefully coordinated crashes were conducted, and in all but three of them, gas tanks ruptured and often burst into flames. In the three tests that didn't result in fires, the cars had prototype safety devices that engineers had developed while working with suppliers."[5] A rubber bladder/liner protected the tank, so no fuel was spilled, and no fire resulted. The unit cost of bladders amounted to $5.08 per car. A second method was to add an extra steel plate attached to the rear of the car just behind the bumper; experts calculated that the part cost up to $11 per car to install the plastic insulator.

Ford determined that the ruptures were caused by two factors: 1) the filler neck breaking off and allowing fuel to pour out, exposing it to an ignition source; and 2) tank penetration by contact with the differential mounting bolts and right shock absorber.[6]

Ford memos discussed these remedies and concluded that shutting down production and retooling was too expensive. These Ford memos detailed a cost analysis in the event of compensating crash victims. Ford valued a human life at $200,000, with a serious burn injury at $67,000; Ford estimated 180 deaths and 180 serious burns, but the cost to redesign and rework the Pinto's gas tank cost about $137 million, while liability costs worked out to around $49 million.[7]

Mark Dowrie in his Fall 1997 article in *Mother Jones* dropped the gauntlet on the Pinto's design in an article entitled "Pinto Madness," "A *Mother Jones* Classic: For seven years the Ford Motor Company sold cars in which it knew hundreds of people would needlessly burn to death."[8] This was about the same time that the *Grimshaw* case was going to trial. *Grimshaw* involved a Pinto rear-end fire that killed the driver and severely injured the passenger; plaintiffs were awarded $6.6 million in damages.[9] *Mother Jones*, "[i]n order to draw attention to the publication of a story that it believed was a political blockbuster . . . held a press conference . . . at which Mark Dowrie . . . was accompanied by Ralph Nader. The *Mother Jones* article was later awarded a Pulitzer Prize."[10]

Mark Dowrie's *Mother Jones* article indicated that Ford rushed the Pinto into production to counter strong competition from Volkswagen for the lucrative small car-market. Preproduction crash tests proved that rear-end collisions would rupture the Pinto's gas tank, but since it was already in production, Ford continued manufacturing it as is, even though Ford owned the patent to a safer fuel tank. Ford lobbied and lied for eight years to thwart the government from changing a safety standard that would have forced Ford to modify the exploding gas tank.[11]

Mother Jones was able to exclusively prove that if you ran into a Pinto, which they labeled a "death trap," at 30 miles per hour, the rear-end would buckle like an accordion, right up to the back seat. Inevitably, the tube leading to the gas tank would rip away and gas would immediately slosh onto the road. The now-buckled tank is jammed up against the differential housing, which contains four sharp protruding bolts that gash holes in the tank and spills more gas. Any spark from scraping metal ignition or a lit cigarette would engulf both cars in flames. "If you gave the Pinto a really good whack . . . say, at 40 mph . . . chances are excellent that its door would jam and you would have to stand by and watch its trapped passengers burn to death."[12]

> Internal documents . . . show that Ford has crash-tested the Pinto at a top-secret site more than 40 times and that every crash made at over 25 mph without special structural alteration . . . resulted in a ruptured fuel tank. Despite this, Ford officials denied under oath having crash-tested the Pinto.[13]

The permanent production goal was for the Pinto to weigh less than 2000 pounds and sell for less than $2,000. These limits were enforced with an iron hand. "So, even when a crash test showed that a one-pound, one-dollar piece of plastic stopped the puncture of the gas tank, it was thrown out as extra cost and extra weight."[14]

Legal liability was assumed and anticipated by Ford; their initial plan was to go to a jury, confident that it could hide the deadly results of the Pinto crash tests. "Ford thought that juries would buy the industry doctrine that drivers, not cars, cause accidents." "It didn't work, juries began ruling against the company and granting million-dollar awards to plaintiffs."[15]

Ford then turned to settlement negotiation, which "involves less cash, smaller legal fees, and less publicity, but it is an indication of the weakness of their case."[16]

> [W]hatever the costs of these settlements, it was not enough to seriously cut into Pinto's enormous profits. The cost of retooling Pinto assembly lines and of equipping each car with a safety gadget . . . was . . . greater . . . than . . . paying out millions to survivors. . . .The bottom line ruled, and inflammable Pintos kept rolling out of the factories.[17]

The *Mother Jones* piece mesmerized American consumers and lawyers by emphasizing that Ford *calculated* the cost-valuing of human life into the design, production, and marketing of the seriously flawed "fire-ball" Pinto.[18]

COST-BENEFIT ANALYSIS

Ford's cost-benefit analysis of the Pinto's relative risk places a dollar value on human life. The *Mother Jones* article exposed the element of corporate greed. The cost-benefit analysis became the basis for Ford's argument against a safer car design; "[c]ost-benefit analysis says that if the cost is greater than the benefit the project is not worth it--no matter what the benefit. Examine the cost of every action, decision, contract, part or change. . . then carefully evaluate the benefits (in dollars) to be certain that they exceed the cost before you begin a program. . ." In this analysis, Ford calculated that a life is worth $200,000.[19] An internal Ford memo entitled *Fatalities Associated with Crash-Induced Fuel Leakage and Fires* "argues that there is no financial benefit in complying with proposed safety standards that would admittedly result in lower auto fires, fewer burn deaths and fewer burn injuries." This is correct, even though Ford already possessed the patented technology that could save 70 or more lives that are burned in a Pinto each year for $11 a car.[20] Within Ford's internal memo was Christopher Leggett's paper entitled, "The Ford Case: The Valuation of Life as it Applies to the Negligence-Efficiency Argument" and "Exhibit Four: What Is a Life Worth?" valuated a life at $200,725.00.[21]

Grimshaw v. FMC

The Ford Pinto case, *Grimshaw v. Ford Motor Company*, was decided by an Orange County jury in February 1978; the jury's award was affirmed by a California appellate court in May 1981.[22] In May 1972, Lily Gray and her Orange County neighbor, 13-year old Richard Grimshaw, left for a trip in Lily's 1972 Pinto. The Pinto stalled and rolled to a halt in the middle lane of the freeway and was struck by another car, which was traveling at about 50 miles per hour but then decreased speed to 30 miles per hour at the point of impact. The resulting rear-end fire killed Mrs. Gray and left Richard Grimshaw with disastrous injuries. In the lawsuit against Ford, the jury, after deliberating for eight hours, awarded the Gray family wrongful death damages of $560,000; Grimshaw was awarded over $2.5 million in compensatory damages and $3.5 million as a condition for denying a new trial. Two years later the court of appeals affirmed, and the state supreme court denied a hearing.[23]

Ford showed a reckless disregard for consumer safety proven by certain facts as indicated in the *Grimshaw* record: Fact One: Ford conducted at least 50 tests that showed a serious gasoline leakage in the *Grimshaw* problem; Fact Two: Ford considered different methods to reduce the risks of gasoline leakage, and even though they produced positive results, it was decided that these alternatives added to production costs; Fact Three: Cost-benefit analyses of the changed location and rubber bladder alternatives would add only $15.03, but it was decided that implementation costs far outweighed expected benefits; Fact Four: Ford continued to manufacture the faulty design even in the face of growing evidence of the design's defects; Fact Five: Ford did not issue recall notices to correct the Pinto gas tanks until eight years after it was designed and tested; Fact Six: At least 32 deaths have resulted from Pinto fires; Fact Seven: Ford appealed punitive damages on the grounds that there was no malicious intent and no evidence that Ford has the power to bind Ford to authorize its decision to produce Pintos without the available safety features; Fact Eight: Ford was indicted with violating Indiana's reckless homicide statute for the design, manufacture, and sale of the Pinto.[24]

PUNITIVE DAMAGES

Punitive damages are damages over and above the sum that will compensate a person for his actual loss. The purpose is to punish the wrongdoer in the future. The wrongful act must be characterized by some circumstance of aggravation, such as willfulness, recklessness, maliciousness, outrageous conduct, oppression, or fraud. The courts must establish a mechanism to assess punitive damages against manufacturers of defective products. The usual causes of actions are negligent design, negligent failure to warn of defects, strict liability and breach of warranty.[25]

In *Wangen v. Ford Motor Co.*, lawsuits were filed against Ford as a result of an accident in which a 1967 Ford Mustang's fuel tank ruptured and burned causing severe injuries to two occupants and death to the other occupants. The court held

that the complaints state a claim for (1) punitive damages in the products liability action predicated on negligence or strict liability in tort; (2) punitive damages in the action survives the death of the injured person; (3) punitive damages in the actions by the parents for damages for loss of society and companionship of child and for loss of the minor's earning capacity and medical expenses. [But], complaints fail to state a claim for punitive damages in the wrongful death action.[26]

American Motors Corp. v. Ellis involved a 1974 AMC Ambassador which exploded and caught fire allegedly caused by a defect in the fuel system. Like *Grimshaw*, the plaintiff was able to prove that American Motors was aware of the defective fuel tank but chose not to seek safer alternative designs, which was enough to allow the jury to consider punitive damages.[27]

Grimshaw allows for punitive damages to be properly awarded in a strict products liability suit.

> Through the results of the crash tests Ford knew that the Pinto's fuel tank and rear structure would expose consumers to serious injury or death in a 20 to 30 mile-per-hour collision. There was evidence that Ford could have corrected the hazardous design defects at minimal cost but decided to defer correction of the shortcomings by engaging in a cost-benefit analysis balancing human lives and limbs against corporate profits. Ford's institutional mentality was shown to be one of callous indifference to public safety. There was substantial evidence that Ford's conduct constituted "conscious disregard" of the probability of injury to members of the consuming public.[28]

The *Grimshaw* case held that "[t]here is substantial evidence that management was aware of the crash tests showing the vulnerability of the Pinto's fuel tank to rupture at low speed rear impacts with consequent significant risk of injury or death of the occupants by fire." This callous awareness of the Pinto's rupture vulnerability allowed plaintiff's lawyers to successfully argue for punitive damages.[29]

Nowak v. Ford Motor Company is a product liability suit arising from a fatal accident of a 1977 Ford whose transmission control system was defectively designed. The jury found that the manufacturer failed to provide adequate warning that the gear shift lever might shift into reverse. The jury awarded total damages of $4,400,000 in punitive damages.[30]

> The settlement summary of *Toyota Motor Co., Ltd. v. Moll* which involved a 1973 Toyota Corolla whose fuel tank exploded upon impact indicated that three sisters, ages 23, 18, and 16, were killed when their vehicle was struck from behind and burst into flames. The plaintiff contends that the manufacturer of the dangerous automobile knew that the gas tank was a design-defect and did nothing to correct the product before offering it for sale to the public. The defendant manufacturer contended that the gas tank was safe. The $5,004,886 verdict included $3,000,000 for punitive damages, and $2,004,886 for compensatory damages.[31]

Similarly, the court in *Wolmer v. Chrysler Corp.* found that the fuel tank of a 1977 Plymouth Volare station wagon was defective and that Chrysler Corp. was liable for wrongful death of $4,000,000 in damages including $3,000,000 in punitive damages on the basis that they knew that the fuel system was inherently dangerous but continued to market the Volare station wagon. The settlement summary indicated that

[a] female back seat passenger burned to death when the vehicle she was rid-ing in was struck from behind and ignited after impact. The decedent's estate contended that the station wagon manufacturer was negligent in designing and producing the vehicle since low-impact tests had shown that the shock absorber often pierced the gas tank and the filler neck gave away during rear-end col-lisions. The plaintiff further contended that although the vehicle passed low-speed tests, the defendant manufacturer should have foreseen the effects at higher speeds.[32]

Criminal Lawsuit

The defective Pinto was the "defendant" in a criminal case where the Ford Motor Company was prosecuted for reckless homicide in Pulaski County Court, Indiana. Three young women were killed in a rear-end collision with a 1973 Ford Pinto that burst into flames.[33] The gist of the indictment was that Ford recklessly authorized and approved the design of the Pinto which would burst into flames thus causing the three deaths. "There were major disputes between the parties about the authentication and relevance of docu-ments. And the defense won a major, if questionable, victory in securing a ruling that Ford's own test results on pre–1973 cars were not admissible into evidence because of the differences in design between the 1973 Pinto and the earlier models."[34] The court battle lasted two months, and after several days of deliberation, the jury acquitted Ford. "[T]he charge of recklessness rested on two separate types of allegations: first, the knowledge of Ford's officials that some burn injuries could be avoided by redesigning or relocating the gas tanks; second, that with this knowledge, Ford acted in conscious disregard of human life by reducing costs instead of saving lives."[35] Professor Richard A. Epstein surmised that "[w]hat was needed at the very least was a showing that Ford acted in bad faith by marketing the car as it stood, because its own officials in fact believed that its design was unreasonably dangerous."[36] But, it certainly can be said that a criminal case based on "crash worthiness" against a corporation for defective design reinforced Ford's potential legal liability and blame for these fiery deaths.

The Pinto lawsuits produced individual lawsuits, class actions, and crimi-nal complaints, which were all legal mechanisms to rectify Ford's faulty cost-benefit analysis. Class actions are used to effectuate positive change against racism, sexism, and corporate greed; one can think of class actions as similarly-situated plaintiffs joining together to fight injustice.

Doctor Leslie Ball, the retired NASA safety chief, averred that

[t]he release to production of the Pinto was the most reprehensible deci-sion in the history of American engineering. . . . Ball name[d] more than 40 European and Japanese models in the Pinto price and weight range with safer

gas tank positioning. Ironically, many of them, like the Ford Capri, contain a "saddle-type" gas tank riding over the back axle. *The patent on the saddle-type tank is owned by Ford Motor Co.* The Pinto fuel system has been called "a catastrophic blunder."[37]

Safety expert Byron Blooh said that "Ford made an extremely irresponsible decision when they placed such a weak tank in such a ridiculous location in such a soft rear-end. It's almost designed to blow up-premeditated."[38]

The Pinto was not an isolated case of corporate malpractice in the auto industry; also, cost-valuing human life was not used by Ford alone.[39] "Ford was just the only company careless enough to let such an embarrassing calculation slip into public records. The process of willfully trading lives for profit is built into corporate capitalism."[40] Corporate malpractice and indifference to consumer safety as a basis for mass tort litigation segued into the pharmaceutical industry with the advent of the Bendectin scandal.

NOTES

1. Posted by Deep State Special Legal Counsel to Faculty Lounge, www.thefacultylounge.org (Dec. 19, 2017, @ 10:24 a.m.).

2. Consumer Guide Auto Editors, *The Pinto Fire Controversy,* HowStuffWorks at http://auto.howstuffworks.com/1971=1980-ford-pinto12.htm.

3. Gary T. Schwartz, *The Myth of the Ford Pinto Case,* 43 Rutgers L. Rev. 1013, 1015–1016 (Sum. 1991) (footnotes omitted).

4. Consumers Guide, *Pinto Fire Controversy,* How Stuff Works.

5. *Id.*

6. *Id.*; see also Mark Dowrie, *Pinto Madness,* A Mother Jones Classic 1 (Sept./ Oct. 1977); *For Seven Years the Ford Motor Company Sold Cars in Which It Knew Hundreds of People Would Needlessly Burn to Death,* Mother Jones 1 (Sept./ Oct. 1977) at https://www.motherjones.com/politics/1977/09/pinto-madness/; and Schwartz *The Myth of the Ford Pinto Case,* 43 Rutgers L. Rev 1013 (Sum. 1991).

7. *Ibid.,* see generally George Eads and Peter Reuter, *Designing Safer Products: Corporate Responses to Product Liability Law and Regulation* (Santa Monica, CA: Rand Institute for Civil Justice, 1983); and Douglas Birsch and John Fielder, *The Ford Pinto Case: A Study in Applied Ethics, Business, and Technology* (Albany: State University of New York Press, 1994).

8. Dowrie, *Pinto Madness,* Mother Jones 1 (Sept./Oct. 1977).

9. *Grimshaw v. FMC,* 119 Cal. App. 3d 757, 174 Cal. Rptr. 348 (1981).

10. Schwartz, *The Myth of the Ford Pinto Case,* 43 Rutgers L. Rev. 1013, 1017.

11. Dowrie, *Pinto Madness,* Mother Jones at 2–3 (emphasis in original).

12. *Id.* at 3.

13. *Id.* at 3.

14. *Id.* at 5.

15. *Id* at 10.

16. Id.

17. *Id.* at 11.

18. *Id.* at 12.

19. *Id.* at 7.

20. *Id.*

21. Christopher Leggett, *The Ford Pinto Case: The Valuation of Life as It Applies to the Negligence Efficiency Argument,* Law & Valuation, Prof. Palmiter (Spr., 1999) at http://users.wfu.edu/palmiter/Law&Valuation/Papers/1999/Leggett-pinto-htm1#2.

22. *Grimshaw v. Ford Motor Co.*, 119 Cal App. 3d 757, 174 Cal. Rptr. 348 (Cal. App., 4th Dist. 1981). See also Michael Schmitt and William May, *Beyond Products Liability: The Legal Social, and Ethical Problems Facing the Automobile Industry in Producing Safe Products,* 56 J. Urban L. Rev. 1021 (1979); and Schwartz, *The Myth of the Ford Pinto Case,* 43 Rutgers L. Rev. 1013.

23. *Id.* at 1016–17 (footnote omitted).

24. See Record at 570, 636.848–50,1120. *Grimshaw v. Ford Motor Co.*, No. 1977 (Super Ct. Orange County, Cal., Feb. 6, 1978); Schmitt and May, *Beyond Products Liability,* 56 J. Urban L. Rev. 1021, 1022-25; and *Indiana v. Ford Motor Co.*, Crim. Compl., No. 11–341 (Cir. Ct. Pulaski, Ind. 1979).

25. *American Motors Corp. v. Ellis*, 403 So.2d 459, 467 (Fla. App. 5th Dist. 1981) (footnotes omitted). See generally David G. Owen, *Problems in Assessing Punitive Damages Against Manufacturers of Defective Products*, 49 Univ. Chicago L. Rev. 1 (Wntr. 1982).

26. *Wangen v. Ford Motor Co.*, 294 N.W.2d 437, 466–67 (Wis. 1980).

27. *American Motors Corp. v. Ellis,* 403 So. 2d 459 (Fla. App. 5th Dist. 1981).

28. *Grimshaw*, 119 Cal. App. 3d 757, 813 (footnotes omitted).

29. *Ibid.* at 814.

30. *Ford Motor Co. v. Nowak,* 638 S.W.2d 582 (Tex. App—Corpus Christi-Edinburg 1982). See also *Nowak v. FMC,* JVR No. 8574, 1980 WL 163824 (Matagorda Cnty., April 1980) Verdict and Settlement Summary.

31. *Moll v. Toyota Motor Co.*, JVR No. 10969, 1981 WL 207077 (Broward Cnty. Cir. Ct., Sept. 1981) Verdict and Settlement Summary. See also *Toyota Motor Co., Ltd. v. Moll,* 438 So.2d 192 (Fla. App. 4th Dist. 1983).

32. *Wolmer v. Chrysler Corp.*, JVR No. 31232, 1985 WL 352656 (Broward Cnty Cir. Ct., date of trial, Jan. 1985) Verdict and Settlement Summary. See also *Wolmer v. Chrysler Corp.*, 474 So.2d 834 (Fla. App. 4th Dist.) rem' d 499 So.2d 823 (Fla. 1986).

33. See Richard A. Epstein, *Is Pinto a Criminal*, Regulation at 15, 15–16 (March/April 1980).

34. *Id.* at 16.

35. *Id.* at 19.

36. *Id.* (emphasis in original).

37. Dowrie, *Pinto Madness,* Mother Jones at 5 (emphasis in original).

38. *Id.*

39. *Id.*

40. *Id.* at 12.

Chapter 4

Bendectin and Birth Defects

Bendectin was developed in the mid-1950s by Wm. S. Merrell Co. of Cincinnati Ohio.[1] "Bendectin is a prescription drug developed to relieve morning sickness in pregnant women. Numerous plaintiffs have filed claims in both federal and state court, alleging that they suffered from birth defects as a result of their in utero exposure to Bendectin."[2]

"Bendectin became the leading treatment for nausea and vomiting of pregnancy."[3] "The product was approved by the FDA in 1956."[4] Bendectin is "a combination drug made up of three ingredients, each of which had been marketed separately—dicyclomine hydrochloride (an antispasmodic), doxylamine succinate (an antihistamine acting as an anti-nauseant), and pyridoxine hydrochloride [pyridoxine is vitamin B-6]. . . ."[5] "Bendectin first reached the market in 1956. . . over the next two decades it became the leading drug for morning sickness and one of Merrell's leading products."[6]

The question is whether Merrell utilized improper practices in the research and development and marketing of their drug. Merrell did *no* premarketing animal clinical tests for the safety of the unborn. Merrell also withheld troubling animal test data from the Food & Drug Administration (FDA) and concealed reports on human birth deformities from inquiring physicians. Drugs of *any* kind should never be prescribed during pregnancy unless essential. Also, there are effective homeopathic alternatives including dry crackers, and particularly in the early morning, drinking no liquids that are either very hot or very cold.[7] Bendectin "was widely suspected of causing birth defects (of a teratogenic nature). It was removed from the market. Over a thousand drug product liability cases were commenced."[8] Bendectin was linked with Thalidomide, which "was a sleeping pill that was . . . used abroad . . . and studied in the United States . . . when it was discovered that it was teratogenic, that is, that it could harm a fetus when taken by pregnant women. . . . The drug affected normal growth of the fetus and could result in abnormally shortened limbs of the newborn; phocomelia or seal-like."[9]

Bendectin was routinely prescribed by doctors for 27 years; an estimated 33 million women around the world took Bendectin—before it was withdrawn from the market in 1983. In January 1987, a Philadelphia jury found that Merrell Dow recklessly disregarded the consequences to the unborn children. The jury awarded $1 million in punitive damages for a club foot, with another $1 million in compensation damages. After the verdict, Merrell Dow continued to maintain that no scientifically acceptable evidence supports claims that Bendectin causes birth defects. The decision to stop making Bendectin was allegedly done *only* because of "compelling non-medical reasons," particularly the cost of defending about 300 lawsuits.[10]

THE *NATIONAL ENQUIRER* ARTICLE

"Some studies had emerged in the late 1970s and early 1980s, which associated Bendectin to some specific malformations. Following an article published in the National Enquirer (1979) which stated that Bendectin could cause birth defects, many women wanted to abort their babies."[11] In 1975, Bendectin was not a suspect drug. In 1977, the situation changed when the first lawsuit was filed against Merrell alleging that Bendectin had caused a birth defect. While Merrell ultimately prevailed in this first lawsuit, more soon followed.[12] The litigation continued with a plaintiff's verdict of $19.2 million in 1994.[13]

David Mekdeci was one of thousands of children born in 1975 with a "limb reduction" birth defect. He was born with a shortened right forearm and a malformed right hand as well as missing pectoral muscles in his chest. David's injury sent his mother, Betty Mekdeci, on a several-year search for an explanation. The precise causes of most birth defects are unknown, perhaps 70 percent of all defects cannot be attributed to any specific cause. As many as 20 percent of defects may be attributed to genetic factors, but David's injury did not appear to fall in this category.[14]

In her search for legal representation, Betty reached out to "Melvin Belli, the self-proclaimed King of Torts. . . . Belli agreed to represent the Mekdecis in the summer of 1976."[15] Their lawsuit, *Mekdeci v. Merrell National Laboratories* was postponed to January 1980.

The delay was just long enough for Bendectin to break into the news and become an important example in disputes about the pharmaceutical industry, drug safety availability, and the short-comings of tort law. In October 1979, the *National Enquirer* published a story with the headline, "*New Thalidomide Scandal Experts Reveal*." The article put Bendectin in the worst possible light, "a new thalidomide that produced monsters."[16]

Belli dropped the Mekdecis as clients because he wanted to concentrate on the other 200 Debendox cases that his firm had acquired. Some of these potential clients were attracted by the publicity surrounding the *Mekdeci* trial, including sympathetic articles in the *New York Times Sunday Magazine* (de St. Jore, 1980), and *Mother Jones* (Dowrie and Marshall, 1980). The publicity generated many inquiries. In addition, the lawyers were actively soliciting cases. Some clients were probably attracted to Belli because of the following thinly disguised advertisement that appeared in the *San Francisco Chronicle* in January and February 1980.

Bendectin Taken For Morning Sickness

Causing Malformed Children

We have a number of these cases and we are trying one now in Federal Court, Florida. We need your help for epidemiological and statistical purposes. If you have any information, please call or write:

Melvin M. Belli, Belli Building

San Francisco, CA 94111

(415) 981 – 1849[17]

The *Mekdeci* Case

Although *Mekdeci* was the first case, it was not the best first case.[18] Unfortunately for the purity of her case, Betty took many other additional drugs during her pregnancy; she was prescribed Actifed, Hemocyte, Erythromycin, Myostatin and Mycolog, Penbritin, and Azo Gantrisin, and an over-the-counter vitamin supplement.[19] The Food, Drug and Cosmetic Act Amendments of 1962 dictated that all drugs marketed before 1962 be examined for efficacy.[20] *Mekdeci v. Merrell National Laboratories* took six years and two trials to complete. After five days of deliberation, the first jury returned a verdict for the plaintiff, but "[a]s to damages it left unchanged the paragraph in the verdict that stipulated $20,000 as out-of-pocket costs owed to the Mekdecis for their reasonable care of their injured son," but as to the amount of David's damages, the jury wrote "Nothing." Since the jury's compromise lies outside the boundaries of permissible trial outcomes, the judge was obligated to order a new trial.[21]

"The second trial lasted nine weeks, but this time it took the jury only two hours to return a verdict for Merrell. Appeals based on, among other things, inadequate representation by counsel were to no avail. Round one was finally over." But the "defense victory in *Mekdeci* . . . [did not] deter the plaintiff's bar from pursuing other cases. The Bendectin litigation had just begun."[22] "The Mekdeci suit evolved into a nasty fight among plaintiff lawyers after

Betty Mekdeci charged that Cohen and Kokus and California plaintiff's attorney Melvin Belli were trying to drop her case for easier Bendectin cases."[23]

The second Bendectin case to go to trial, *Koller v. Richardson*, was every bit as controversial as *Mekdeci*. The reputation of two major plaintiffs' law firms and the viability of a multimillion-dollar product liability suit were called into question by "a legal secretary's allegations that her former employers and their client may have been engaged in a massive fraud."[24] *Koller* was originally very attractive "to the *Mekdeci* lawyers . . . because the plaintiff's mother had not taken other drugs during her pregnancy . . . the . . . . injuries were severe, and the case was to be tried in Washington, D.C. . . . . [which is] a plaintiff-friendly jurisdiction."[25]

> The next Bendectin trial in May 1983 also was in Washington, D.C. Joan Oxendine had read about Bendectin in the *National Enquirer* . . . her daughter Mary was born in 1971 with limb reduction defect. The suit was filed early in 1982, lasting one month and resulting in a plaintiff's verdict for $750,000 with a punitive damages trial scheduled to follow. However, the trial judge granted a judgment notwithstanding the verdict (J.N.O.V.) in favor of Merrell, finding the verdict to be against the great weight of the evidence. The District of Columbia Court of Appeals reversed, concluding that a dismissal was an abuse of trial court discretion and reinstated the verdict.[26]

"The outcome was a clear victory for plaintiffs and sent a signal that there was a substantial likelihood that future cases would succeed and that awards could well justify the costs of litigation. Merrell, recognizing the potential adverse effect of the case relentlessly fought the verdict."[27]

Merrell accused one of the plaintiff's experts, Alan Done, of testifying falsely at trial and filed a motion for a new trial. The trial judge granted the motion in February 1988. However, in August of 1989, the D.C. Court of Appeals again reversed, reinstating the original verdict. Defendant's petition for a writ of certiorari to the U.S. Supreme Court was denied in 1990.[28] The appellate court ruled in 1991 that the trial court could not enter an enforceable and appealable "final judgment" on the $750,000 compensatory damage award until the punitive damage phase of the trial was completed.[29] In a tactical maneuver, the plaintiff abandoned her punitive damage claim and moved for summary judgment on compensatory damages. The motion was denied, and the appellate court ordered a trial court to consider Merrell's post-judgment motion, asking for relief based on new evidence that Bendectin's teratogenicity developed subsequent to the original *Oxendine* trial.[30]

In the autumn of 1996, the trial judge entered an order granting Merrell a judgment as a matter of law concluding that the plaintiffs could not produce admissible evidence that Bendectin is a teratogen.[31] Merrell's legal strategy appears to have paid off in that after years of litigation, only two verdicts were not overturned.[32] "Merrell's relentless effort to overturn the *Oxendine* verdict was driven in part by its desire to avoid an adverse judgment. The efforts also reflect the fact that *Oxendine* did not stand alone, but rather was one of the Bendectin cases. The stakes in the case reached beyond *Oxendine* itself."[33] As a trial tactic, Merrell was a "repeat player" but, "*Oxendine* served as an incentive for plaintiffs to continue to litigate. Even if most cases are successfully defended, an occasional plaintiff success will encourage other suits and eventually spell doom for a defendant."[34] In the end, "Oxendine represented a clear victory for a Bendectin claimant, with a dramatic increase in filings, from less than 100 cases filed in 1981, to over 500 filing in 1984."[35]

Causation

Merrell's preeminent argument was that the plaintiff failed to present statistically significant epidemiological proof that Bendectin causes limb reduction defects.[36] But, proving that a drug is a necessary link in the causal chain to a specific deformity is at best problematic. It is a futile task "at least given the current state of scientific affairs."[37] One judge sardonically observed that "what scientists know about the causes of cancer is how limited is their knowledge."[38] "In the absence of direct evidence, scientific methods that permit causal inference . . . are employed."[39]

"In the science of toxicology, there are five different types of evidence that may contribute to an inference of causation: epidemiology, animal toxicology, in vitro testing, chemical structural analysis, and case reports."[40] "The vast majority of birth defects are apparent at birth, which means that the latency period from exposure to disease is less than nine months. Hospital records document birth defects, and a number of databases involving births had been developed for research purposes."[41]

The proof of causation in mass tort cases comes in two parts, general causation, and specific causation. "General causation asks whether exposure to a substance causes harm to anyone. Specific causation asks whether exposure to a substance caused the plaintiff's injury. Under traditional tort theory, a plaintiff must prevail by a preponderance of the evidence on both questions to succeed. Epidemiological studies can answer both questions."[42] "Epidemiological studies that show a statistically significant correlation between a substance and an injury are usually sufficient to allow a plaintiff to prevail on the issue of general causation."[43] The Fifth Circuit Court of Appeals in *Brock v. Merrell Dow Pharmaceuticals* holds that a plaintiff cannot prevail on a claim based on epidemiological data absent statistically significant findings.[44] Commentators have identified two problems with *Brock*'s reliance on statistical significance. The first concerns the appropriate measure of statistical significance.[45]

"Second, the *Brock* opinion fails to recognize that all studies can fall prey to two types of errors. Alpha values guard only against Type I error, the error of finding false positives. Type II error, or findings of false negatives, conclude that no relationship exists when one in fact does."[46] "A plaintiff can prove specific causation by preponderance of the evidence by providing epidemiological evidence that indicates a relative risk greater than 2.0; that is, the people exposed to the substance suffer injuries more than twice as frequently as those not exposed."[47] However, in the Bendectin cases the court held that the question of proximate causation can be tried separately, which does not favor plaintiff since it now must prove "but for" causation as opposed to the weaker "substantial factor" test.[48]

JUNK SCIENCE

In the late 1980s, scientific fraud complaints were brought against Dr. William Griffin McBride, who was convicted of deliberately falsifying data. Dr. McBride . . . took the stand in the 1980s as an expert witness in several highly-publicized U.S. cases and raised doubt about the safety of Bendectin based on the "Debendox experiment" he claimed to have performed but which later was proven to be false.[49]

The U.S. Supreme court in *Daubert v. Merrell Dow* established a standard for admissibility of scientific testimony.[50] "In that case, plaintiff alleged that Bendectin . . . caused limb reduction birth defects. Plaintiffs' experts, through what was . . . [allegedly] deemed to be 'junk science,' failed to present any study in support of plaintiffs' theory that Bendectin could cause malformations in human fetuses."[51] But, in *Hoffman* there was expert testimony to the effect that, if nothing else, synergistic responses create the possibility of birth defects.[52] The *Hoffman* court incorrectly summarizes that Dr. Swan's testimony has no relevance unless the plaintiffs can show that Bendectin by itself caused birth defects.[53]

Bendectin proponents allege that plaintiffs' "experts were able to exploit the inevitable residual doubt concerning the drug's safety, and through a process of moving toward the most favorable type of evidence and deconstructing opposing studies they were able to present a plausible case that persuaded many juries that Bendectin was a teratogen."[54] A jury in Corpus Christi, Texas, on September 26, 1991, awarded $3.75 million to Kelly Havner for birth defects caused to her right hand by her mother's use of Bendectin. Seven days later, the jury added $30 million in punitive damages.[55] The key to the jury's deliberations is "the importance of scientific and statistical evidence for proving the causal link between the alleged toxin and the plaintiff's injury."[56] Even proponents of Bendectin's safety admit that "[s]ome *in vivo* studies *have* a teratogenic effect [and that] . . .six epidemiological studies have found statistically significant correlations between Bendectin and some type of defect."[57] Bendectin plaintiffs want to believe that Merrell negligently tested and marketed its product knowing that it was intended solely for a physically and emotionally vulnerable subclass of women. If nothing else, Bendectin should have been marketed with better warnings.[58]

PUNITIVE DAMAGES

Punitive or exemplary damages are assessed in addition to compensatory damages to punish and deter the defendant from outrageous acts of misconduct; a jury in its discretion will render such an award.[59] For example in *Toole v. Richardson-Merrell, Inc.*, the defendant disregarded the possibility of injury in its eagerness to market their blood cholesterol wonder drug Mer/29 to the point of falsifying test records to ensure FDA approval and representing it as proven safe, when it was not. The defendant knew the drug posed a risk to consumers; disregarding their safety is reckless and should warrant the jury's award of punitive damages.[60] The defendant's actions showed a sinister economic desire to profit at any cost.[61] "THE MER/29 STORY is a case history of the legal response to the problems of mass litigation. It shows how plaintiffs' attorneys banded together voluntarily and without court control to dispose of approximately fifteen hundred civil suits filed by injured drug users who sought aggregate punitive damages. . . ."[62] The success of the MER/29 litigation is comparable to Bendectin since punitive damages were based on the drug manufacturer's duplicity. The manufacturer's outrageous conduct *must* warrant punitive damages.[63]

In 1984, the Bendectin lawsuits were settled for $120 million.[64] Juries usually awarded plaintiffs both compensatory and punitive damages but were often initially overturned by trial judge's granting of judgment notwithstanding the verdict (J.N.O.V.). Luckily, the Appeals Court would just as often reverse and remand J.N.O.V. on the basis that the jury's verdict was not against the weight of the evidence or an abuse of the trial court's discretion. Defendant's argument centered on the testimony of expert witnesses or the viability of scientific studies that tend to indicate that Merrell Dow knew that Bendectin was a teratogen but continued to manufacture and market it to a medically vulnerable subgroup.[65]

Bendectin litigation is a precursor to Agent Orange and Big Pharma feeding frenzies. The key to Bendectin litigation was proving a causal link between Merrell Dow's fraudulent concealment and birth defects. Agent Orange plaintiffs must also prove that defendant's negligence caused cancers and later birth defects.

NOTES

1. *Bendectin History,* Home Page at 1, https://www.bendectin.com/en/ (footnotes omitted).

2. *In re Bendectin Products Liability Litigation,* 749 F.2d 300, 301–2 (6th Cir. 1984) (footnotes omitted).

3. *Bendectin History,* Bendectin Home Page, at 1.

4. *Ibid.* (footnote omitted).

5. Joseph Sanders, *Bendectin on Trial: A Study of Mass Tort Litigation,* p. 1 (Ann Arbor: University of Michigan Press, 1998).

6. *Ibid.*

7. See generally Morton Mintz, *Drug for Morning Sickness Is Suspected in Birth Defects,* Washington Post at 1 (Feb. 11, 1980). Douglas Peters, *Bendectin* 1980 Trial 56.

8. Charles Krause and Alfred Gans, *Bendectin; Thalidomide,* 6A American Law of Torts §18:401; See generally David Owen, *The Highly Blameworthy Manufacturer: Implications on Rules of Liability and Defense in Products Liability Actions,* 10 Ind. L. Rev. 769 (1977); Wayne Brazil, *The Adversary Chapter of Civil Discovery: A Critique and Proposals for Change,* 31 Vand. L. Rev. 1295 (1978); Michael Saks and Robert Kidd, *Human Information Processing and Adjudication: Trial by Heuristics,* 15 Law & Soc'y Rev. 123 (1980); David Owen, *Rethinking the Policies of Strict Products Liability,* 33 Vand. L. Rev. 681 (1980); John Wade, *On Product Design Defects and Their Actionability,* 33 Vand. L. Rev. 551 (1980); Sheila Birnbaum, *Unmasking the Test for Design Defect: From Negligence [to Warranty] to Strict Liability to Negligence,* 33 Vand. L. Rev. 593 (1980); Herbert Kritzen, W. A. Bogant, and Neil Vidman, *The Aftermath of Injury: Cultural Factors in Compensation Seeking in Canada and the United States,* 25 Law & Soc'y Rev. 499 (1991); Michael D. Green, *Bendectin and Birth Defects: The Challenges of Mass Toxic Substances Litigation* (Philadelphia: University of Pennsylvania Press, 1996); and Wendy Wager, *Choosing Ignorance in the Manufacture of Toxic Products,* 82 Cornell L. Rev. 773 (1997).

9. 6A America Law of Torts §18:40 at 1 (footnotes omitted).

10. Beth Gillen, *Jury Awards $1 Million in Bendectin Lawsuits,* JOC.com, https://www.joc.com/jury-awards-1million-bendectin-lawsuit_1988 (Jan. 28, 1987).

11. *Bendectin History,* Bendectin Home Page at 1 (footnotes omitted).

12. Sanders, *Bendectin on Trial* at 1 (footnote omitted).

13. *Id.* at 1–2 (footnotes omitted).

14. *Id.* at 2 (footnotes omitted).

15. *Id.* at 6.

16. *Id.* at 10.

17. *Id.* at 27.

18. *Mekdeci v. Merrell National Laboratories* (A Division of Richardson-Merrell, Inc.), 711 F.2d 1150 (11th Cir. 1983).

19. Sanders, *Bendectin on Trial* at 3.

20. *Id.* at 4.

21. *Id.* at 12.

22. *Id.* at 15 (footnote omitted).

23. David Lanter, *Benedictine Trial Disintegrates; Allegations of Misconduct Made,* 5 Nat' L. J 6 (Feb. 21, 1983).

24. *Id.* See *Koller v. Richardson-Merrell Inc.,* 737 F.2d 1038 (D.C. Cir. 1984), vacated 472 U.S. 424 (1985).

25. Sanders, *Bendectin on Trial* at 28.

26. *Oxendine v. Merrell Dow Pharmaceuticals,* 506 A.2d 1100, 1114 (D.C. App. 1986).

27. Sanders, *Bendectin on Trial* at 29.

28. *Oxendine v. Merrell Dow Pharmaceuticals,* 506 A.2d 330, 332 (D.C. 1991), cert. den. 110 S.Ct. 1121 (1990).

29. *Merrell Dow Pharmaceuticals, Inc. v. Oxendine,* 593 A.2d 1023 (D.C. 1991).

30. *Merrell Dow Pharmaceuticals, Inc. v. Oxendine,* 649 A.2d 825 (D.C. App. 1994).

31. *Oxendine v. Merrell Dow Pharmaceuticals, Inc.,* 1998 WL 680992 (D.C. Super. 1996).

32. Sanders, *Bendectin on Trial* at 29.

33. *Id.*

34. *Id.* at 30.

35. *Id.*

36. *Brock v. Merrell Dow Pharmaceuticals, Inc.,* 874 F. 2d 307 (5th Cir. 1989), modified 884 F.2d 166 (5th Cir. 1989), cert. den. 110 S.Ct. 1511 (1990).

37. Green, *Expert Witnesses and Sufficiency of Evidence in Toxic Substances Litigation,* 86 NW U. L. Rev. 643, 645 (footnote omitted).

38. *Environmental Defense Fund v. EPA,* 598 F.2d 02, 89 (D.C. Cin. 1978), as quoted in Green, *Expert Witnesses,* 86 NW U. L. Rev. 643, 645.

39. See generally David Owen, *The Highly Blameworthy Manufacturer: Implications on Rules of Liability and Defense in Products Liability Actions,* 10 Ind. L. Rev. 769 (1977); John Wade, *On Product Design Defects and Their Actionability,* 33 Vand. L. Rev. 551 (1980); David Owen, *Rethinking the Policies of Strict Products Liability,* 33 Vand. L. Rev. 68 1 (1980); Sheila Birnbaum, *Unmasking the Test for Design Defect: From Negligence [to Warranty] to Strict Liability to Negligence,* 33 Vand. L. Rev. 593 (1980); David Bernstein, *Out of the Frying Pan and Into the Fire: The Expert Witness Problem in Toxic Tort Litigation,* 10 Law Rev. of Litig. 117 (1990); Joseph Sanders, *The Bendectin Litigation, A Case Study in the Life Cycle of Mass Torts,* 43 Hastings L. J. 301 (Jan. 1992); Joseph Sanders, *From Science to Evidence: The Testimony on Causation in the Bendectin Cases,* 46 Stan. L. Rev 1 (Nov. 1993); and Robert Brent, *Bendectin and Birth Defects: Hopefully, the Final Chapter,* 67 Birth Defects Research (Part A) 79 (2003).

40. Green, *Expert Witnesses,* 86 NW. U. L. Rev. at 646 (footnote omitted).

41. *Id.* at 678.

42. Joseph Sanders, *From Science to Evidence: The Testimony on Causation in the Bendectin Cases,* 46 Stan. L. Rev. 1, 14 (Nov. 1993) (footnote omitted).

43. *Id.* (footnote omitted).

44. *Brock v. Merrell Dow Pharmaceuticals,* 874 F. 2d 307, 311-12 (5th Cir.) modified 884 F.2d 166 (5th Cir. 1989), cert. den. 494 U.S. 1047 (1990).

45. Sanders, *From Science to Evidence.*

46. *Id.* (footnotes omitted).

47. *Id.* at 16 (footnotes omitted).

48. In re Bendectin Litigation, *Hoffman v. Merrell Dow Pharmaceuticals,* 857 F.2d 290, 308–309 (6th Cir. 1988).

49. *Bendectin History,* Bendectin home page at 2 (footnotes omitted).

50. *Daubert v. Merrell Dow,* 509 U.S. 579 (1993).

51. *Bendectin History,* Bendectin home page at 2 (footnotes omitted). See generally Michael Saks and Richard Van Duizend, *The Use of Scientific Evidence in Litigation* (Williamsburg, VA; National Center for State Counts, 1983); Peter Huber, *Galileo's Revenge: Junk Science in the Court Room* (New York: Basic Books, 1991); David Faigman, *Struggling to Stop the Flood of Unreliable Expert Testimony,* 76 Minn. L. Rev. 877 (Feb. 1992); David Faigman, Elise Porter, and Michael Saks, *Check Your Crystal Ball at the Courthouse Door, Please: Exploring the Past, Understanding the Present, and Worrying About the Future of Scientific Evidence,* Cardozo L. Rev. 1 799 (April 1994); Faigman, *Mapping the Labyrinth of Scientific Evidence,* 46 Hastings L. J. 555 (Jan. 1995); Trent Stephens and Rock Bryner, *Dark Remedy: The Impact of Thalidomide and Its Revival as a Vital Medicine* (Cambridge, MA: Presents Pub. 2001); and Faigman et al., *Modern Scientific Evidence* (Thomason /West 2006).

52. *Hoffman,* 857 F.2d 290, 311.

53. *Id.*

54. Sanders, *Bendectin on Trial* at 115.

55. *Haver v. Merrell Dow Pharm,* No. 88–3915-F (S.D. Tex. 1991).

56. Sanders, *From Science to Evidence,* 46 Stan. L. Rev. 1, 3.

57. *Id.* at 25 (emphasis in original) (footnotes omitted).

58. *Id.* at 51–52.

59. See David Owen, *Punitive Damages in Products Liability Litigation,* Mich. L. Rev. 12 58, 1265 (June 1976). See generally Douglas Garden, *Punitive Damages in Products Liability Cases,* 16 Santa Clara L. Rev. 895 (1976); Grant DuBois, *Punitive Damages in Personal Injury Products Liability and Professional Malpractice Cases: Bonanza or Disaster,* 43 Ins. Counsel J. 344 (1976); John Fulton, *Punitive Damages in Products Liability Cases,* 15 Forum 117 (1979).

60. See *Toole v. Richardson-Merrell, Inc.,* 251 Cal. App 2d 689, 60 Cal. Rptr. 398 (1967); *G.D. Searle & Co. v. Superior Court,* 49 Cal. App.3d 22, 31, 122 Cal. Rptr. 218, 224 (1975), citing *Donnelly v. Southern Pacific Co.,* 18 Cal.2d 863, 869, 118 P.2d 465, 468 (1974); Garden, *Punitive Damages,* 16 Santa Clara L. Rev. at 914; and Paul Rheingold, *The MER/29 Story—An Instance of Successful Mass Disaster Litigation,* 56 Cal. L. Rev. 116 (1968).

61. *Toole*, 251 Cal. App.3d 689, 714–15, 60 Cal. Rptr. 398, 416 (1967).

62. Rheingold, *The Mer 129 Story*, 56 Cal. L. Rev. at 116.

63. See also *Wussiow v. Commercial Mechanisms*, 97 Wis.2d 136 (1980) (faulty manufacture of baseball pitching machine); and *Leichtamen v. American Motors Corp.*, 67 Ohio F.2d 45,69 (1981) (faulty manufacture of "Off-the-Road" vehicle); and *Grue v. Dayton-Hudson Corp.*, 297 N.W.2d. 727 (Minn. 1980) (manufacture of flammable "Flannelette" pajamas).

64. Mintz, *Bendectin Lawsuits Are Settled*, Washington Post at 1 (July 15, 1984).

65. *Oxendine v. Merrell Dow Pharmaceuticals*, 506 A.2d 110 (D.C. App 1986).

Chapter 5

Agent Orange

"I Love the Smell of Napalm in the Morning" (Lt. Col. Bill Kilgore as portrayed by Robert Duvall in *Apocalypse Now*, produced by Omni Zoetrope; distributed by United Artists, 1979). In March 1975, the United States fled from Vietnam but "left behind . . . a once fertile land now defoliated by millions of gallons of Agent Orange--a deadly herbicide that causes cancer, neurological damages and birth defects."[1] Agent Orange killed and injured thousands of Vietnamese civilians and both Vietnamese and American servicemen. Agent Orange also entered the food system and the DNA of those affected, causing birth defects.

American veterans of the Vietnamese War in 1978 "sued a number of chemical manufacturers, blaming them for various diseases and traumas that they and their families had allegedly suffered because of exposure to Agent Orange."[2] Agent Orange "evolved into an offensive strategy [known as Operation Ranch Hand] designed to destroy enemy crops as well as to clear roads and communication lines."[3] The use of Agent Orange ended in April 1970, but in "the five years of the program, some 112 million of gallons of it had been sprayed [by low-flying C-123 aircraft] over as much as 10 percent of South Vietnam's land area."[4]

Agent Orange's toxicity was well-known before its use in Vietnam: "As early as 1952, army officials had been informed by Monsanto Chemicals Companies, later a major manufacturer of Agent Orange, that [the defoliant] . . . was contaminated by a toxic substance."[5] In 1963, the "President's Science Advisory Committee reported to the Joint Chiefs of Staff on the possible health damages of herbicide use."[6]

Seven years after Agent Orange was first used in the conflict, the American military discontinued its use when published documents reported that exposure could cause birth defects. Ongoing research has provided conclusive evidence that compounds in Agent Orange are causally related to various types of cancer, as well as fatal metabolic disorders, damage to the nervous system, and skin disorders. In 2002, U.S. researchers observed that populations in Vietnam that suffered a high degree of exposure have dioxin levels thirty-three times higher than average, and up to 206 times higher in individual cases. In some villages, one in every ten children suffers a serious birth defect, including physical and mental retardation, missing or malformed limbs, and conditions such as spinal bifida and cerebral palsy.[7]

The manufacture of Agent Orange, by one of many manufacturers, with the complicit authorization of their preeminent defoliant purchaser, the United States of America, created a by-product called TCDD, which is "perhaps the most toxic molecule very synthesized by man." "Agent Orange produced by different manufacturers was often mixed rather indiscriminately in Vietnam before. . . . As a result, the herbicide sprayed there had TCDD concentrations ranging from one part per million to 140 parts per million."[8]

The legal response to Agent Orange was just as daunting as the epidemiology of cancers and birth defects that is at the root of exposure to this defoliant. The first claim was in 1978, and in 1979, the Judicial Panel on multi-district litigation chose Judge Jack B. Weinstein (E.D.N.Y) who certified a voluntary class to decide liability and causation and a mandatory class for punitive damages. Two-hundred fifty-thousand claimants were included, but on the eve of trial in Spring 1984, the manufacturers agreed to pay $180 million. "In July 1993, the Institute of Medicine concluded that there is sufficient evidence to link exposure to Agent Orange to Hodgkin's disease and to a rare liver disorder. . . . [T]he Secretary of Veterans Affairs announced that Vietnam veterans suffering from these diseases would be eligible for special disability payments."[9]

Additionally, on June 18, 2015, the U.S. government in a rule approved by the White House Office of Management and Budget, agreed to pay millions of dollars in disability payments to 2100 Air Force reservists and active-duty forces exposed to Agent Orange residue on airplanes used in the Vietnam War.[10]

LONG-TERM IMPACT

Judge Jack Weinstein in 1994 used class action law to resolve tens of thousands of veterans' claims for Agent Orange exposure.[11] "Under the terms of the settlement, all veterans who had been exposed to Agent Orange, including so-called 'future' victims who did not yet know that they were injured, were included in a class-wide resolution of the case."[12]

A class at risk, not covered by Judge Weinstein's settlement, are living veterans who are currently without symptoms, but still at risk of genetic and somatic damage. These at-risk would-be plaintiffs served in Vietnam and were exposed to Agent Orange, but do not presently exhibit symptoms of dioxin-related medical problems.[13]

Two Navy veterans, Ivy and Hartman, brought class actions in state court for injuries that were manifested after the settlement date. Defendants countered by removal to federal court where the claims were barred by the original settlement. The Second Circuit Court of Appeals affirmed the dismissal holding that injury occurs when the toxin enters the body even though its adverse effects are not immediately apparent.[14]

Two Vietnam veterans, Stephenson and Isaacson, who both suffered from cancers, filed lawsuits in 1988 that were joined and transferred to Judge Weinstein's Court.[15] Both veterans manifested their injuries only after the settlement period ended and its funds were depleted.[16]

The district court dismissed the case, but the Second Circuit Court of Appeals vacated and remanded, holding that the suit was a permissible collateral attack.[17] The court gave two reasons for this conclusion: (1) neither the Supreme Court nor the district court has considered the adequacy of representation for plaintiffs whose injuries manifested after the depletion of the settlement fund; and (2) collateral attacks on the adequacy of representation have been allowed in other circuits.[18] The Second Circuit held that plaintiffs were not adequately represented at trial because it included only currently injured plaintiffs.[19]

The Supreme Court held that "with respect to respondent Daniel Raymond Stephenson . . . the judgment is affirmed by an equally divided court." The Supreme Court remanded Isaacson's claim, but allowed Stephenson's case to proceed. The Supreme Court affirmed the Second Circuit's opinion as to Stephenson in a 4–4 split, with Justice Stevens taking no part in the decision on the basis that his son had served in Vietnam.[20]

The Fifth Circuit Court of Appeals began their opinion in *Winters v. Diamond Shamrock Chemical* with this sobering introduction: "Margaret Winters now taken from this world by disease allegedly cause by Agent Orange."[21] Margaret Winters was a registered nurse who worked for the United States Agency for International Development in Vietnam as a nurse from August 1966 to October 1967. Within several months of her arrival in Vietnam, she developed eye blisters. She returned to the United States in 1967 after 14 months in Vietnam. Eye blisters and tumors were present in both eyes. "In August of 1983, Winters developed a lump under her arm which was subsequently diagnosed as non-Hodgkin's lymphoma."[22]

Winters insisted that no medical doctor ever told her that her NHL was even possibly connected to Agent Orange before 1991. She filed suit in 1993 alleging a link between Agent Orange exposure and her lymphoma. Although a cause of action usually accrues when a wrongful act causes an injury, there is an exception when claimant is unable to know of the cause of the injury at the time it occurred. The two-year statute of limitations for personal injuries under Texas law begins under the exception, when plaintiff "discovers . . . through the exercise of reasonable care and diligence . . . the nature of her injury and its cause in fact."[23] The court denied her estate's claims while blaming Nurse Winters for not connecting her non-Hodgkin's lymphoma to Agent Orange exposure. "Moreover, Winters was a registered nurse." The court charged Winters with the quantum of knowledge and experience that would alert her of the possible health effects of Agent Orange exposure.[24] Sadly, Winters was not alive at the time of the summary judgment against her to refute these assumptions. Not every medical professional has the cool detachment to accurately diagnose the epidemiology of the specific cancer that kills her.

MULTI-DISTRICT LITIGATION (MDL)

Agent Orange was a "new kind" of case; "millions of American soldiers . . . returned from . . . [the Vietnam] charnel house. . . with bitterness, dread, controversy, and debilitating illness."[25] In 1978, the veterans, suffering from a myriad of cancers associated with Agent Orange exposure sued a number of chemical manufacturers. The disabled veterans hoped that "[t]he laws . . . would assuage their pain and vindicate their sacrifices."[26]

> The Agent Orange case bears little resemblance to traditional tort adjudication. Its magnitude and complexity beggar the imagination with more than 600 separate actions originally filed by more than 15,000 named individuals. The parties consisting of some 2.4 million Vietnam veterans, their wives, children born and unborn, seven (originally twenty-four) corporate defendants, and the United States government.[27]

Since financial and personnel demands of litigating this case are staggering, plaintiffs "are represented by a network of law firms that numbered almost 1,500 by May 1984, located in every region of the country. . . [T]he case resulted in the largest tort settlement in history. The settlement, reached in May 1984 after almost six years of litigation, created a fund of $180 million," not to mention the interest that accrued daily.[28] "The two lawyers petitioned the Judicial multi-district Litigation Panel, a group of federal judges who decide whether to consolidate a series of closely related cases (and if so, in what judicial district) originally brought in disparate jurisdictions for discovery purposes and perhaps for trial as well."[29] The Judicial Panel determines the appropriateness of transferring a group of cases, called a "docket," [30] to a single district for pretrial proceedings, selects a transfer district and judge to hear consolidated cases, and orders the remand of the cases to their original districts for trial, if appropriate.[31] The panel lacks power to consolidate cases for trial. In most MDLs, there is a pool of money that lead counsel and the steering committee expect will be utilized so that they get paid for their services.[32] However, the financing of Agent Orange litigation has come mostly from private sources.[33]

IN RE AGENT ORANGE PRODUCTS LIABILITY LITIGATION

"The Agent Orange litigation raised the dual problem of the undetermined plaintiff and the indeterminate defendant."[34] This case is the first to confront an unprecedented challenge to the legal system—"a future in which the law must grapple with the chemical revolution and . . . live comfortable with it."[35] "In re Agent Orange Prod. Liab. Litig. represented the collectivized claims of Vietnam veterans, their spouses, their parents, and their children in a class action against the manufacturers of Agent Orange . . . the Judicial Panel on multi-district Litigation ordered all Agent Orange cases consolidated and transferred to the District Court of the Eastern District of New York . . ."[36] "The settlement of $180 million was upheld after seven years of litigation."[37]

> The U.S. Department of Veteran Affairs produced an informational flier that explained available benefits from the Agent Orange Settlement Fund which was created as a result of In re Agent Orange Prod. Liab. Litig—the Fund Closed in 1997—The Settlement Fund was distributed to class members in accordance with a distribution plan established by United States District Court Judge Jack B. Weinstein, who presided over the litigation and the settlement. Because the plaintiff class was so large (an estimated 10 million people), the Fund was distributed to class members in the United States through two separate programs designed to provide maximum benefits to Vietnam Veterans and their families most in need of assistance.[38]

Government Contractor Defense

"Who is to blame for the calamitous consequences of the Agent Orange operation?"[39] *In re "Agent Orange" Product Liability Litigation* (Agent Orange I) sought to blame the chemical companies who manufactured the herbicide.[40] "The manufacturers used the government contractor defense which relies on the contention that since the government controlled the design and manufacture of Agent Orange, therefore, it immunized the manufacturers from liability."[41] "Although the United States District Court for the Eastern District of

New York recognized that the contractors in Agent Orange I are protected by the government contract defense, it refused to grant the chemical companies a summary judgment because too many material facts relevant to the companies' defense remain unresolved."[42]

The logic supporting the defense is that "[o]nce the Department of Defense makes a decision to order production of a certain weapon to certain specifications; reevaluation of that decision by contractors or courts is destructive to our government's ability to wage war."[43]

The modern form of the government contractor defense was created by Judge Pratt during the Agent Orange litigation.[44] The contractor must prove that the government established the product's specifications, that the manufactured product met the government's specifications, and that the government knew about the potential hazards to product users.[45] To Judge Pratt, all that was necessary for the defense to be employed was to show that the government set the specifications and the manufacturer followed those specifications.[46] However, the defense is more limited if the government merely supplies "performance specifications"[47] rather than a "specified product."[48] "Some Courts demand that the injury-causing aspect of the product be mandated by the specifications or the terms of the contract if the defense is to attach."[49] In *Johnston v. United States*,[50] four civilian aircraft workers sued the manufacturers of aircraft instruments constructed with luminous radioactive compounds.[51] The plaintiffs developed cancers allegedly caused by exposure to the luminous radioactive substances painted on the faces of the aircraft instruments.[52] The *Johnston* court found that the government contract defense was inapplicable, because the government specifications did not mandate the use of Radium 226.[53] "The court reasoned that the manufacturer should not be able to escape liability since it could have used a less dangerous compound."[54]

The government contractor defense should be eliminated since "between the government contractors and the injured servicemen, the government contractors are more able to afford the loss. . . . Furthermore, the contractors appear to be the more morally culpable party."[55]

IS ROUNDUP THE NEXT AGENT ORANGE?

There are similarities between Agent Orange and the latest feeding frenzy, Roundup herbicide litigation, since both are manufactured by Monsanto Corp. Agent Orange stopped production in 1972, and Roundup was introduced in 1974. Monsanto allegedly falsified data on the safety of Roundup. Ironically, Monsanto is now selling Roundup in Vietnam. Roundup litigation was centralized in the Northern District of California for purposes of MDL alleging that the widely used herbicide Roundup, could cause non-Hodgkin's lymphoma and that the manufacturer failed to warn consumers about risks. The World Health Organization now considers the glyphosate-based herbicide Roundup to be a "possible human carcinogen" and a cause of non-Hodgkin's lymphoma (NHL).[56] The legal wrangling has been intense, so far Roundup litigation has been allowed to continue. The Court held that plaintiff's medical expert opinion proving that glyphosate was a substantial factor in causing plaintiff's NHL satisfied requirements for admissibility.[57] Plaintiffs were also allowed to continue their claims based on failure to warn and failure to properly label risks from any foreseeable use.[58]

On July 15, 2019, the United States District Court for the Northern District of California held that the jury award for Edwin Hardeman of $3,066,667 in past economic damages was not excessive, considering the terror of being diagnosed with NHL, the uncertainty of his long-term prognosis, and debilitating effects of chemotherapy. Also, the award of $2 million in future economic damages was not excessive even though he was currently in remission. The court, however, reduced the jury's punitive award from $75 million to $20 million for a total award of $25,267,634.10. The Court concluded that although Monsanto's approach to the safety of Roundup was reprehensible, and that this jury concluded that it was more likely than not that Roundup caused Mr. Hardeman's NHL, the jury still has not determined whether glyphosate causes NHL.[59]

The tragedy of Vietnam was further exacerbated by devastating illnesses that mysteriously affected veterans and their families. Additionally, Vietnam nationals and their families were excluded from the settlement fund.[60] Legally, the United States with its sovereign immunity protection, which ironically means that "The King Can Do No Wrong," could not be a defendant even though they ordered the manufacture of toxic defoliants like Agent Orange and napalm ("sticky fire"), and then used them indiscriminately and negligently. The "research" for these toxic war crimes was partially completed with Army funds at American universities.

So, how do you achieve satisfaction for an egregious wrong that continues in your children? The veterans sued the manufacturers in a class action suit but were handicapped from the beginning because of the problem of the unidentified tortfeasor and the government contractor defense. The Agent Orange Settlement Fund was a great legal and social achievement but did not cover those who failed to show "timely" symptoms, and, of course, Vietnamese nationals.[61] The Agent Orange nightmare is perfectly characterized in Freda Wilcox's book title, *Waiting for an Army to Die: The Tragedy of Agent Orange* (Santa Ana, CA: Seven Locks Press, 1999). Agent Orange was described as "Vietnam's Deadly Fog." Paul Sutton, former chairman of Vietnam Veterans of America, ruefully reflected that "About a million and a half of us are already gone" (Chicago Tribune, 2009). The first lawsuit was filed by 28-year-old Paul Reuters, founder and chairman of Vietnam Veterans Against Agent Orange, who claimed his abdominal cancer was caused by Agent Orange. Paul appeared on the *Today Show* in Spring 1978 and prophetically stated that "I died in Vietnam, but I didn't even know it"—although his symbolic death was in Vietnam years earlier, his actual death was on December 14, 1978. Paul was a helicopter crew chief who flew behind the planes that sprayed Agent Orange.[62]

On August 9, 2019, Bayer Ag, who purchased Roundup, proposed to pay as much as $8 billion to settle more than 18,000 U.S. lawsuits alleging that its Roundup herbicide causes cancer.

Dalkon Shield litigation was another mass tort that involved defective contraceptive devices. As with Agent Orange, the manufacturer of the Dalkon Shield produced a dangerously defective product and targeted a specific demographic segment of the population, then lied about it.

NOTES

1. Kathleen Rogers and Heidi Kuhn, *Agent Orange and Millions of Land Mines,* Houston Chronicle at A29 (October 1, 2017).

2. Peter H. Schuck, *Agent Orange on Trial: Mass Toxic Disasters in the Courts*, p. 3 (Cambridge, MA: Belknap Press Enlarged Edition, 1987)

3. *Id.* at 16.

4. *Id.* at 17.

5. *Id.*

6. *Id.*

7. Lisa Toohey, *Compensation for Agent Orange Damage in Vietnam,* 13 Willamette J. Int'l L. & Disp. Resol. 287, 288 (2005) (footnotes omitted).

8. Richard Marcus, Book Review, *Apocalypse Now? Agent an Orange on Trial! Mass Toxic Disaster in the Courts,* 85 Mich. L. Rev. 1267, 1270 (April/ May 1987).

9. Deborah Henslen and Mark Peterson, *Understanding Mass Personal Injury Litigation: A Socio-Legal Analysis,* 59 Brook. L. Rev. 961, 1002–1003 (Fall 1993) (footnotes omitted). See generally Charles Krause and Alfred Gans, *Agent Orange Litigation,* 6A American Law of Torts 18:433 (Dec. 2017 update).

10. Hope Yen, AP, *U.S. to Pay Millions for Agent Orange Claims,* Washington Times at https://www.washingtontimes.com/news/2015/jun/18/opnewsbreak-u (June 18, 2015).

11. *In re "Agent Orange" Prod. Liab. Litig.* (Agent Orange I), 611 F. Supp. 1396 (E.D.N.Y. 1985).

12. Anne Bloom, *From Justice to Global Peace: (Brief) Genealogy of the Class Action Crisis,* 39 Loy. L.A. L. Rev. 719, 721–22 (Aug. 2006) (footnotes omitted). See generally Bruce Meyers, *Soldiers of Orange: The Administrative, Diplomatic, Legislative and Litigation Impact of Herbicide Agent Orange in South Vietnam,* 8 B.C. Envt'l. Aff. L. Rev. 159 (1979); Paul Sherman, *Agent Orange and the Problem*

of the Indeterminate Plaintiff, 52 Brook. L. Rev. 369 (1986); and Michael D. Green, *Expert Witnesses and Sufficiency of Evidence in Toxic Substances Litigation; The Legacy of Agent Orange and Bendectin Litigation,* 86 NW. U. L. Rev. 643 (Spr. 1992).

13. *In re Agent Orange,* MDL No. 38, Docket No. 79C-1195, Plaintiff's Third Amended Verified Complaint at 5 (E.D. N.Y. 1979). See also Sara Maurer, *Dow Chemical Co. v. Stephenson: Class Action Catch 22,* 55 S.C. L. Rev. 467, 471–72 (Spr. 2004).

14. *In re Agent Orange Prod. Liab. Litig.,* 996 F.2d 1425, 1430, 1433 (2d. Cir. 1993).

15. *Stephenson v. Dow Chem. Co.,* 273 F.3d 249, 255–56 (2d. Cir. 2001). See also Maurer, *Dow Chemical Co. v. Stephenson.*

16. *Dow Chem. v. Stephenson,* 123 S. Ct. 1261, 1262 (2003).

17. *Stephenson v. Dow,* 273 F.3d 249 261.

18. Maurer, *Dow Chemical,* 55 S.C. L. Rev. 467, 474 (footnotes omitted). See *Stephenson v. Dow,* 273 F.3d 249, 257–59.

19. *Id.* at 260–61.

20. *Dow v. Stephenson,* 123 S.Ct. 2161, 126–62 (2003). See also Kevin Bernier *The Inadequacy of the Broad Collateral Attack:* Stephenson v. Dow Chemical Company *and Its Effect on Class Action Settlements,* 84 B.U. L. Rev. 1023, 1028 (Oct. 2004).

21. *Winters v. Diamond Shamrock Chemical Company,* 941 F. Supp. 617 (E.D. Tex. 1998).

22. *Id.* at 619.

23. *Id.* at 621 (footnotes omitted).

24. *Id.* at 622.

25. Schuck, *Agent Orange on Trial,* p. 3.

26. *Id.*

27. *Id.* at 4–5 (footnotes omitted).

28. *Id.* at 5.

29. *Id.* at 49. See generally Francis E. McGovern, *Toward a Functional Approach for Managing Complex Litigation,* 53 U. Chi. L. Rev. 440 (Spr. 1986); Shira Scheindlin, *Discovering the Discoverable: A Bird's Eye View of Discovery in a Complex Multi-District Class Action Litigation,* 52 Brook. L. Rev. 397 (1986); Robert Rabin, *Some Thoughts of the Efficiency of Mass Toxic Administrative Compensation Scheme,* 52 Md. L. Rev. 951 (1993); and McGovern, *An Analysis of Mass Torts for Judges,* 73 Tex. L. Rev. 1821 (June 1995).

30. Susan M. Olson, *Federal Multi-District Litigation: Its Impact on Litigants,* 13 Just. Sys. J. 341, 341 (1988–1989).

31. *Id.* at 343 (footnote omitted).

32. Paul Rheingold, *The Development of Litigation Groups,* 6 Am. J. Trial Advoc. 1, 10 (1982).

33. *Id.* at 12.

34. Aaron Twerski, *With Liberty and Justice for All: An Essay on Agent Orange and Choice of Law,* 52 Brook. L. Rev. 341, 353 (1986). See generally *Procedural History of the Agent Orange Product Liability Ellen Tannenbaum, Litigation,* 52 Brook. L. Rev. 335 (1986); *Pratt-Weinstein Approach to Mass Tort Litigation,* 52 Brook. L. Rev.

455 (1986); and Michael D. Green, *Expert Witness and Sufficiency of Evidence in Toxic Substances Litigation; The Legacy of Agent Orange and Bendectin Litigation*, 86 NWU. L. Rev. 645 (Spr. 1992).

35. Schuck, *Agent Orange on Trial*, 6.

36. Mary Cathern Hensinger, *Agent Orange and Boyle: Leading the Way in Mass Toxic Tort Actions*, 65 Contemp. Health L. & Policy 359, 363 (Spr. 1990) (footnotes omitted). See *In re Agent Orange Prod. Liab. Litig.*, 506 F. Supp. 762, 768–69 (E.D. N.Y. 1980).

37. *In re Agent Orange Prod. Liab. Litig.*, 818 F.2d 187 (2d Cir. 1987).

38. U.S. Dept. of Veteran Affairs, *Agent Orange Settlement Fund*, https://www.benefits.va.gov/compensation/claims-postservice-agent. See also Harvey Bernom, *The Agent Orange Veteran Payment Program*, 53 Law & Contemp. Probs. 49 (1990).

39. William Blechman, *Agent Orange and the Government Contract Defense; Are Military Manufacturers Immune from Products Liability?*, 36 U. Miami L. Rev. 489, 491 (May 1982).

40. *In re Agent Orange Products Liability Litigation*, 506 F. Supp. 762 (E.D. N.Y.), rev'd, 635 F.2d 987 (2d Cir. 1980), cert. den., sub. nom. *Chapman v. Dow Chem Co.*, 454 U.S. 1128 (1981).

41. See Blechman, *Agent Orange and the Government Contractor Defense*, 36 U. Miami L. Rev. 489, 491–92.

42. *Id.* at 492. See generally R. Todd Johnson, *In Defense of the Government Contractor Defense*, 36 Cath. U. L. Rev. 219 (Fall 1986); Neil G. Woff, *Boyle v. United Technologies Corp.: A Reasonably Precise Immunity—Specifying the Defense Contractor's Shield*, 39 DePaul L. Rev. 825 (Spr. 1990); and David G. Owen, *Special Defenses in Modern Products Liability Law*, 70 Mo. L. Rev. 1 (Wntr. 2005).

43. Jonathan Glasser, *The Government Contractor Defense: Is Sovereign Immunity A Necessary Prerequisite?*, 52 Brook. L. Rev. 495, 499–500 (1986).

44. *In re Agent Orange Product Liability Litigation*, 534 F. Supp. 1046, 1055 (E.D. N.Y. 1982).

45. *Id.* See Glasser, *The Government Contractor Defense*, 52 Brook. L. Rev. 495, 506–7.

46. 534 F. Supp. at 1056.

47. *Id.*

48. *Id.* See Glasser, *Government Contractor Defense*, 52 Brook. L. Rev. 495, 507.

49. *Id.* at 49.

50. *Johnston v. United States*, 568 F. Supp. 351 (D. Kan. 1983).

51. *Id.* at 353.

52. *Id.*

53. *Id.* at. 355–59.

54. Glasser, *Government Contractor Defense*, 52 Brook. L. Rev. 495, 508.

55. Richard A. Rotin, *The Essence of The Agent Orange Litigation: The Government Contractor Defense*, 12 Hofstra L. Rev. 983, 985 (Summer 1984).

56. See *In re Roundup Products Litigation*, MDL No. 2741, 214 F. Supp. 3d 1346 (MDL 2016); *Id.*, Pretrial Order No. 1, 2016 WL 9276118 (N.D. Cal.) (Trial Filing); and *Id.*, 2018 WL 3368534 (C.D. Cal.).

57. *In re Roundup Products Liability Litigation*, 358 F.Supp.3d 956 (N.D. Cal. 2019); See also Testimony of Plaintiffs Expert Witness, Dennis Weisenburger, M.D.; and *In re Roundup Products Liability Litigation*, 2018 WL 8193838 (N.D. Cal. 2019) (Expert Testimony).

58. *In re Roundup Products Liability Litigation*, 364 F. Supp. 3d 1085 (N.D. Cal. 2019).

59. *Id.* 385 F. Supp. 3d 1042 (N.D. Cal., July 15, 2019).

60. See *Vietnam Association for Victims of Agent Orange*, 517 F.3d 104 (2d Cir. 2008) (essentially, government contractor defense banned state laws claims). See also *Supreme Court Won't Review Agent Orange Cases. Vietnam Ass'n for Victims of* Agent Orange vs. Dow Chem. Co., 22 Andrews Gov't Cont. Litig. Rptr. 4 (No. 23) March 23, 2009); and Lisa Toohey, *Compensation for Agent Orange Damage in Vietnam,* 13 Willamette J. Int'l L. & Disp. Resol. 287 (No. 2, 2005).

61. See generally, Harvey P. Bernman, *The Agent Orange Veteran Payment Program,* 53 Law & Contempt Probs. 49, 58 (1990); and Kristine Karnezis, *Construction and Application of Agent Orange Act of 1991,* Pub. L. No. 102–104, 105 Stat. 11. . ., 49 A.L.R. Fed. 2d 439 (original published in 2010).

62. *Waiting for an Army to Die?,* Agent Orange Record, http://www.agentorangerecord.com/information/thequestforaddit.

Chapter 6

Dalkon Shield Litigation

Judge Miles Lord categorized the Dalkon Shield IUD as a "Monstrous Mischief" perpetrated by A. H. Robins, Inc., who marketed a defective and dangerous contraceptive device for millions of women.[1] However, the patient brochure for the Dalkon Shield bragged that "Most women find the Dalkon Shield the safest and most satisfying method of contraception they have ever used."[2] Although IUDs these days are safe and highly effective contraceptives, previous generations of birth control users associated IUDs with dangerous pelvic infections and miscarriages. That's because the Dalkon Shield unfairly tainted the reputation of all IUDs since in the late 1960s and early 1970s there were no FDA or FTC regulations that pertained to contraceptive devices, but it was the Dalkon Shield particular "string" that was made with a material and by method that hasn't been used before or since, that made the Dalkon Shield particularly dangerous.[3]

By mid-1972, the Shield had a growing reputation for higher-than-average rates of failure and a substantiated linkage to pelvic inflammatory disease.

In October 1984, Robins set up a multimillion-dollar program to remove Shields from women who were still wearing them after all those years. Of the more than 400,000 lawsuits filed against Robins, 9500 were litigated or settled, and Robins declared bankruptcy in 1985. In 1986, it was estimated that 100,000 Americans still had Dalkon Shields installed in their uteruses. That same year, all but one IUD had been taken off the market due to the plummeting popularity of that particular form of contraception.[4]

A 37-year old woman became pregnant and died after her uterus spontaneously aborted. An FDA study showed 14 other septic abortions among women using the Shield; of the 287 septic abortions related to IUDs, 219 were Shield users. At the request of the FDA, Robins suspended domestic sales in June 1974. But the company continued to market the Shield abroad in 79 other countries. By the time Robins suspended sales, the company had been sued by 47 Shield users.[5]

CASE STUDY

On January 16, 1973, Carrie Palmer, who was then a twenty-four-year-old wife and mother, was fitted by her obstetrician-gynecologist, Dr. Kenneth Petri, with a shield. Palmer, who wanted to wait several years before having more children, chose this device as a birth control method on the advice of Dr. Petri and based on Robins' promotional materials describing the superior contraceptive and safety features of the shield. Dr. Petri had specifically relied on promotional claims made by Robins as to the safety and effectiveness of the shield in pre-scribing this device. After having been fitted with the shield, Palmer continued to use it as a method of contraception because, based on her review of Robins' promotional literature given to her by Dr. Petri, she believed the shield to be 98.9% effective in preventing pregnancy and safer than the birth control pill.

In August 1973 Palmer became pregnant. Dr. Petri, believing that removal of the shield might cause a spontaneous abortion, whereas leaving it in place could cause no harm, did not remove the device. Palmer's pregnancy progressed nor-mally until November 18, 1973, when she became violently ill with influenza-like symptoms. Within hours of her admission into the hospital, she suffered a spon-taneous septic abortion, an involuntary miscarriage caused by a blood borne bacterial infection centered in the uterine area. Palmer subsequently went into septic shock, a condition resulting from a massive infection with a concomitant fall in blood pressure to a dangerously low level. She also developed a blood disorder which impeded natural blood clotting ability. In order to save her life, it was necessary to perform a total hysterectomy in which her uterus, fallopian tubes and ovaries were removed. It was Dr. Petri's expert opinion that Palmer's uterine infection and the septic abortion were caused by the shield. . . . Palmer filed suit against Robins in December 1975.[6]

MULTIDISTRICT LITIGATION (MDL)

In 1975, a jury awarded a Shield plaintiff $10,000 in compensatory damages and $75,000 in punitive damages. By 1979, three thousand cases had been filed against Robins. . . . Most of these early cases settled for an average cost of $11,000. . . . Early in the litigation, federal suits were transferred to the Western District of Kansas for Multi-district Litigation processing. After substantial discovery, the MDL Judge transferred the cases back to the originating courts.[7]

Four years later, A.H. Robins again tried to form a mandatory federal class action for punitive damage claims. . . . During the period Robins faced sharply increasing numbers of claims and judgments and paid increasingly larger amounts to settle claims. . . . In order to limit its liability for Dalkon Shield claims, Robins launched a $5 million worldwide advertising campaign to alert potential claimants of the bankruptcy bar date.[8]

"In the Dalkon Shield MDL, there was a lead counsel who turned out to be the sole counsel with no committee to back him up on work or decision making."[9] "In the Dalkon Shield Litigation, lawyers [were] . . . witnesses before Congressional committees and . . . made presentations to the Food and Drug Administration relating to IUDs."[10] "[I]n the Dalkon Shield litigation, the manufacturer, A. H. Robins, voluntarily agreed to apply to the state court cases the MDL discovery taken in the federal cases. This again gave the defendant surcease from multiple discoveries. . . . Over 150 Dalkon Shield lawyers . . . participated in this state court plan."[11]

THE FDA STRIKES BACK

"The late Mari Aguirrez (not her real name) woke up on the morning of June 5, 1977, she was, at first, too drenched with sweat to feel the blood. . . . Dimly, Maria must have realized that the baby was already awake and fussing. He was still fussing an hour later when Maria's sister, summoned by the older children, came running in." Maria died as a result of the unsafe Dalkon shield.[12]

> The dangers of the Dalkon Shield IUD were well known before the dump began in 1972. Only a few months after the Dalkon Shield went on the market in 1971, reports of adverse reactions began pouring into the headquarters of the manufacturer. . . . In several cases, the damage was so severe as to require a hysterectomy. There were even medical reports of Dalkon Shields ripping their way through the walls of the uterus and being found floating free in the abdominal cavity far from the uterus.

The Dalkon Shield caused over 200,000 cases of serious uterine infections with 17 deaths attributed to its use.[13]

The Food and Drug Administration (FDA), in August of 1974, opened its hearings on the Dalkon Shield. "At that time, the FDA had little jurisdiction over medical devices like IUDs; they could investigate their safety, but . . . could not ban them from the market. Despite the FDA's lack of [actual] authority, the hearings were held . . . because . . . the carnage had become too gruesome to ignore." The overwhelming evidence at the hearings clearly undercut Robins' defenses in future product liability suits. "Only then did the company give up. Robins made no attempt to resume its domestic sales, suspended at the FDA's urging." Another devious aspect of the Shield was its dumping in "third-world" countries; this practice also ended with the capitulation of A.H. Robbins.[14] "Anyone . . . it doesn't even have to be a doctor—can go down to his basement, get a few hairpins, stick them together, and call it an IUD. There's nothing we can do about it until someone is injured or dies—Joseph Mamana, Chief of the FDA's Office of Medical Devices Compliance Section, as quoted in the *National Observer*, September 8, 1973."[15]

The problem was that IUDs were originally classified as "devices," not "drugs," an unfortunate distinction made in the Food, Drug, and Cosmetic Act of 1938, which was badly outdated by the end of the 1960s. Because of blatant carnage and zero oversight, the FDA was advised to reconsider their regulatory policy concerning IUDs. Without regulation, unscrupulous manu- facturers could have their way with fraudulent marketing, slipshod testing, and unsterile packaging and insertion techniques.[16] "[T]he IUD resulted in broadening the Food and Drug Administration's oversight of medical devices, brought needed transparency to physicians' conflicts of interests, uncovered a corporate scandal with a whistleblower that led to a major pharmaceutical bankruptcy, and involved 327,000 women (though only 195,000 met strict criteria for claims) in the largest U.S. personal injury case."[17]

Activist Judge Miles Lord of the federal district of Minnesota, while overseeing 23 Dalkon Shield cases in 1984, accused Robins of a corporate cover-up. He was concerned about reports that Robins executives had sup- pressed, lost, or destroyed internal documents that indicated that the Shield was defective. In 1984, Robins' former lawyer, Roger Tuttle, who had left the company 10 years earlier and was now a law professor at Oral Roberts Law School, came forward with confirmation that there was an organized cover-up in the form of highly incriminating copies of documents that he made before destroying the originals.[18]

Judge Miles Lord:

"Thou shall not steal applies to every corporate official who sells shoddy, dangerous, or unusable merchandise in the name of profit. Thou shall not kill applies to the corporations and agencies of those who are killing and maiming through industrial pollution. . . . They should appear [in church]with the same attitude of contrition and humility which accompanies every other sin."[19] Judge Lord consolidated all the cases for one trial and convened a jury of 28 people.

This expanded jury would first decide the question of liability, in other words, was A.H. Robins negligent? Then the jurors would be split into three groups to decide, case by case, if the Shield caused the women's specific injuries and, if so, how much each woman should be compensated. When all of the cases were concluded, the jurors would then join together and decide whether A.H. Robins should pay punitive damages as well.[20]

In his consolidation meeting on December 9, 1983, where he met with attorneys for both sides, he also announced that he would allow plaintiffs' attorneys to depose Robins' top officials about what they knew and when they knew it. Depositions began in January 1984, where one-by-one each executive claimed absolutely no knowledge of, nor any responsibility for the Dalkon Shield tragedy. Judge Lord ordered A. H. Robins to produce thousands of new documents in ten carefully detailed categories which were to be supervised by two special court masters to weed through the documents and decide which were privileged and which should be made available to plaintiffs' attorneys. Judge Lord's techniques produced results; by February 23, 1984, when the appeals court upheld his document production order, only two of the original 23 Dalkon Shield cases remained to be tried before Judge Lord, since Robins had gradually settled the cases since January. Eventually, on February 29, 1984, A. H. Robins agreed to pay $4.6 million to settle those two cases and another five cases represented by plaintiffs' lead attorney.[21] Judge Lord demanded that the three most senior A. H. Robins executives attend the settlement hearing on February 29, 1984; he personally reprimanded these officials:

> Today as you sit here attempting once more to extricate yourselves from the legal consequences of your acts, none of you has faced up to the fact that more than 9,000 women have made claims that they gave up part of their womanhood so that your company might prosper. . . . You've got lives out there, people, women, wives, moms, and some who will never be moms. . . . You are the corporate conscience. Please, in the name of humanity, lift your eyes above the bottom line.[22]

THE BANKRUPTCY OF A. H. ROBINS, INC.

> The A.H. Robins Co. filed for bankruptcy on August 21, 1985. Robins had been sued by approximately 16,000 plaintiffs; almost 9,500 cases were settled for approximately $530 million with 60 cases tried to a jury verdict in a 33 to 27 split favoring plaintiffs. Among the jury awards were two large judgments for punitive damages--one for $7.6 million and one for $6.2 million. . . . Robins desired to establish a close-ended fund to compensate those claimants who had not been barred. All liabilities from Dalkon Shield related claims would rest with a trust fund while the company could proceed unencumbered in its normal business operations.[23]

District Judge Merhige of Richmond, Virginia, took a two-pronged approach. "In August 1986, he appointed an examiner, former U.S. Bankruptcy Judge Ralph R. Mabey, to facilitate negotiations by increasing the total value of the company. . . . On July 27, 1987, Judge Merhige scheduled a hearing to estimate the total value of the Dalkon Shield related claims in accordance with Section 502(c) of the Bankruptcy Code."[24] "Judge Merhige conducted an estimation hearing from November 5 through November 11, 1987 . . . concerning the total value of pending claims . . . varied from $1.0 billion to $7.3 billion, with the second highest estimate at $2.5 billion."[25] From a litigation standpoint, the exposed corporate cover-up was the final blow for A. H. Robins Company's defense strategy. After the cover-up, more women filed lawsuits. Robins turned to bankruptcy as a strategy since it was still financially sound. A bankruptcy with reorganization could protect their remaining assets and prevent women with yet unknown problems such as infertility from filing future claims. Reorganization occurred and a $2.5 billion trust fund was established. As a result, Robins' stock increased four-fold and it was sold in 1989 to American Home Products (now Wyeth). Although this was a "successful" business tactic, injured women did not have their day in court, and individual claimants were paid less than $1,000. The settlement in no way adequately compensated those who were severely damaged both physically and psychologically.[26] However, the court concluded that the proposed settlement was reasonable, adequate, and fair.[27]

The Dalkon Shield is an American nightmare that continues today. It is a story of falsified marketing initiated by corporate greed, duplicity, and deceit, with A. H. Robins shielding its litigation costs to entice wealthy buy-out suitors—all for a profit.

> Despite Robins' knowledge of the septic abortion danger, it did not immediately alert the medical community to that danger. In October 1972, Robins revised its patient brochure, stating that "if a woman becomes pregnant while wearing a Shield, the bag of water pushes the IUD to one side and the developing baby is not really touching the devices at all." Also, as late as April 1973 Robins continued to advise physicians to leave the shield in place in the event the user became pregnant and desired the pregnancy to go to term.[28]

> In the fall of 1973 Robins had become aware that Dr. C. D. Christian, a professor of obstetrics and gynecology at the University of Arizona, was writing an article on the danger of mid-trimester septic abortions posed by IUDs, particularly the Shield. Subsequently, in February 1974, Robins called a conference to examine the problem. The conference led to a "Dear Doctor letter," dated May 8, 1974, to 120,000 doctors throughout the United States, warning them of the hazards associated with the Shield in cases of unplanned pregnancies. . . . Robins ultimately took the shield off the market in June 1974, at the request of the Food and Drug Administration.[29]

None of the previous feeding frenzies could prepare the consumer or the legal community for the litigation that is related to asbestos exposure. Most of the previous frenzies were limited to specialized usage of consumer products; asbestos, however, was deemed to be a miracle fiber that revolutionized insulation.

NOTES

1. Susan Perry and Jim Dawson, *Nightmare: Women and the Dalkon Shield* (New York: Macmillan Publishing Co. 1985).

2. *Id.* at 1.

3. Planned Parenthood Advocates of Arizona, *Instrument of Torture: The Dalkon Shield Disaster,* http://advocatesaz.org/2016/03/28/instrument-of-torture-the-dalkon-shield-disaster/.

4. *Id.*

5. Deborah Hensler and Mark Peterson, *Understanding Mass Personal Injury Litigation: A Socio-Legal Analysis,* 59 Brook L. Rev. 961 (Fall 1993) (footnotes omitted). See generally Gina Kolata, *The Sad Legacy of the Dalkon Shield,* New York Times at Sci. 1 (Dec. 6, 1987); and Carol Krismann, *Dalkon Shield Birth Control Device,* www.Britannica.com at http://www.britannica.com/topic/dalkon-shield.

6. *Palmer v. A. H. Robins Co., Inc.,* 684 P.2d 187, 196–97 (Colo 1984).

7. Hensler and Peterson, *Understanding Mass Personal Injury Litigation,* 59 Brock L. Rev. 961, 985 (footnotes omitted). See also *In re A. H. Robins Co., "Dalkon Shield" IUD Products Liability Litigation (No. 11),* 610 F. Supp. 1099 (Jud. Panel On MDL, 1985).

8. Hensler and Peterson, *Understanding Mass Personal Injury Litigation,* 59 Brook L. Rev. 961, 985-86 (footnotes omitted).

9. Paul Rheingold, *The Development of Litigation Groups,* 6 Am. J. of Trial Advocacy 1, 4 (1982).

10. *Id.* at 6.

11. *Id.* at 7 (footnotes omitted).

12. Mark Dowrie, Barbara Ehrenreich, and Stephen Minkin, "The Charge: Genocide. The Accused: The U.S. Government," *Mother Jones* 1–2 (Nov./Dec. 1979) at http://www.motherjones.com/politics/1979/1 1/charge-gynocide./2/.

13. *Id.* at 2.

14. *Id.* at 4.

15. As quoted in Perry and Dawson, *Nightmare* at 124.

16. *Id.* at 126-35.

17. Abstract from Clare L. Roepke and Eric A. Schaff, *Long Trail Strings: Impact of the Dalkon Shield 40 Years Later,* 4 Open J. Obstetrics & Gynecology 996 (2014) at http://dx.doi.org/1 0.423/ojog.2014.416140.

18. *Id.* at 1000.

19. U.S. District Judge Miles Lord in a speech before the Minnesota Council of Churches, 1981, as quoted in Perry and Dawson, *Nightmare* at 198.

20. *Id.* at 201.

21. *Id.* at 201–6.

22. As quoted in *Id.*, at 207–8. See generally Sheldon Engelmayer and Robert Wagman, *Lord's Justice: One Judge's Battle to Expose the Deadly Dalkon Shield I.U.D.* (New York: Anchor Press/Doubleday, 1985).

23. Francis McGovern, *Resolving Mass Tort Litigation*, 69 B.U. L. Rev. 659 (1989) (footnotes omitted); See generally Sharon Youdelman, *Strategic Bankruptcies: Class Actions, Classification & the Dalkon Shield Cases,* 7 Cardozo L. Rev. 817 (Spr. 1986); Georgene Vairo, *The Dalkon Shield Claimants Trust: Paradigm Lost (or Found)?,* 61 Fordham L. Rev. 617 (Dec. 1992); Georgene Vairo, *The Dalkon Shield Claimants Trust, and the Rhetoric of Mass Tort Claims Resolution,* 31 Loy. L.A. L. Rev. 79 (Nov. 1997); C. Gavin Shepherd, *Transvaginal Mesh Litigation: A New Opportunity to Resolve Mass Medical Device Failure Claims,* 80 Tenn. L. Rev. 477 (Wntr. 2013); and Kenneth Feinberg, *The Dalkon Shield Claimants Trust,* 53 Law & Contemp. Probs. 79 (Autumn 1990).

24. McGovern, *Resolving Mass Tort Litigation,* 69 B.U.L. Rev. 659, 680 (footnotes omitted).

25. *Id.* at 684–86 (footnotes omitted).

26. Roepke and Schaff, *Long Tail Strings,* 4 Open. J. Obstet. & Gyn. at 1001. *See* Linda Williams, *$2.4. Billion Dalkon Shield Payout Options Disclosed,* LA Times at 3 (March 18, 1990).

27. *Dalkon Shield Claimants, Inc. v. A. H. Robins Co., Inc.*, 88 B.R. 755, 763 (E.D. Va. 1988).

28. *Palmer v. A. H. Robins Co., Inc.*, 684 P.2d 187, 196 (Colo. 1984).

29. *Id.* at 197.

Chapter 7

Asbestos Exposure

Asbestos is known to cause cancer and yet it is still legal. Asbestos is one of the most effective insulation materials and was used for many years, in ships and homes; use grew steadily through World War II and peaked in 1974. However, it was generally unknown that inhalation of asbestos fibers can cause asbestosis, lung cancer, and mesothelioma. There is little doubt that exposure was widespread. Legally, sickened employees were barred from suing employers by the workers' compensation exclusivity doctrine, therefore, asbestos workers sued asbestos manufacturers for compensation. In 1973, the Fifth Circuit ruled that manufacturers could be held strictly liable for injuries caused by asbestos exposure. By 1992, an estimated 200,000 asbestos personal injury claims were filed or pending. Asbestos manufacturers countered by seeking bankruptcy protection.[1]

Harvard Law Professors Christopher Edley and Paul Weiler surveyed the legal problem of asbestos exposure in 1993—Federal and state courts are clogged with 100,000 asbestos suits and that number is rising every month. The primary early targets of asbestos litigation—the major suppliers of asbestos and asbestos-related products sixty years ago—paid billions of dollars in tort damages. Then, facing many more billions of dollars in prospective tort liability, more than a dozen major American corporations went bankrupt. "Former President George Bush . . . continually harped on a litigation Explosion they attribute to personal injury lawyers wearing tasseled Loafers."[2]

Barry I. Castleman in his epochal book, *Asbestos: Medical and Legal Aspects*, acknowledged that there was alarming evidence in the early 1930s that breathing asbestos caused asbestosis and cancer. But industry trade groups withheld this information although it was known by asbestos mining and manufacturers that asbestos was deadly; no warning labels were affixed to asbestos products until late 1962.[3] There was a delay in the public to fully realize that dangerous asbestos exposure stalled "public efforts to regulate the asbestos industry, compensate affected members of society, and ultimately conduct independent, thorough (animal inhalation, epidemiological, and pathological) studies to determine just how deadly asbestos was. The substitution of asbestos by safer material was likewise long delayed."[4] "Prior to 1970, the field of industrial medicine and hygiene was dominated by industry."[5] "However, most of this changed dramatically since 1970, with the enactment of federal environmental and occupational health legislation and the establishment of research agencies at the state and federal levels."[6] "The asbestos disease catastrophe of today resulted in part because of inadequate social measures to protect the public health. But asbestos is only one of many well-recognized, hazardous materials upon whose use the world appeared increasingly to depend."[7] The lesson that must be learned is to be diligent about potential health disasters and not ignore overwhelming evidence, even *if* the benefits of the allegedly dangerous product appear too good to ignore.

Asbestos Exposure Causes Cancer—The Environmental Protection Agency believes that a single asbestos fiber can cause cancer. The first recorded death due to pulmonary asbestosis was the unfortunate 33-year-old Nellie Kershaw of Rochdale, UK, who worked in an asbestos company and was diagnosed by her physician as "asbestos poisoning." She was denied both National Health Insurance and workers' compensation benefits. "By not acknowledging the possibility of asbestos–related illnesses, her employer lost an important opportunity to alert employers, factory floor supervisors, and management of the hazards of asbestos and seek effective controls."[8] The historic 1930 British survey of Disease in Asbestos Factories by Merewether and Price "studied workers . . . who were actively employed in the asbestos textile industry."[9] The survey also showed that at an early stage, asbestos might not be clearly recognized from chest x-rays.

> In summary, asbestosis was by 1935 widely recognized as a mortal threat affecting a large fraction of those who had regularly worked with the material. It was known that the disease process would not become evident for the first few years of exposure no matter how intense the exposure was. Yet slowly but surely, the lung scarring would develop as the mineral fibers accumulated in the lungs and had time to provoke the characteristic response.[10]

> The sudden change which has taken place in the conditions of life consequent upon the development of modern industry has been associated with a rapid increase in cancer mortality, and this rise is greatest where modern industry is most developed.[11]

The Metropolitan life Insurance Co. Report of 1935 indicated that "x-ray films were made of 126 persons (108 men, 18 women) working in asbestos plants in the United States. . . . The cases were selected at random from among those having more than 3 years of employment in the industry. In other words, 53 percent of the workers had asbestosis by a conservative reading of the X-rays, and another 31 percent had some X-ray signs or disease (doubtful)."[12]

> The carcinogenicity of asbestos was recognized in Germany in 1938. British and American authors contributed additional case reports and analyses and were expressing positive views on the association of asbestos and lung cancer in the 1940s. . . . Indeed, these autopsy studies comprised the earliest epidemiologic support for the relation between asbestos and cancer.[13]

Asbestos was originally "touted as a miracle substance—able to withstand punishing forces of fire, corrosion, and acid, while also versatile enough to weave into textiles, line automobile brakes, retard shipboard fires, and bind rockets together. In its most important use, asbestos was the designated substance incorporated in Navy warships to protect American seamen from fires caused by enemy bombers and submarines in World War II."[14] "In automobile brake work, the mechanic cleans the drums and wheels by blowing . . . [asbestos] the dust with a high-pressure air hose. The mechanic inhales this during the blowing procedure and again when dusting."[15]

In addition to primary reports of asbestosis in product users, abstracts, review articles, government reports, and medical textbooks, it became known that there was an asbestosis "hazard to insulators and/or asbestos product users where the hazard was described as breathing asbestos dust."[16] "The tragedy of asbestos exposure is that only after so much death and disease have occurred and been set in motion did industrial nations turn away from the use of asbestos. The opportunity to take direct preventive action by the establishment of and adherence to truly health-based standards was hardly given a chance."[17]

Castleman stresses, however, that there were always alternatives to asbestos insulation. "Asbestos was used in magnesia and calcium silicate insulations as a reinforcing agent in the finished product. . . . Not only were magnesia products disclosed in numerous patents using alternative fibers such as animal hair, mineral wool, fiberglass, wood, and cotton; but also, other types of insulation, such as fiberglass, vermiculite, and rigid glass, could have replaced asbestos-reinforced magnesia insulations."[18]

In *Tina Herford and Douglas Herford v. AT&T Corp., Bristol-Myers Squibb Co.*[19] Plaintiffs allege that Tina Herford's use of Johnson & Johnson's talcum powder for feminine hygiene caused her cancer on the basis that Johnson & Johnson knew that their product contained asbestos. Plaintiffs further allege that Johnson & Johnson baby powder is hazardous to the health and safety since the dangerous propensities of their product was known to defendants since 1930.

Plaintiff TINA HERFORD suffers from malignant pleural mesothelioma caused by exposure to asbestos from Defendants' Products. . . . As a direct and proximate result of the . . . conduct of Defendants. . . .

Plaintiff TINA HERFORD has suffered and will continue to suffer permanent injuries and future injuries to her person, body and health including, but not limited to, pain, discomfort, loss of weight, loss of appetite, fatigue, somnolence, lethargy, dyspnea, dysphagia, and other physical symptoms, and the mental and emotional distress attendant thereto, as Plaintiff's malignant mesothelioma progresses, . . .

"Bystander" Asbestos Disease—

We now recognize that the threat to life from breathing asbestos extends in some degree even to individuals only slightly exposed to the dust. We also know that levels of exposure insufficient to produce asbestosis can nonetheless cause cancer; moreover, the exposures that can cause asbestosis are not as great as once imagined. On the continuum of risk were, roughly speaking, the asbestos handing workers ("direct" occupational exposure), others who worked nearby but did little or no work with asbestos themselves ("indirect" occupational exposure), asbestos workers' family members (household contact exposure), and neighbors of sources of asbestos air pollution and solid wastes.[20]

Bystander asbestos disease can also be carried through air pollution. In a 1936 North Carolina investigation of textile employees, "the dust inside the plant was so thick at times that one could not see across the room."[21] "Some of the dust was sucked out by a few fans in the plant and drifted over to nearby homes."[22]

"The families of asbestos workers have sustained significant exposure over the years due to dust brought home by the workers on their clothes, shoes, hair, toolboxes, lunch boxes, and more recently, automobiles."[23] "Since the 1930s, it has been known that, even with low levels of exposure to asbestos, the lung defenses were inadequate to totally remove the inhaled fibers."[24]

The asbestos litigation was different from the standard manufacturing product defect liability case before asbestos, since asbestos affected an entire product line and users of the product, including miners, insulation workers, shipyard workers, brake mechanics, and school children. The Ford Pinto fireball created an obvious awareness of the potential for risk of defective, dangerous products. However, with asbestos, the feedback might be glacial, and exposure could take decades before the risk became apparent. The backlog of exposures and the disease gestation period ultimately created a wave of cases. Since any compensation paid is long after the initial exposure, the companies' incentives for safety is diminished. Companies were probably not fully aware of the extent of the cancer's hazards. The magnitude of the compensation may exceed a company's ability to pay. You can only cover risk exposure if these costs were anticipated at the initial exposure. Asbestos litigation exceeded the total financial resources of the asbestos industry. But the plaintiff must show that it is unreasonably dangerous, and that it was the disease's proximate cause. Mesothelioma is a signature disease that occurs only with asbestos exposures. But lung cancer is more problematic since there can be multiple causes, of which asbestos is just one of the possibilities.[25]

The ABA's Commission on Asbestos Litigation recommended to the House of Delegates that the American Bar Association adopt the "ABA Standard for Non-Malignant Asbestos-Related Disease Claims" dated February 2003; and that the American Bar association supports enactment of federal legislation consistent with the ABA Standard that would: (1) allow those alleging non-malignant asbestos-related disease claims file a cause of action in state or federal court only if they meet the medical criteria in the ABA Standard; (2) toll all applicable statutes of limitations until such time as the medical criteria in the ABA Standard are met. A federal jury awarded nearly $31 million on Jan. 23, 1991, in consolidated asbestos cases from the massive Brooklyn Navy Yard personal injury litigation.

> In the first verdicts made public in the litigation, the jury found for the plaintiffs in 52 cases and for the defense in 12, according to court records. . . [Cases] were consolidated into a federal-state litigation under Judge Jack B. Weinstein of U.S. District Court for the Eastern District of New York and Justice Helen E. Freedman of the Supreme Court for New York County. The suits alleged the plaintiffs' sole or principal exposure came at the Navy Yard, where battleships and aircraft carriers were produced during and after World War II.[26]

The personal injury suits alleged that the asbestos manufacturers failed to adequately test for potential dangers to consumers and for failures to properly label the product with appropriate warnings about the dangers of asbestos and ways to minimize that danger.[27] In *Borel vs. Fiberboard,* the Fifth Circuit concluded that a duty to warn attaches whenever a reasonable man would want to be informed of the risk in order to decide whether to be subjected to exposure.[28]

The massive asbestos litigation caused many of the manufacturers to seek bankruptcy protection. Johns-Manville was the largest manufacturer of asbestos–containing products and the largest supplier of asbestos in the United States. Johns-Manville filed for bankruptcy. The company had 16,500 outstanding asbestos-related claims for $12.5 billion in damages. The filing was unusual since its business was generally sound. In declaring bankruptcy, Manville used bankruptcy to control its burgeoning liability claims.[29] "The

Asbestos Claims Facility (ACF) and the Center for Claims Resolution (CCR) were organized to administer and arrange for evaluation, settlement, payment or defense of all asbestos–related personal injury claims against their members."[30] The asbestos litigation "picture is not a pretty one. Decisions concerning thousands of deaths, millions of injuries, and billions of dollars are entangled in a litigation system whose strengths have increasingly been overshadowed by its weaknesses."[31]

Asbestos cases

> [i]n major jurisdictions, are concentrated in the hands of relatively few law firms: on average, 20 defense firms and 3 to 5 plaintiff firms per site. Some plaintiff lawyers have multijurisdictional practices; many are members of a nationwide organization that shares evidentiary information. During the early phases of the litigation, the small size and cohesiveness of the plaintiff bar contributed significantly to plaintiff victories.[32]

By the 1930s, principal asbestos mining corporations and asbestos production manufacturers were aware that breathing asbestos causes potentially fatal pneumoconiosis. It was estimated that 131,000 deaths from asbestos-associated cancer occurred in the United States between 1985 and 2009. Deaths will continue to rise in all parts of the world and in the future from "bystander" exposure.[33]

The asbestos disease epidemic will continue worldwide. "In every industrial nation it has long been acknowledged that social order and welfare exists, because of the working man and woman. . . . [S]ocieties both East and West [must] take reasonable steps to protect the health of workers against a long–recognized, insidious threat to life. This menace had carried over from the workplace to endanger society at large."[34]

The next asbestos litigation cluster can be found in talc that is an active ingredient in Johnson & Johnson's Baby Powder. The plaintiff's bar argues that there was a failure to warn about the risk of ovarian cancer when used for feminine hygiene. Silicosis litigation was a derivative of asbestos lawsuits, but was unable to gain traction, and is mostly viewed as a failed feeding frenzy.

NOTES

1. Deborah Hensler and Mark Peterson, *Understanding Mass Personal Injury Litigation: A Social-Legal Analysis,* 59 Brook. L. Rev. 961, 962 (Fall 1993) (footnotes omitted). See generally Steve Gold, *Causation in Toxic Torts: Burdens of Proof, Standards of Reservations, and Statistical Evidence,* 99 Yale L. 376 (Dec. 1986); Michael Scadron, *The New Government Contractor Defense: Will It Insulate Asbestos*

Manufactures from Liability for The Harm Caused by Their Insulation Products?; 25 Idaho L. Rev. 375 (1988/1989); Alani Golanski, *Judicial Scrutiny of Expert Testimony in Environmental Tort Litigation,* 9 Pace Envt'l. H. L. Rev. 399 (Spr. 1992); *Injunctions in Mass Tort Cases in Bankruptcy,* Hrg. before The Subcomm. on the Judiciary, 103rd Cong. (1992); *The Need for Supplemental Permanent Injunctions in Bankruptcy,* Hrg. before the Subcomm. on Courts and Admin. Practice of the Senate on the Judiciary 103rd Cong. (1993); Christopher Edley and Paul Weiler, *Asbestos; A Multi-Billion Dollar Crisis,* 30 Harv. J. on Leg. 383 (1993); W. Kip Viscusi, *Alterative Institutional Responses to Asbestos,* 12 J. Risk & Uncertainty 147 (1996); Lloyd Tataryn, *Dying for a Living* (Ottawa: Denean & Greenley, 1979); Richard Solomon, *Cleaning the Air; Resolving the Asbestos Personal Injury Litigation,* 2 Fordham Envt'l. H. L. Rev. 125 (1991); Lori Khan, *Untangling the Insurance Fibers in Asbestos Litigation: Toward a National Solution to the Asbestos Injury Crisis,* 68 Tul. L Rev. 19 5 (Nov. 1993); Victor Schwartz, Mark Behrens, and Rochellele Tedesco, *Addressing the "Elephantine Mass" of Asbestos Cases: Consolidated v. Inactive Dockets (Pleural Registries) and Case Management Plans That Defer Claims Filed by the Non-sick,* 31 Pepp. L. Rev. 271 (2003); Mark Reeves, *Makes Sense to Me: How Moderate, Targeted Federal Tort Reform Legislation Could Solve the Nation's Asbestos Litigation; The Untold Story of Asbestos: Why it is Still Legal and Still Killing* (Emmaus, PA: Rodale, 2003) 323; Wendy Wagner, *Choosing Ignorance in the Manufacture of Toxic Products,* 82 Cornell L. Rev. 773 (May 1997); G. Marcus Cole, *A Calculus without Consent; Mass Tort Bankruptcies Future Claims and the Problem of Third Party Non-Debtor Discharge,* 84 Iowa L. Rev. 753 (1999); and ABA, Comm on Asbestos Litigation, Report to the House of Delegates 8–9 (Feb. 2003).

2. Christopher Edley and Paul Weiler, *Asbestos: A Multi-Billion-Dollar Crisis,* 30 Harv. J. on Legis. 383, 383-84 (Summer 1993) (footnote omitted).

3. Barry I. Castleman, *Asbestos: Medical and Legal Aspects,* 726 (Frederick, MD: Aspen Publishers, 5th ed. 2005).

4. *Id.* at 727.

5. *Id.*

6. *Id.*

7. *Id.*

8. Irving Selikoff and Morris Greenberg, *A Landmark Case in Asbestosis,* 265 JAMA 898 (No. 7, Feb. 20, 1991).

9. E. R. A. Merewether and C. W. Price, *Report of the Effect of Asbestos Dust on the Lungs and Dust Superstation in the Asbestos Industry,* H.M. Stationery Of. (1930), as quoted in Castleman, *Asbestos: Medical and Legal Aspects,* 11-12.

10. *Id.* at 33.

11. Edgar L. Collis and Major Greenwood, *The Health of the Industrial Worker* 160 (London: J. & A. Churchill, 1921), as quoted in Castleman, *Asbestos,* 4.

12. *Id.* at 26–27 (footnote omitted) (emphasis in original).

13. *Id.* at 113–14.

14. Edley and Weiler, *Asbestos,* 30 Harv. J. on Legis. 383, 387.

15. Mrs. Arthur G. McLeod, *Asbestos and Cancer (Letter),* 93 Canad. Med Assoc. J. 278 (Aug. 7, 1965) as quoted in Castleman, *Asbestos,* 451.

16. *Id.* at 322.

17. *Id.* at 299.

18. *Id.* at 385–86.

19. *Herford v. AT&T Corp.*, Compl. Case No. BC 646 (Cal. Sup. Ct., L.A. Cnty. Jan. 10, 2017).

20. Castleman, *Asbestos,* 429–30.

21. *Id.* at 433.

22. *Id.* (footnote omitted).

23. *Id.* at 437.

24. *Id.* at 443–44.

25. W. Kip Viscusi, *Alternative Institutional Responses to Asbestos,* 12 J. Risk & Uncertainty 147, 183 (1996).

26. *Federal Jury in New York Awards $31 Million in Consolidated Brooklyn Navy Yard Lawsuits, Verdicts and Settlement:* Toxics Law Reporter (BNA) (Feb. 6, 1991).

27. Castleman, *Asbestos,* 317.

28. *Borel v. Fiberboard,* 493 F.2d 1076 (5th Cir. 1973).

29. Frederick Dunbar, Denise Martin, and Phoebus Dhrymes, *Estimating Future Claims: Case Studies from Mass Tort and Product Liability,* 110 (Wayne, PA; Anderson Professional Books, 1996).

30. *Id.* at 111 (footnote omitted).

31. Deborah Hensler, William Felstiner, Molly Selvin, Patricia Ebener, *Asbestos in the Courts, the Challenge of Mass Toxic Torts III* (Santa Monica, CA: Rand Institute for Civil Justice, 1985).

32. *Id.* at viii.

33. Castleman, *Asbestos*, 725, 728.

34. *Id.* at 817.

Chapter 8

The Silicosis Bust

Vioxx is a drug that about 20 million Americans took between 1999 and 2004, but Merck stopped selling it after a clinical trial linked the drug to heart attacks and strokes in patients who used it for 18 months or longer. Company documents suggest that Merck scientists were worried about Vioxx's potential heart dangers as early as 1997. Vioxx is a manufacturer-initiated and controlled "feeding frenzy."[1]

In contrast to Vioxx is litigation involving silicosis, which at one time also engendered its own "feeding frenzy."[2] It has been alleged that the silicosis "crisis" was created by "'[m]ad-dog' lawyers, abetted by serial plaintiffs hunting for someone to sue at every, opportunity . . . [that] are allegedly killing research and development and leading multinational corporations to cower in fear."[3] Trial lawyers segued their successful techniques in asbestos lawsuits to silicosis. US District Judge Janis Jack found that plaintiffs were being recruited even though they likely had suffered no harm.[4] Silicosis was a publicity nightmare for trial lawyers.

In *In re Silica Products Liability Litigation*, Judge Jack engineered a sea change in how the plaintiffs' bar evaluates potential mass tort and class-action suits.[5] Judge Jack's decision had major repercussions on both silicosis and asbestos litigation, where cases often featured "many of the same plaintiffs' lawyers, doctors and even plaintiffs."[6]

About 60 percent of the silicosis plaintiffs had previously been asbestos plaintiffs, despite the fact that it is "extremely rare" for one to be stricken with both diseases.[7] The shift orchestrated by Judge Jack follows a lengthy period of plaintiffs' lawyers' mass recruitment of clients and subsequent settlement attempts with pharmaceutical companies.[8] Some critics claimed these practices led to numerous lawsuits involving "dubious claims," leaving less money for people who "were truly harmed" by prescription drugs.[9] The plaintiffs' bar counters that such arguments make it more difficult for those who have been "truly harmed" to hold the pharmaceutical companies accountable.[10]

SILICOSIS AND THE SPECTER OF ASBESTOS

Silica litigation involved personal injury suits filed by "workers who allegedly developed silicosis after being exposed to silica on the job."[11] "Some plaintiffs' lawyers appear to have modified their 'asbestos litigation kits' to address silica litigation."[12]

In a 2005 ruling, District Court Judge Jack noted that recorded cases of silicosis dated back to the sixteenth century, making it "one of the oldest recognized occupational diseases." Abrasive blasting, mining, quarrying, and rock drilling are all occupations that could expose one to silica. Judge Jack further noted that such "continued exposure is tragic, because while silicosis is incurable, it is also 100 percent preventable." This information provides the backdrop for the issue of immediate concern to her Court: namely, silicosis lawsuits, especially in Mississippi. In 2000, approximately forty plaintiffs filed silicosis claims in Mississippi courts. In 2001, approximately 76 plaintiffs filed silicosis claims in Mississippi courts. However, in 2002, the number of new Mississippi silicosis claims skyrocketed to approximately 10,642.[13] But, the silicosis claims presented in her courtroom did not "look anything like what one would expect from an industrial disaster."[14]

Given the large number of claims, Judge Jack surmised that the Center for Disease Control or the National Institute for Occupational Safety and Health would be involved to effectively respond to the silicosis epidemic. But neither organization became involved in the so-called crises.[15] "In short, this appears to be a phantom epidemic, unnoticed by everyone other than those enmeshed in the legal system."[16] A *Wall Street Journal* article reports that "[a]sbestos attorneys are using the same legal machinery to generate silicosis claims, relying on a huge network of chest X-ray screeners, medical experts and local labor unions involved in asbestos litigation."[17]

In "double-dipping," when lawyers file claims at multiple bankruptcy trusts on a plaintiff's behalf, the trusts are each told different stories regarding the origins of the plaintiff's illness, and the plaintiff ultimately collects from each trust. For example, Harry Kananian and mesothelioma. He met with an attorney before he died, who submitted different claims with special asbestos trusts, developing different stories about how Harry met asbestos for each trust. The firms collected $700,000 for Kananian's estate.[18]

The exposure of the Kananian scam began to bolster greater oversight by the courts. Judges looked closer at silicosis claims and the accompanying bankruptcies, which were described by a reporter as "cash cows for the trial bar." Commentators noted that the practice of plaintiffs' lawyers cashing in repeatedly for healthy clients "often leaves little for those who are truly ill."[19]

Bankruptcy courts also began to closely scrutinize "prepackaged" filings. Other judges, "perhaps inspired by the scathing silicosis opinion . . . of federal Judge Janis Graham Jack," began to demand more evidence that plaintiffs were truly ill.[20] The attorneys behind the rise in silicosis filings were summoned to appear before the House Oversight and Investigation Subcommittee.[21] Subcommittee members discovered important new details about how the legal community developed silicosis suits, including the possibility of "double-dipping."[22] "Although the hearing left many questions unanswered, it focused the silicosis scam investigations away from the doctors and onto those who were allegedly directing the doctors: The lawyers."[23]

JUDGE JACK EFFECTIVELY ENDS
ANOTHER "LITIGATION CRISIS"

In Schwartz and Lorber's letter to trial judges, they urged the judges to "avoid another litigation crisis" as they claimed to "have witnessed a new, marked increase in litigation against industrial sand manufacturers and . . . industrial minerals companies."[24] They accused the plaintiffs' bar of modifying their "asbestos litigation kits to address silica litigation."[25] The point is, however, that asbestosis really was a health care disaster, whereas silicosis lawsuits are part of an allegedly manufactured litigation crisis.[26] The asbestos nightmare was real and pandemic in certain isolated locations like Libby, Montana. A television review in the *New York Times* reported that the PBS production of "Libby" tells the story of how an entire town in Montana was exposed to asbestos for decades without its knowledge, resulting in an estimated 1,500 cases of lung abnormalities and how the W. R. Gravel & Co. knew the asbestos was there.[27]

As with asbestos litigation, defendants in silica cases argue that plaintiffs' attorneys recruit healthy clients by holding "mass screenings in which hired doctors review chest X-rays for slight lung changes that could indicate dust exposure. Some doctors have generated two separate reports for a single X-ray . . . one for asbestosis and one for silicosis."[28]

Texas federal Judge Janis Graham Jack effectively ended the "silicosis revolution" on June 30, 2005, with an extraordinary 249-page decision.[29] Judge Jack blasted nearly every one of the 10,000 silicosis claims in her court.[30] She also documented the fraudulent means by which lawyers, doctors, and screening companies had manufactured the claims.[31] "[T]hese diagnoses were about litigation rather than health care," wrote Judge Jack, stating further that the diagnoses were "manufactured for money."[32] In response to Judge Jack's comments, an editorial in the *Wall Street Journal* stated that "the trial bar revved up the same machinery for silicosis, an occupational lung disease that can be fatal but has been in decline for decades."[33]

As a former nurse, Judge Jack was at a loss to explain how a disease that leads to fewer than 200 deaths year in the United States could suddenly result in more than 20,000 claims from Mississippi and the surrounding areas. The judge accused the plaintiff's counsel of creating a "phantom epidemic" of silicosis,[34] effectively ending the disease as a legitimate cause of action. "So, what evidence of fraud did Judge Jack discover? . . . In many cases, the doctors never saw the patients, the people who did the X-rays were not radiologists, and one doctor performed more than 1,200 diagnostic evaluations in 72 hours. . . . Judge Jack blasted the lawyers [and] . . . charged that their 'clear motivation' was 'to inflate the number of plaintiffs and overwhelm the defendants and the judicial system."[35]

In June of 2007, a grand jury indicted a Houston-area lawyer and two employees of the Hartford Insurance Company, charging them with an alleged kickback scheme that involved millions of dollars already received from silicosis settlements.[36] After Judge Jack's decision in June 2005, reverberations were felt throughout the legal community.[37] In March 2006, the House Oversight and Investigations Subcommittee heard testimony from doctors who were singled out by Judge Jack for supporting 10,000 phony silicosis claims that she said had been "manufactured for money."[38] George Martindale testified that he diagnosed more than 3,600 plaintiffs with silicosis, also admitting that he did not know the criteria for a silicosis diagnosis.[39] As noted in the *Wall Street Journal*, the House testimony and its revelations were unprecedented.[40] Judge Jack's practice of permitting the defendant to extensively question the doctors who had diagnosed the alleged injuries was an unusual one.[41] One commentator noted that Judge Jack's "decision has had a major chilling effect on litigation involving both silicosis and asbestos, which features many of the same plaintiffs' lawyers, doctors, and even plaintiffs."[42]

THE MYTH OF THE "FEEDING FRENZY": A POSTMORTEM?

After Judge Jack debunked the so-called silicosis "crisis," the question remains whether the "feeding frenzy" phenomenon still exists. Professor Lester Brickman suggest that judges now "approach mass tort litigation with a healthy skepticism when mass claims have been generated by the type of litigation screening used in asbestos, silica, fen-phen and breast implant litigations."[43] In his article, Professor Brickman outlined the impact of asbestos claims in the 1980s that were paid out without requiring proof of injury or liability. Most of the 600,000 plaintiffs suffered no real symptoms or impairment. In reality, according to Professor Brickman, asbestosis is a "disappearing disease." Many states adopted "comprehensive asbestos litigation reform" packages, which combined with a victims' fund created by Congress to effectively remove asbestos from tort litigation.[44]

Another indication of the demise of the "feeding frenzy" was *In re Vioxx Products Liability Litigation*, in which the Eastern District of Louisiana denied the plaintiffs' steering committee's request for certification as a nationwide class of Vioxx users who claimed either personal injury or wrongful death.[45] Similarity, on September 6, 2007, the Supreme Court of New Jersey rejected a class-action lawsuit against Merck over Vioxx.[46]

Around the time of Merck's victory in *Ernst v. Merck*,[47] the plaintiff's bar took greater interest in other potential mass tort issues, such as the prevailing use of drug-coated-stents,[48] even though bare-metal stents are safer.[49]

Another potential mass tort involves Gardasil, a drug from Merck that inoculates young women against the human papilloma virus, which can cause cervical cancer.[50]

In 2006, the federal government and a respirator manufacturer agreed to a deal that would supply the United States with 60 million disposable masks to be used in the event of a terrorist attack.[51] Plaintiffs' attorneys soon claimed "the masks had defective designs or warnings" and were responsible for a new silicosis epidemic.[52]

In a 2006 newspaper editorial, a concerned writer pondered where the trial bar would look to next after the asbestos and silicosis claims began to unravel.[53] The author noted that a Rhode Island jury found three paint companies liable for creating a "public nuisance" by selling lead paint many decades ago, but this case did not prove to be effective in terms of creating a new area for mass torts.[54] Despite all this, it appears that Merck's successful defense strategy of refusing to settle any Vioxx claims has had a chilling effect on the creation of any other "block-buster torts."

In 2007, when a medical journal article linked Avandia, a popular diabetes drug, with elevated heart risks, both the pharmaceutical business and the lawyers that sue them sprang into action.[55] The manufacturer of Avandia, GlaxoSmithKline, bought full-page ads in the *Houston Chronicle* and other large newspapers, reassuring diabetics that Avandia was safe.[56] A few pages later, *Houston Chronicle* readers saw an attorney's ad soliciting Avandia users who wanted to sue.[57]

Having been through Vioxx, Fen-Phen, the Ortho Evra Patch and many other drugs before Avandia, the legal machine that sues over undisclosed potential drug side effects is well oiled . . . [including] Websites. . . . The Internet solicitations appeared instantaneously, the newspaper and TV ads running now, and at least two seminars are in the works to instruct plaintiffs' lawyers on how to handle Avandia lawsuits.[58]

The report, published in the May 21, 2007, edition of the *New England Journal of Medicine*, suggested that Avandia could "raise the risk of heart attack by 43 percent and of cardiac-related death by 64 percent."[59] After the study was published, Avandia's prescriptions and Glaxo's stock prices dropped sharply.[60]

Judge Jack's scathing response to the so-called silicosis crisis empowered and enabled Merck's Vioxx defense team. Judge Jack acted as if she was a member of the defense team—in fact, she questioned some of the doctors herself.[61]

The threat of "feeding frenzies" among plaintiffs' attorneys have been limited at least in part by Judge Jack's opinion and Merck's novel legal defense of Vioxx. The trial bar attempted to use their "asbestos-kit," for the newly rediscovered silicosis litigation crisis. Judge Jack made sure that this approach did not work.

However, it appeared that the plaintiff's bar might try again to use their "asbestos-kit" to recreate their asbestos litigation strategy with the Vioxx crisis. The difference here was the approach of Merck's attorneys. At first, Merck's strategy was thought to be extremely risky. But by not conceding cases and settlements, the plaintiffs' bar was unable to create momentum, even after the *Ernst* decision. Merck's case-by-case approach guaranteed that the Vioxx litigation would be slowed down to a snail's pace thus negating the possibility of "stampede justice." In the interim, the FDA Revitalization Act was passed, raising the possibility that the FDA was a silent, co-culprit with Merck behind the Vioxx scandal. The pace of "feeding frenzies" has slowed and the likelihood of future drug scandals resulting in similar action by plaintiff attorneys has diminished.

However, corporate greed and its acknowledged concealment of safety concerns will invariably create opportunities for trial lawyers, such as with the opioid epidemic. A precursor to opioid litigation is litigation against the tobacco industry and the acknowledgment that nicotine is a dangerous and addictive drug. The tobacco industry is constantly changing to ensnare younger clients, with vaping yet another marketing ploy to sell nicotine-based products. The plaintiff's bar will react to tobacco's most current legerdemain and initiate appropriate class-action lawsuits.

NOTES

1. Mark Stein, *Pain Relief,* New York Times at C2 (Nov. 5, 2005).

2. Paul Davies, *Class In-Action: Plaintiffs Lawsuits against Companies Sharply Decline—Court Rulings, Legislators Curb Asbestos, Silicosis Claims, Judicated Firm Cuts Filings—Questioning "Jackpot Justice,"* Wall Street Journal Al (Aug. 26, 2006).

3. Bill Straub, *The Gloves Are Off,* 42 T. L. J. 24, 26 (July 2006); see accord *In re Silica Prod. Liab. Litig.*, 398 F. Supp. 2d 563, 673-75 (S.D. Tex. 2005); Victoria Slind-Flor, *Judge Slams Law Firm in Silicosis Case: Multi-District Suit Created a "Phantom Epidemic," She Says,* 29 ABA J. eReport 1 (July 15. 2005).

4. Paul Davies, *Class In-Action, Wall Street Journal* A1 (Aug. 28, 2006).

5. 398 F. Supp. 2d 563.

6. Davies, *Class In-Action,* Wall Street Journal A1 (Aug. 26, 2006).

7. *Id.* "One doctor has made roughly 88,000 asbestos diagnoses over the years and diagnosed about 70% of the 10,000 silicosis cases that Judge Jack found fraudulent. Her ruling also prompted congressional hearings and state and federal criminal investigations," and *Id.*, generally.

8. *Id.* "Law firms reaped the benefit, often pocketing up to a third of any resulting settlement," and *Id.*, generally.

9. *Id.*

10. *Id.*; Melissa Shapiro, *Student Author: Is Silica the Next Asbestos? An Analysis of Silica Litigation and the Sudden Resurgence of Silica Lawsuits Filings,* 32 Pepp. L. Rev. 983, 1014–16 (2015).

11. Victor Schwartz and Leah Lorber, *A Letter to the Trial Judges of America: Help the True Victims of Silica Injuries and Avoid Another Litigation Crisis,* 28 Am. J. Trial Advoc. 295, 296 (2004); see, e.g., *In re Silica Prod. Litig.*, 398 F. Supp. 2d 569 (S.D. Tex. 2005).

12. Schwartz & Lorber, *Help the True Victims,* 28 Am. J. Trial Advoc. 295, 296 (citation omitted); Thomas A. Gilligan, Jr., *Silica Litigation from Both Sides of the Bar: Is Silica the Next Asbestos? The Defendant's Perspective,* 1 Mealey's Litig. Rptr. 19 (Jan 2003).

13. *In re Silica Prod.*, 398 F. Supp. 2d at 570.

14. *Ibid.* at 572 (for example, the asbestos crisis); see generally John G. George, *Sandbagging Closed Texas Courtrooms with Senate Bill 15: The Texas Legislature's Attempt to Control Frivolous Silicosis Claims without Restricting the Constitutional Rights of Silicosis Sufferers,* 37 St. Mary's L.J. 849 (2006).

15. *In re Silica Prod.*, 398 F. Supp. 2d at 572.

16. *Id.* at 572–73.

17. Susan Warren, *Silicosis Suits Rise Like Dust-Lawyers in Asbestos Cases Target Many of the Same Companies,* Wall Street Journal 135 (Sept. 4, 2003).

18. Kimberly A. Strassel, *Trusts Busted,* Wall Street Journal A18 (Dec. 5, 2006).

19. *Id.*

20. *Unbundling Asbestos,* Wall Street Journal Al (Aug. 21, 2006).

21. *The Asbestos Waterloo,* Wall Street Journal A12 (Jun. 10, 2006).

22. *The Silicosis Bar Association,* Wall Street Journal A10 (Aug. 2, 2006).

23. *Id.* See *Very Rough Justice,* Wall Street Journal A12 (May 22, 2006); *Litigosis,* Wall Street Journal A16 (Apr. 26, 2006); Strassel, *Trusts Busted.*

24. Schwartz and Lorber, *Help the True Victims,* 28 Am. J. Trial Advocacy at 296. See also Victor E. Schwartz & Leah Lorber, *A Letter to the Nation's Trial Judges: How the Focus on Efficiency is Hurting You and Innocent Victims in Asbestos Liability Cases,* 24 Am. J. Tr. Advoc. 247 (2000).

25. *Id.* See also Gilligan, *Silica Litigation from Both Sides,* 1 Mealey's Litig. Rptr. 19; Shapiro, *Is Silica the Next Asbestos?,* 32 Pepp. L. Rev. at 1014–16. See generally Griffin B. Bell, *Asbestos and the Sleeping Constitution,* 31 Pepp. L. Rev. 1 (2003); Andrew B. Morris and Susan E. Dudley, *Defining What to Regulate: Silica and the Problem of Regulatory Categorization,* 58 Admin. Rev. 271, 278 (2006); Victor E. Schwartz, Mark A. Behrens, and Andrews W. Crouse, *Getting the Sand Out of the Eyes of the Law: The Need for a Clear Rule for Sand Suppliers in Texas after Humble Sand & Gravel, Inc. v. Gomez,* 37 St. Mary's L.J. 283 (2006); Victor E. Schwartz, Mark A. Behrens, and Rochelle M. Tedesco, *Addressing the "Elephantine Mass" of Asbestos Cases: Consolidation Versus Inactive Dockets (Pleural Registries) and Case Management Plans That Defer Claims Filed by the Non-Sick,* 31 Pepp. L. Rev. 271, 278 (2003); Victor E. Schwartz and Rochelle M. Tedesco, *The Law of Unintended Consequences in Asbestos Litigation: How Efforts to Streamline the Litigation have Fueled More Complains,* 71 Miss. L.J. 531 (2001) (for more information on the asbestos and silica crisis).

26. Schwartz and Lorber, *Help the True Victims,* 28 Am. J. Tr. Advoc. at 332.

27. Mike Hale, *Hidden in Plain Sight, Asbestos Haunts a Town*, New York Times E2 (Apr. 28, 2007).

28. Warren, *Silicosis Suits Rise Like Dust,* Wall Street Journal 135 (Sept. 4, 2003).

29. See *In re Silica Prod. Liab. Litig.,* 398 F. Supp. 2d 563 (S.D. Tex. 2005).

30. *Id.* at 571–72.

31. *Id.* at 633–36.

32. *Id.* at 633–36.

33. *The Silicosis Sheriff,* Wall Street Journal A10 (Jul. 14, 2005).

34. *Id.*

35. Roger Aronoff, *A Dark Day for Ambulance Chasers,* http://www.aim.org/media-monitor/a-dark-day-for-ambulance-chasers (Aug. 17, 2005).

36. Mike Tolson, *Local Lawyer is Indicted in Alleged Plot for Kickbacks,* Houston Chronicle A1 (Jan. 28, 2007).

37. *Two Screen for Corruption,* Wall Street Journal A10 (Dec. 2, 2005).

38. *Silicosis Clam-Up,* Wall Street Journal A18, 19 (Mar. 13, 2006).

39. *Id.*; see also Kimberly A., Strassel, *The Great Asbestos Scam,* Wall Street Journal A18 (Apr. 10, 2006).

40. *The Asbestos Waterloo,* Wall Street Journal A12 (Jun. 10, 2006).

41. Lester Brickman, *False Witness,* Wall Street Journal A9 (Dec. 2, 2006).

42. Davies, *Class In-Action,* Wall Street Journal A1 (Aug. 26, 2006).

43. *Id.*; see Lester Brickman, *What Did Those Asbestos X-Rays Really Show?,* Wall Street Journal A9 (Nov. 5, 2005).

44. *Id.*; see also Davis, *Class In-Action,* Wall Street Journal A1 (Aug. 26, 2006); John E. George, *Sandbagging Closed Texas Courtrooms with Senate Bill 15: Texas Legislature's Attempt to Control Frivolous Silicosis Claims without Restricting the Constitutional Rights of Silicosis Sufferers,* 37 St. Mary's L.J. 849, 950–54 (2006); Shapiro, *Is Silica the Next Asbestos?,* 32 Pepp. L. Rev. at 985–86, 1015–19; Warren, *Silicosis Suits Rise Like Dust,* Wall Street Journal A18 (Dec. 05, 2006).

45. *In re Vioxx Prod. Liab. Litig.,* 239 F.R.D. 450, 452 (E.D. La. 2006); Associated Press, *Judge Denies Class Status for Plaintiffs against Merck,* New York Times C2 (Nov. 23, 2006).

46. Associated Press, *Court Denies Class Status for Plaintiffs Against Merck,* New York Times C2 (Sept. 7, 2007).

47. *Merck v. Ernst,* 2009 WL 1677857; Mike Tolson, *Vioxx Maker Notches Gains with Strategy; Merck Fights Each Lawsuit, But the Cost Run $1 Million a Day,* Houston Chronicle B1 (Nov. 28, 2006).

48. Barnaby J. Feder, *Newer Stents Pose Dangers, Two Doctors Say,* New York Times A22 (Oct. 12, 2016).

49. *Id.*

50. Stephanie Saul and Andrew Pollack, *Furor on Rush to Require Cervical Cancer Vaccine,* New York Times A1 (Feb. 17, 2007).

51. *Litigosis, supra* n. 23.

52. *Id.*

53. *Motley Legal Crew,* Wall Street Journal A14 (Feb. 27, 2006).

54. *Id.* (quotations omitted).

55. Mary Flood, *Drug Doubts Put Lawyers in Motion: Pharmaceutical Companies Also Move Quickly When Studies Hit,* Houston Chronicle B1 (Jun. 10, 2007).

56. *Id.*

57. *Id.*

58. *Id.* See Jeanne Whalen, *Shareholders Sue Glaxo Over Avandia Disclosure,* Wall Street Journal D7 (Jun. 13, 2007).

59. Flood, *Drug Doubts,* Houston Chronicle B1 (Jun. 16, 2007).

60. Whalen, *Shareholders Sue,* Wall Street Journal D7 (Jun. 13, 2007).

61. See *In Re Silica Prod. Liab. Litig.,* 398 F. Supp. 2d 563, 617.

Chapter 9

Tobacco Industry Litigation

The tobacco industry, in the guise of Philip Morris International, initiated a campaign to legally threaten "third world" countries, such as Togo, to ward off more stringent regulations on cigarettes, such as laws that require cigarette boxes to feature pictures of diseased body parts with warnings of smoking's health consequences. "[A] division of Philip Morris has threatened to sue the Australian government, alleging that the country's requirement that cigarette boxes not bear brand logos or imagery—such as the Marlboro Man—will reduce the value of the brand's trademark and intellectual property." However, the sad truth is that at least four Marlboro Men have died of smoking-related diseases.[1]

> There are about one billion smokers in the world, and they are mostly male especially in poorer countries. Worldwide, in rich Western countries, smoking rates have been decreasing since 2000, thanks to stringent anti-smoking policies, and the health benefits of this have been enormous. On the other hand, in low-and middle-income countries, the number of smokers has increased substantially.[2]

"The World Health Organization (WHO) estimates that eighty percent of all premature deaths from smoking—now about five million per year, and likely up to eight million in 2030—occurs in developing countries." "Handing out free cigarettes—now banned in the West—is still done in countries such as Nigeria, Vietnam and Lebanon. Sexy young ladies in Marlboro clothing give away free packets to young people."[3]

The following is the Tobacco Control Legal Consortium's July 2009 summary of the Federal Regulation of Tobacco, hopefully envisioning a sea change when on June 22, 2009, President Barack Obama signed into law the Family Smoking Prevention and Tobacco Control Act, which gave the FDA comprehensive authority to regulate the manufacturing, marketing, and sale of tobacco products.

The Act adds a new Chapter IX to the Food, Drug, and Cosmetic Act, governing the regulation of tobacco products and created a new Center for Tobacco Products to establish tobacco product standards. The FDA can now "regulate both current and new tobacco products and restrict tobacco product marketing, while also directly implementing provisions that will . . . restrict tobacco product marketing and advertising, strengthen cigarette and smoke-less tobacco warning labels . . . and increase nationwide efforts to block tobacco product sales to youth."[4]

In their July 2009 summary, the Tobacco Control Legal Consortium hoped that society would reap the beneficial effects of the Family Smoking Prevention and Tobacco Control Act. However, by September 6, 2013, they sadly concluded that the FDA exhibited a lack of progress in regulating other tobacco products. In a Dear Colleague letter the consortium reminded their colleagues that the FDA

> now regulates cigarettes, smokeless tobacco, and roll-your-own tobacco. But, shockingly, more than four years after Congress granted the FDA the power to regulate other tobacco products, the agency has yet to act: e-cigarettes, cigars, "little cigars," dissolvable products, hookah, and other products [e.g., vaping] remain totally free of federal regulation. This half-way approach is confound-ing state and local enforcement efforts and creating the false impression that unregulated products are safe.[5]

The U.S. Department of Justice (DOJ) in 1999 sued several major tobacco companies for fraudulent and unlawful conduct and also demanded reim-bursement for tobacco-related medical expenses. The district court judge dismissed the DOJ's claim for reimbursement but allowed the DOJ to sue under RICO (Racketeer Influenced and Corrupt Organizations Act). The DOJ insisted that the tobacco companies had engaged in a decades-long conspiracy to (1) mislead the public about the risks of smoking; (2) mis-lead the public about the danger of secondhand smoke; (3) misrepresent the addictiveness of nicotine; (4) manipulate the nicotine delivery of cigarettes; (5) deceptively market cigarettes "light"; (6) target the youth market; and (7) not produce safer cigarettes. In July 2005, the district court allowed health group organizations to intervene in the lawsuit for the purpose of indicating permissible and appropriate remedies. On August 17, 2006, Judge Kessler issued an opinion of 1,683 pages that held that the tobacco companies were liable for violating RICO by fraudulently covering up the health risks and for marketing their products to children. The judge concluded that defendants have engaged in, executed, and continue to engage in and execute, a massive 50-year scheme to defraud the public, in violation of RICO. The tobacco companies filed an appeal to the U.S. Court of Appeals. The court granted the motion, and on May 22, 2009, the three–judge-panel unanimously upheld Judge Kessler's decision to find the tobacco companies liable. The court upheld most of the ordered remedies but denied additional remedies sought by public health interveners and the Department of Justice. The court also found that the First Amendment does not protect fraudulent statements.[6]

STATE LAWSUITS

The states initiated lawsuits against the tobacco industry to recoup their losses for medical services, etc., caused by tobacco use. In the 1950s, cigarette tar was linked to tumors. The Tobacco Industry Research Committee issued a statement that cigarette products were not injurious to a person's health. In 1964, U.S. Surgeon General Report cited health risks associated with smoking. In 1965, Congress passed the Federal Cigarette Label and Advertising Act, requiring a Surgeon's General warning on cigarette packs. In 1971, all broadcast advertising for cigarettes is banned. In 1982, U.S. Surgeon General C. Everett Koop finds that secondhand smoke may cause lung cancer. In 1992, Wayne McLaren, who modeled as the "Marlboro Man," dies of lung cancer. Jeffrey Wigand, who was formerly the Vice President of Scientific Research for Brown & Williamson becomes a whistleblower. Most states file lawsuits to recoup the billions of dollars spent on treating sick smokers; states settle with the tobacco industry for large amounts; Texas, in 1998, settles for a record $14.5 billion.[7]

> The Master Settlement Agreement (MSA) is an accord reached in November 1998 between the state Attorney Generals of 46 states, five U.S. territories, the District of Columbia and the five largest tobacco companies in America concerning the advertising, marketing, and promotion of tobacco products. In addition to requiring the tobacco industry to pay the settling states approximately $10 billion annually for the indefinite future, the MSA also set standards for, and imposed restrictions on, the sale and marketing of cigarettes by participating cigarette manufacturers.

Over the years, the states have collected record amounts of tobacco revenue, but are spending less of it on tobacco prevention programs.[8]

BIG TOBACCO ON THE DEFENSE

A Federal Court has ordered Lorillard, Altria, Philip Morris USA, and R.J. Reynolds Tobacco to make this statement about designing cigarettes to enhance the delivery of nicotine: "Cigarette companies control the impact and delivery of nicotine in many ways, including designing filters and selecting cigarette paper to maximize the ingestion of nicotine, adding ammonia to make the cigarette taste less harsh, and controlling the physical and chemical make-up of the tobacco blend. When you smoke, the nicotine changes the brain--that's why quitting is so hard."[9]

The tobacco industry has attempted to fight back and the U.S. Supreme Court in *FDA v. Brown & Williamson Tobacco Corp.*[10] seems to agree with them. However, the Family Smoking Prevention & Tobacco Control Act (FSPTA) was signed into law by President Obama in 2009 and gave the FDA the ability to regulate tobacco products. It changed the scope of tobacco policy by giving the FDA the ability to regulate tobacco products, like it has regulated food and pharmaceuticals since the passing of the Pure Food and Drug Act in 1906. The FSPTA gives FDA comprehensive control on tobacco products including to regulate tobacco companies to submit an ingredients list; regulate tobacco companies to make public nicotine content; enlarge warnings on packaging; regulate use of terms such as "mild" or "light"; and create a Tobacco Product Scientific Advisory Committee to help inform the FDA on tobacco issues. The Center for Tobacco Products was implemented as a branch of the FDA, and, as such, banned flavored tobacco.[11] Ironically, Philip Morris supported the legislation since the Act, by significantly reducing the tobacco companies' ability to advertise, increased the marketing impact of top dog Philip Morris as the reduction only solidified its 50 percent market share.

Philip Morris doesn't give up easily. It says it has created a less toxic cigarette which it claims could save lives and eliminate smoking. "The new technology, called IQOS, consists of a tube that gently heats up sticks of tobacco instead of burning them. By using heat instead of flame, the company says, IQOS eradicates 90 to 95 percent of toxic compounds in cigarette smoke." "Fueling such doubts is the fact that many of America's leading health organizations and experts remain deeply suspicious of Philip Morris." "This is the company, they point out, that makes Marlboro—the world's best-selling cigarette—and misled the public for years about the hazards of smoking." "They are masterful liars. That's not an exaggeration—that's fact proven by decades of evidence. IQOS technology deliberately uses tobacco, unlike vaping machines, which use a liquid solution to deliver nicotine. Philip Morris scientists argue that for smokers to quit, you need to offer something with the same buzz and taste of tobacco."[12] Like tobacco, guns kill people. Also, like big tobacco, the National Rifle Association is a formidable lobbyist with deep pockets. Both fields have been fertile grounds for feeding frenzies, with the spate of pointless mass murders emphasizing the need for legal monitoring.

NOTES

1. Ryan Parker, *John Oliver Targets Cigarettes on Last Week's Tonight; Philip Morris Reacts,* Feedback at http://www.latimes.com/enterainment/tv/showtraker. la-et-st-philip-morrisiohn-oliver-20150216-story.html (Feb. 16, 2016).
2. Sybilla Claus, Premium Times Opinion (July 31, 2016) at https://opinion. premiumtimesng.com/2016/07/31/170.
3. *Id.*
4. Tobacco Control Legal Consortium et al., Federal Regulation of Tobacco: A Summary (2007), from TCLC's Facts sheets on the proposed Regulation of Tobacco products by the U.S. Food and Drug Administration: S. 625/H.R. 1108 (August 2007) at 2–3.
5. Tobacco Control Legal Consorting et al., Citizen Petition to U.S. Food & Drug Administration to Assert Jurisdiction over and Regulate All Tobaccos Products (Sep. 6, 2013) at 1. See generally M. Timothy O'Keefe, *The Anti-Smoking Commercials: Study of Television's Impact on Behavior,* 35 Public Opin. Q 242 (2001); Kathleen Mcleed, *The Great American Smoke Out: Holding Cigarette Manufacturers Liable for Failing to Provide Adequate Warnings of the Hazards of Smoking,* 27 B.C.L. Rev. 1033 (1986); Raymond Ganarosa, Frank Vandell, Brian Willis, *Suits by Public Hospitals to Recover Expenditures for the Treatment of Disease, Injury and Disability Caused by Tobacco and Alcohol,* 22 Fordham Urban L. Rev. 81 (Fall 1994); Ellen Wertheimer, *The Smoke Get in Their Eyes: Products Category Liability and Alternative Feasibility Designs in the Third Restatement,* 61 Tenn. L. Rev. 1429 (Sum.1994); William Pryor et al., *Report of the Task Force of Tobacco Litigation Submitted to Governor James and Attorney General Sessions,* 27 Columbia L. Rev. 577 (1996–1997); W. Kip Viscusi, *The Governmental Composition of the Insurance Cost of Smoking,* 42 J. L. & Econ. 575 (Oct. 1999); Gary T. Schwarz, *Cigarette Litigation's Offspring Controversial Products in Light of the Tobacco Wars,* 27 Pepp. L. Rev. 751 (2000); and Anthony Sebok, *Pretext, Transparency and Motive in Mass Restitution Litigation,* 57 Vand. L. Rev. 21 77 (Nov. 2004).
6. *United States v. Philip Morris,* 499 F. Supp. 2d 1 (D.D.C. 2006).
7. Frontline, PBS, *Inside the Tobacco Deal,* https://www.pbs.org./wgbh/pages/ frontline/shows/settlement.timelines/fullindex.html. See generally Donald Garner, *Cigarettes and Welfare Reform,* 26 Emory L. J. 269 (1977); Johnathan Massey, *The Florida Tobacco Law: Fairy Tale Objections to a Reasonable Solution to Florida's Medicaid Crisis,* 46 Fla. L. Rev. 591 (Sept. 1994); Kevin Warsh, *Corporate Spinoffs and Mass Tort Liability,* 1995 Colum. Bus. L. Rev. 675 (1995); Jana Schrink *Settlement, Its Implications for Public Health Policy—An Executive Summary of a Conference at the University of Wisconsin Law School,* 22 5 Ill. U. L. J. 705 (Spr. 1998); Richard Daynard and Graham Kelden, *The Many Virtues of Tobaccos Litigation. In the Failed Global Settlement, the Tobacco Industry Almost Freed Itself from the Civil Justice System,* 34 Trial 34 (Nov. 1998); Doug Rendleman, *Common Law Restitution in the Mississippi Tobacco Settlement; Did the Smoke Get in Their Eyes,* 33 Ga. L. Rev. 847 (Spr. 1999); Gary Wilson and Jason Gillmer, *Minnesota's Tobacco Case: Recovering Damages without Individual Proof of Reliance under*

Minnesota's Consumer Protection Statutes, 25 Wm. Mitchell L. Rev. 507 (1999); and Michael DeBow, *The State Tobacco Litigation and the Separation of Powers in State Governments: Repairing the Damages,* 31 Seton Hall L. Rev. 563 (2001).

8. Public Health Law Center, *Master Settlement Agreement,* http://www.public healthlawcenter.org/topics/tobacco-control-litigation/mastersettlementagreement.

9. *Id.*

10. *FDA v. Brown & Williamson Tobacco Corp.,* 120 S.Ct. 1291, 1294 (2000).

11. Family Smoking Prevention & Tobacco Control Act, P.L. 111–31, Title 21 U.S.C. §301: Food and Drugs.

12. William Wan, Wash. Post, *Big Tobacco Touts New Cigarette Technology. Company: Product Eliminates Majority of Toxins from Smoke,* Houston Chronicle at A5 (Aug. 13, 2017).

Chapter 10

Lawyers, Guns, and Money

America is still reeling from the senseless murder of 17 students and faculty at Marjory Stoneman Douglas High School in Parkland, Florida, on February 14, 2018. The shooter, 19-year-old Nikolas Cruz, was an expelled student who used an AR-15, a semiautomatic assault rifle, to kill and wound defenseless students. Unlike Columbine, he was quietly captured and will stand trial for capital murder. The Parkland survivors have aggressively challenged legislators to ban semiautomatic weapons and bump stocks, which turn semiautomatic weapons into automatic weapons. "Never Again MSD" is a rallying cry for gun control and the elimination of the sale of assault rifles. Mass shootings can be another potential feeding frenzy.[1]

There have been many lawsuits and class actions against gun manufacturers based on product liability. However, the gun lobby, especially the National Rifle Association (NRA) has vigorously fought against these lawsuits and all attempts to regulate the sale and use of any firearm based on the Second Amendment to the U.S. Constitution and the so-called right to bear arms. Attorney Stuart Speiser laments the failure of American lawyers to effectuate product safety for handguns that their owners intend to use as instruments of deliberate harm. "There are of course laws against shooting people with guns. But it is obvious that these laws are not furnishing a deterrent enough to keep America from becoming a shooting gallery, with all of our citizens serving as targets for an army of illegal gun users." Although there has been some gun control legislation, the gun lobby has always been too powerful to permit effective regulation.[2] Attorney Speiser sees the problem as a fatal flaw in the distribution chain and a natural effect of corporate greed. Strict product liability should be extended to the entire chain of distribution, including distributors, wholesalers, importers, dealers, retailers, and trade associations. "If handgun manufacturers could be sued directly by gunshot victims where the gun was bought by an obviously irresponsible person, and where it could be shown that the manufacturer did not take reasonable steps to prevent the distribution of his guns to such persons . . . and, the victims of illegal shootings would be compensated . . . through liability insurance and later by the gun manufacturers themselves."[3] Another relevant question is whether some guns are good *only* for murder. It is undisputed that the United States has more firearms in civilian hands than any other nation.[4]

GUN CONTROL

"The AR-15 rifle has become known as the powerful weapon used by a number of gunmen to slaughter scores of people in Newtown, San Bernardino, Las Vegas, Parkland, and beyond. This style of rifle was designed originally for troops to kill enemy fighters. The gun fires a small-caliber, high-velocity bullet that can cause especially damaging soft tissue wounds."[5]

While being stared down from the gallery by surviving Marjory Stoneman Douglas High School students, the Florida State Senate voted to approve a two-year moratorium on sales of AR-15 semiautomatic rifles, going far beyond the gun-related measures that Republican legislative leaders said they would consider. But that two-year moratorium lasted only 15 minutes. It had been approved by a voice vote, and opponents quickly insisted on reconsidering it. In the rare Saturday session, the Senate debated a Republican-sponsored bill that would raise the minimum age to purchase a firearm to 21 from 18; mandate a three-day waiting period for most gun purchases; ban bump stocks, which enable semiautomatic rifles to fire much faster; and set up a voluntary program to arm trained schoolteachers and pay them a stipend to participate. The Democrats lost. As a result, Democrats managed to get just one amendment passed; adding 12 hours of required diversity training for participants in the program to arm teachers.[6]

"Every constitutional right that we hold dear has a limitation," Democratic Sen. Gary Farmer said. "These are just military-style killing machines and the right of self-defense and the ability to hunt will go on." Republicans argued that banning such weapons would violate the Second Amendment right to bear arms.[7]

Surprisingly, Florida signed into law on March 9, 2018, the Marjory Stoneman Douglas Public Safety Act which established new firearm regulations and created a program for arming some school employees in a rare show of compromise by Republicans on gun control in the wake of the Parkland massacre. The new law imposes a three-day waiting period for most purchases of long guns and raises the minimum age for purchasing these weapons to twenty-one. The legislation also includes millions of dollars to arm some school employees and a ban on the possession and sale of bump stocks, which can make guns shoot with the speed of automatic weapons. The act would temporarily allow the state to remove weapons from people who are deemed to be a risk and initiate a new judicial process to remove guns and ammunition from people who are determined to be a threat to themselves or to others.[8]

The preeminent force against gun control is the NRA, which is a virtual subsidiary of the gun industry. The NRA was founded in 1871—some call it a terrorist organization for advocating the widespread distribution and sale of assault-style weapons. It is the best-funded lobbyist organization in the United States. Dr. Frank Ochberg, a professor in psychiatry at Michigan State University, and a leading expert on PTSD asserts that "we have obviously failed on guns. . . . 'Good people have tried to do good things, but no policy has been enacted to reduce access of military weapons to kids,' he said. 'No leader has the guts to take on the NRA.' Nor has its own membership."[9] President Trump, however, while talking to lawmakers, said he was willing to take on the NRA: "They have great power over you people, they have less power over me." But, of course, he blinked and changed his mind, asserting that his administration would leave it to the states to set an age limit for purchasing assault rifles.[10]

In a *New York Times* editorial, it was noted that lawmakers are facing "intense public pressure to break their decades-long gridlock on gun control, a demand fortified by a bipartisan group of governors calling for Congress to take action to protect against mass shootings." Parkland students have become overnight gun control advocates and media fixtures.[11]

Florida is known as the Gunshine State, and "few places have seen the National Rifle Association wield its might more effectively than in Florida. . . . [T]he NRA derives its political influence . . . from a muscular electioneering machine, fueled by tens of millions of dollars' worth of campaign ads and voter-guide mailings, that scrutinizes candidates for their views on guns and propels members to the polls. . . When candidates waver in their support for sweeping gun rights, the group does not hesitate to turn on them."[12]

In 1994, Congress passed a ban on assault weapons. "At the time, school shootings were still seen as an anomaly, and the ban proved to be short-lived; it expired exactly 10 years later, in accordance with a sunset provision that had been a key condition for its original passage. Left for dead, proposals for a new ban on semiautomatic military-style rifles like the AR-15 that was used in the Valentine's Day school shooting in Parkland, Fla., are suddenly back in the national conversation. Marjory Stoneman Douglas High school shooting survivor Samuel Zeif, one of several victims, and school officials who met with President Donald Trump, summed up the current sentiment: "I don't understand how I can walk into a store and buy a weapon of war"; said Zeif, an 18-year-old senior who lost his best friend in the shooting rampage."[13]

California U.S. Sen. Dianne Feinstein, a Democrat who was the architect of the 1994 ban, "called for a new iteration of her long-stalled bill restricting assault weapons. 'From Aurora to Sandy Hook, San Bernardino to Las Vegas, Sutherland Springs to Parkland, one common thread that runs through mass shootings is the use of the AR-15 military-style assault weapons,' she said. 'These weapons are designed to kill the greatest number of people in the shortest time, and we need to get these weapons of war off our streets.'"[14]

"The rampage at Sandy Hook Elementary School in Newton, Conn., which killed 20 children and six educators in 2012, spurred Connecticut lawmakers to draft some very tough gun measures. Connecticut expanded an existing ban on the sale of assault weapons, prohibiting the sale of higher-capacity magazines and registering existing assault rifles. Individuals admitted to psychiatric hospitals must relinquish their guns, at least temporarily; also, the Department of Mental Health and Addiction Services must be notified to ensure that the gun owner turns in or transfers the weapon. Additionally, former mental patients are not eligible for a gun permit for at least two years after release."[15]

COLUMBINE, SANDY HOOK, AND PARKLAND

The tragedy of Columbine High School on April 20, 1999, introduced to the world a "terrifying affliction [that] had infested America's small towns and suburbs . . . the school shooter."[16] Thirteen students were gunned down by two other students who then killed themselves. The nation asked why?—and the answer inexplicably appeared to be Marilyn Manson and Goths. Interestingly, in Michael Moore's excellent documentary *Bowling for Columbine*, Marilyn Manson was interviewed for the film and was asked what he would say to the killers if he had a chance to talk to them. His answer was that "I wouldn't say a single word to them, I would listen to what they have to say, and that's what no one did."[17]

On December 14, 2012, twenty children and six adult staff members at Sandy Hook Elementary School were gunned down by 20-year-old Adam Lanza who used his recently murdered (by him) mother's Bushmaster AR-15-style semiautomatic rifle. Adam killed his mother first. After killing 27 people, he killed himself, because of a deteriorating internalized mental health and easy access to a semiautomatic weapon. He shot 156 rounds in less than five minutes. Lanza downloaded Columbine videos. The estate of his mother, Nancy Lanza, was sued for allowing her mentally imbalanced son access to her guns. Additionally, suits were filed against the Newton Board of Education and Remington Arms for manufacturing the Bushmaster AR-15 style rifle.[18]

The alleged shooter at Marjory Stoneman Douglas High School, Nikolas Cruz, 19, was a former student who boasted that "I'm going to be a professional school shooter." The *New York Times* on February 21, 2018, ran a full two-page indictment by Moms Demand Action for Gun Sense in America and Everytown for Gun Safety with the names, phone numbers, and NRA money funding of members of Congress with the admonition that "THESE MEMBERS OF CONGRESS TAKE NRA MONEY. BUT REFUSE TO TAKE ACTION TO PASS GUN SAFETY LEGISLATION. TELL YOUR MEMBER OF CONGRESS THAT YOUR VOTE IS GOING ELSEWHERE UNLESS THEY ACT." The piece began with a call to action by a Parkland School shooting survivor—"We're children. You guys are the adults . . . get something done," followed by the iconic photograph of the students walking in line with their hands on the student in front of them and their shadows reflected on the school's wall.[19]

A recently expelled and heavily armed Nikolas Cruz entered the Marjory Stoneman Douglas High School on February 14, 2018, shortly before classes let out and killed 17 people while terrified students barricaded themselves inside classrooms. Cruz was kicked out for "disciplinary reasons." He carried countless magazines and an AR-15 rifle.[20] "Cruz carried a black duffel bag and black backpack, and arrived at the school in an Uber at 2:19 p.m. He pulled out his AR-15 rifle and shot people in the hallways and five classrooms. After discarding the rifle, he blended in with other students and walked to a Walmart and stopped at a McDonald's. The police arrested him on a residential street at 3:41 p.m."[21]

Cruz was violent and unstable, but when notified of his violent behavior, law enforcement did little to ameliorate his dangerous tendencies. Cruz's mother died in November 2017; after that he stayed on a couch at a suburban Palm Beach mobile home of a friend, who gave him an ultimatum—either you go, or your gun goes. He chose the gun. His Broward County Public Defender, Howard Finkelstein, said that Cruz "exhibited every single known red flag from cutting animals to having a cache of weapons to disruptive behavior to saying he wanted to be a school shooter."[22]

The surviving students' activism is focused on fighting for change: "They have won praise for their strength and eloquence on the world's stage. But even as they raise millions of dollars and plan nationwide rallies . . . and spar with politicians and conservative critics, the young survivors . . . are struggling with the loss of their friends and educators and the nightmares that flood back in moments of stillness."[23]

The students returned to Marjory Stoneman Douglas High School on February 28, 2018. The survivors created the #douglasstrong movement.[24] The sheriff's deputy, Scott Peterson, who was assigned as the school resource officer on February 14, 2018, did not enter the school to confront Cruz since he decided that the gunfire came from outside the school. Although he was called a coward, it can be argued that Peterson was only following his training by seeking cover and taking up tactical position, campus lockdown.[25]

Civil lawsuits have been filed as an aftermath to the massacre at the First Baptist Church in Sutherland Springs, Texas, on November 5, 2017, which killed 26 people, and left 20 injured. Relatives of victims filed wrongful death civil claims "against the Air Force for failing to tell the FBI about the shooter's criminal history—an error that allowed him to buy guns from licensed dealers. The Air Force confirmed . . . that it never reported gunman Devin Kelley's 2012 convictions for spousal and child abuse to civilian law enforcement authorities."[26]

In the Marjory Stoneman Douglas murders, wrongful death suits will be based on the alleged negligence of the sheriff's department, the FBI, the Uber driver, and the school district. As a result of the Parkland massacre, the NRA is boycotted by major corporations such as airlines and car rentals. The #BoycottNRA movement exposes the vulnerability of the NRA which seemed impossible before February 14, 2018.[27] Also, First National Bank, the nation's largest privately-owned bank holding company, will stop producing credit cards for the NRA, in response to customer feedback.[28]

The Parkland massacre became a movement that focuses on gun control. Emma Gonzalez, a student at Marjory Stoneman Douglas spoke that "we are going to be the kids you read about in textbooks. Not because we're going to be another statistic about mass shooting in America, but because . . . we are going to be the last mass shooting. Just like *Tinker v. Des Moines*, we are going to change the law. That's going to be Marjory Stoneman Douglas in that textbook, and it's going to be due to the tireless effort of the school board, the faculty members, the family members and, most of all, the students. The students who are dead, the students still in the hospital, the students now suffering PTSD, the students who had panic attacks during the vigil because the helicopters would not leave us alone. . . ."[29]

The MSD students seek to reverse this nation's firearms insanity, like the civil rights movement. The students' fierce determination and moral urgency might just make a difference. "What if the horror they experienced firsthand and their unrelenting grief, anger and frustration fuels a movement that endures? What if images of young pallbearers carrying a beloved teacher and coach to his final resting place, a young man with tears in his eyes pleading with President Trump to help end the madness, a strong, young woman with cropped hair and determination in her voice vowing to continue the fight—what if those powerful images become a galvanizing force?"[30]

Emma Gonzalez is a student leader who has 1.2 million twitter followers. The students are in command of their own stories. "With their consistent tweeting of stories, memos, jokes and video clips, the students have managed to keep the tragedy that their school experienced—and their plan to stop such shootings from happening elsewhere—in the news for weeks, long after past mass shootings have faded from the headlines." On March 9, 2018, their persistent reminders of the tragedy paid off when Governor Rick Scott of Florida signed an array of gun limits into law.[31] This is an unprecedented grass roots movement that has seriously impinged on the NRA's once imperial death grip on gun control. It is a sea-change. Semiautomatic weapons with bump stocks murdered 58 country and western fans in Las Vegas and 22 people in an El Paso Walmart. These weapons are military weapons and inappropriate for civilian life. Mass shootings, sadly, are mass catastrophes like Lockerbie, Katrina, Harvey, and Ethiopian Airlines Flight 302. It is the job of personal injury lawyers to seek redress from negligent defendants.

NOTES

1. See Marjory Stoneman Douglas High School Public Safety Commission, Initial Report Submitted to the Governor, Speaker of the House of Representatives and Senate President (Jan. 1, 2019); Sarah Lerner, MSD teacher, ed., *Parkland Speaks. Survivors from Marjory Stoneman Douglas Share Their Stories* (New York: Crown, 2019); and *L.S. v. Peterson*, 2018 U.S. Dist. LEXIS 210273 (S.D. Fla.) (MSD *Students versus Broward County*).

2. Stuart Speiser, *Lawsuit*, 369 (New York: Horizon Press, 1980). See generally Gary Kleck, *Point Blank, Guns and Violence in America* (New York: Aldine de Gruyter, 1997). For material on our violent society, see generally Hugh Graham & Ted Gurr, eds., *Violence in America. Historical and Comparative Perspectives* (Beverly Hills: Sage Pub., rev. ed., 1979); James Dick, *Violence and Oppression* (Athens, GA: University of Georgia Press, 1979); Jeffrey Goldstein, *Aggression and Crimes of Violence* (New York: Oxford Univ. Press, 1975); Hugh Graham, *Violence: The Crisis of American Confidence* (Baltimore: Johns Hopkins Press, 1971); Monica Blumenthal et al., *More about Justifying Violence: Methodological Studies of Attitudes and Behavior* (Ann Arbor, MI: Institute for Social Research, 1975); Robert Toplin, *Unchallenged Violence, an American Ordeal* (Westport, CT: Greenwood Press, 1975); Robert Putnam, *Our Kids: The American Dream in Crisis* (New York: Simon & Schuster, 2015); Monica Blumenthal et al., *Justifying Violence: Attitudes of American Men* (Ann Arbor, MI: Institute For Social Research, 1972); David Kennedy, *Don't Shoot: One Man, a Street Fellowship, and the End of Violence in Inner-City America* (New York: Bloomsbury, 2011); Diane Ravitch and Joseph Viteritti, eds., *Kid Stuff: Marketing Sex and Violence to America's Children* (Baltimore: Johns Hopkins University Press, 2003); David Cartwright, *Violent Land: Single Men and Social Disorder from the Frontier to the Inner City* (Cambridge, MA: Harvard University Press, 1996); Richard Bloom, *Strain of Violence: Historical Studies of American Violence and Vigilantism* (New York: Oxford University Press, 1975); and George Benson and Thomas Engemann, *Amoral America* (Durham, NC: Carolina Academics Press Rev. ed., 1982).

3. Speiser, *Lawsuit , 370–71.*

4. Kieck, *Targeting Guns,* 63.

5. Jack Healy, *I'm a Very Proud Owner Fans of AR-15 Explain Their Weapon's Appeal,* New York Times at A14 (Feb. 21, 2018).

6. Patricia Mazzei, *Even After a Mass Shooting, Here is Why Florida Has Trouble Passing Gun Laws,* New York Times at A17 (Mar. 5, 2018).

7. Brendan Farrington, AP, *Fla. Senate Debates Guns, School Safety. Bill Would Add Mental Health Programs, Boost Campus Security,* Houston Chronicle at A26 (Mar. 4, 2018).

8. Michael Scherer, Wash. Post, *Fla. Backs New Gun Laws after Parkland Shooting, Legislators Create Program to Enforce School Safety,* Houston Chronicle at A9 (Mar. 6, 2008); and Patricia Mazzei, New York Times, *Florida Governor Signs Gun Limit,* Houston Chronicle at A1 (Mar. 10, 2018).

9. Dave Cullen, *Columbine,* 387 (New York: Twelve 2009).

10. *See* Kevin Diaz, *Pres. Asks Congress to Consider a Variety of Proposals, Including Cornyn's Background Check Reform,* Houston Chronicle at Al (Mar. 1, 2018). However, less than two weeks later he bowed to the NRA and embraced its agenda of armed teachers and incremental improvements to the background check system. See Michael Shear and Sheryl Stolberg, *Trump Retreats from Promises on Gun Control. Conceding to the N.R.A. Cites a Lack of "Political Support" for Raising Rifle-Buying Age,* New York Times at Al (Mar. 13, 2018).

11. Editorial, *Is This the Moment for Gun Control? Congress Feels Pressure,* New York Times at A10 (Feb. 26, 2018).

12. Eric Lipton and Alexander Burns, *N.R.A.'s Muscle Built on Votes, Not Donations,* New York Times at 1 (Feb. 25, 2018).

13. Kevin Diaz, *Critics Point to Past for Gun Ban: Both Sides Appeal to 1994 Law Amid Weapons Debate,* Houston Chronicle at A1 (Feb. 25, 2108). See also Laura Litran, Bloomberg, *Bipartisan Gun Measures Pile Up in Senate—With No Plans to Act,* Houston Chronicle at A12 (Mar. 9, 2018) (Although bipartisan proposals to address gun violence in the U.S. Senate multiply, there are no plans to vote on any of them).

14. *Id.*

15. Lisa Foderaro and Kristen Hussey, New York Times, *State Gives the Nation Gun-Control Lessons. After Newton, Connecticut Drafted Laws That Have Curbed Firearm Deaths,* Houston Chronicle at A27 (Feb. 18, 2018).

16. Cullen, *Columbine,* 14.

17. *Id.,* 317.

18. See Lisa Foderaro and Kristin Hussey, *After Sandy Hook, Connecticut Offers Lessons on Gun Control to Florida,* New York Times at 19 (Sun., Feb. 18, 2018). See also Maureen Dowd, ed., *Appealing to the Gun Gods,* New York Times at SR9 (Feb. 18, 2018).

19. New York Times at A12 & A13 (Feb. 21, 2018).

20. Lori Rosa, Moriah Balingit, William Wan, and Mark Berman, Wash. Post, *Horrific, Horrific Day, Seventeen Slain at Florida School,* Houston Chronicle at A1 (Feb. 15, 2018).

21. Chronicle News Services, *School Shooting Suspect's Life: Guns, Depression and Trouble*, Houston Chronicle at A1 (Feb. 16, 2018).

22. Chronicle Wire Services, AP, *Rage and Pain Fuel Gun Protections in Florida State Agency; Found Suspect Stable Despite Alarming Video, Posts*, Houston Chronicle at A1 (Feb. 18, 2018).

23. Jack Healy, New York Times, *Parkland Teens Spirited by Day, Doleful by Night*, Houston Chronicle at A27 (Feb. 25, 2018).

24. See Terry Spencer, AP, *Parkland Students Make Emotional Return*, Houston Chronicle at 9A (Feb. 26, 2018); and Kelli Kennedy, Terry Spencer and Josh Replogle, AP, *Florida High School Reopens with Hugs, Tears, Police After Shooting*, Houston Chronicle at A8 (March 1, 2018).

25. Kelli Kennedy, Brendan Farrington, and Curt Anderson, AP, *Deputy Thought Gunfire Outside. Trump Criticizes Police Action in School Shooting*, Houston Chronicle at A1 (Feb. 27, 2018).

26. Guillermo Contreras, John Telesco, and Sig Christenson, *Civil Claims Foiled in Church Killings, Relatives Pursue Wrongful Death Action Against Air Force*, Houston Chronicle at A5 (Nov. 29, 2017).

27. Lindsey Beve, Fred Barbosh, and Avi Selk, Wash. Post, *Major Airlines Join Growing NRA Boycott. Companies Follow Other Corporations That Cut Ties with Gun Rights Group*, Houston Chronicle at A28 (Feb. 25, 2018).

28. Grant Shulte, AP, *First National Bank Set to Halt Production of NRA-Branded Credit Cards*, Houston Chronicle at 83 (Feb. 23, 2018); Editorial, *Voice of a Generation. Parkland Students Give Us Hope That Real Change Is Coming to Our Nation's Gun Policy*, Houston Chronicle at A31 (Feb. 25, 2018).

29. *Id.*

30. *Id.*

31. Jonah Bromwich, New York Times, *The Social Media Warriors of Parkland. Florida Students Stake out Twitter to Confront Politicians and Pundits on Guns*, New York Times at 13 (Sun. March 11, 2018). See also *L.S. v. Peterson*, 2018 U.S. Dist. LEXIS 210273 (S.D. Fla.) (MSD students versus Broward County); and Marjory Stoneman Douglas High School Public Safety Commission, Initial Report Submitted to the Governor, Speaker of the House of Representatives and Senate President (Jan. 1, 2019).

Chapter 11

Lockerbie and Mass Disasters

Men and women are responsible for events, technology, and products that cause masses of people to suffer death, disability and large property losses. These disasters are routine in the sense that they are bound to occur-- the only questions are when and how these self-created disasters grow in severity and frequency. Dangers are enhanced by increases in world population, concentration of people in urban areas, manipulation of the environment, creation of new products through chemical and biological engineering, and closer links between various parts of the world through trade and exchange of technology.[1]

"Disasters maintain an especially compelling grip on the popular mind. Evidence of this phenomenon is readily found in the persistent appeal of the so-called disaster movies—films depicting a seemingly endless variety of situations in which massive loss of human life is threatened. It is the potential loss of life on a vast scale, in and of itself, that creates the sense of high drama." Whether the victims are huddled together en masse in a boat or plane, in an unprecedented storm or flash flood, or sealed off in the relative isolation of their homes, or whether the victims are strangers brought together by circumstance, or neighbors with preexisting social and familial bonds, disaster threatens and ultimately breaches our sense of communal security.[2]

The Beverly Hills Supper Club fire in Southgate, Kentucky, on May 28, 1997, killed 162 people and injured another hundred. It resulted in the first tort class-action suit with claims for damages of $2.7 billion. The principal defendants were the club owners, insurers, and aluminum wire manufacturers. By 1982, all the cases in federal and state courts had been settled or dismissed except for a class-action suit against electrical wiring companies.[3]

On July 17, 1981, two skywalks in the lobby of the Hyatt Regency Hotel in Kansas City collapsed on a dance floor crowded with about 1400 people. One hundred thirteen people were killed and another 186 were injured. It was determined that the connection beams were not designed to hold the weight of the thirty-five-ton skywalks. One hundred suits had been filed in state court

101

against twenty defendants, including Hallmark, Hyatt Hotels, the building's architects, structural engineers and contractors, and the city of Kansas City.[4]

On November 21, 1980, faulty wiring in the kitchen of the MGM-Grand Hotel in Las Vegas started a fire that killed 84 people and injured over 500; most deaths and injuries were caused by smoke inhalation. The hotel had no smoke alarms, and sprinklers were located on the casino level and the money counting room, but not the casino itself. There was significant building and fire code violations that contributed to the fire. Over 112 defendants were named, including the MGM-Grand Hotel, Clark County, various subcontractors, construction companies, and suppliers and manufacturers of building materials, equipment, and furnishings. The hotel and other defendants quickly settled over 120 claims; the remaining claims were "multidistrict" and assigned to Judge Bechtle, of the Eastern District of Pennsylvania. The collective nature of Bechtle's process was reinforced by MGM-Grand's position that it would settle none of the remaining claims unless all settled.[5]

Three arsonists on December 31, 1986, set fire to the DuPont Plaza Hotel, in San Juan, Puerto Rico, killing 97 people and injuring several hundred. More than 2,300 plaintiffs filed claims against more than 250 defendants. In June 1989, Bally Manufacturing Corporation, the manufacturer of the hotel's slot machines which, the plaintiffs claimed, had emitted toxic gas during the fire, settled for $2.1 million. The claims against the remaining 80 products and services defendants went to trial in late July 1989.[6]

BUFFALO CREEK

The flood at Buffalo Creek, West Virginia, on February 26, 1972, killed over 125 people and left thousands homeless; 132 million gallons of debris-filled muddy water burst through a make-shift Buffalo Mining Co. dam and roared through Buffalo Creek. The cause of this disaster can be described as lax enforcement of administrative regulations due to industry pressure.

Buffalo Creek is a narrow mountain hollow where some 5,000 inhabitants lived before the flood devastated a series of small villages. These communities were classic company towns where nearly everyone was either employed by the Buffalo Mining Co. or was engaged in services that supported mining.

Since 1960, the Buffalo Mining Company had used the upper reaches of Buffalo Creek as a dual-purpose disposal site. The slag, a by-product of a coal mining operation, had been dumped in the creek bed and had accumulated to form a dam that impounded the grimy black water used in the company's coal-washing operation. By 1968, two smaller impoundments had been filled to capacity and a third, vastly larger slag pile was building up steadily.[7]

The third dam "at the time of the disaster varied from forty-five to sixty feet high as it stretched across the hollow."[8] On the morning of February 26, 1972, the dam collapsed from the weight of the water, freeing a massive accumulation of foul water, slag, and burning debris which tore through the hollow. One victim described it as "a black ocean where the ground had opened up and . . . was coming in big waves . . . the homes went out, like they were nothing . . . [like] a milk carton out in the river . . . the water seemed like the demon itself. It came, destroyed, and left."[9] Clearly,

> the dam violated both federal and state law. In preparing the lawsuit, [Gerald] Stern discovered that a state inspector had warned the Buffalo Mining Company on numerous occasions that it was violating West Virginia law by its failure to construct an emergency spillway. Similarly, Stern's research uncovered knowing violations of federal safety regulations promulgated under the Federal Coal Mine Health and Safety Act, including a provision that refuse piles shall not be used to impede drainage or impound water. Again, the company simply ignored this requirement, as well as other applicable safety standards, with impunity.[10]

As always, "[t]he threat of legal liability remains the primary means of securing implementation of safety measures. Assuming a minimum degree of rationality among top management officials, a spillway would have been constructed without the necessity of government intervention if the Buffalo Mining Company had even a proximate recognition of its potential liability."[11]

Gerald Stern in his book, *The Buffalo Creek Disaster*, argues that the gross indifference of the coal company and administrative officials who looked the other way created the disaster.[12] Stern reinforces his point by relating how four of the top corporate executives met at the Buffalo Mining Company operation two days before the disaster and drove around in the rain discussing a strip-mining permit they were seeking, while ignoring the dangerously rising black lake behind the dam.[13]

> Six hundred twenty-five of the victims joined together to seek the traditional form of relief for accidental injury, compensation in tort. The Buffalo Creek flood was somewhat distinctive among disasters in affording this avenue of relief. . . . [M]any disasters are acts of God; when a hurricane, flood or earthquake strike, there generally is no private party to sue . . . immediate reaction of the mining company was to claim . . . that the flood was an act of God.[14]

Stern represented 625 victims but asserts that there were 4,000 survivors, and 1,000 destroyed homes.[15] "Those tenacious enough to resist the company's initial settlement offers and to relive the tragedy in the pretrial interrogations eventually shared a $13.5 million settlement."[16] However, the tort system failed to deal with the psychic injury of virtually all of the survivors including PTSD and the collective trauma of loss of community.[17]

"Recovery for those plaintiffs who had been in the floodwater at Buffalo Creek, or threatened by it, was relatively easy since they clearly fit into a category in which West Virginia law afforded compensation for emotional distress. Most of the plaintiffs, however, were in a more tenuous legal position. They had suffered psychic harm but had not been threatened by the water; or in some cases, witnessed others in it."[18] The valuation of mental suffering is always highly speculative, "[b]ut the staggering traumatic consequences of the disaster, mass guilt, anxiety, rootlessness, powerlessness, and withdrawal created an Alice-in-Wonderland atmosphere in which the lawyers traded monetary claims made out of whole cloth."[19]

The initial legal issue was whether the plaintiffs could "pierce the corporate veil" and sue Buffalo Mining Co.'s parent company, the Pittston Corporation. Once the corporate veil was "pierced," the recovery of the bulk of the $52 million damage claim, later increased to $64 million, turned on the legal distinction between "negligent" and "reckless" behavior. Psychic harm and punitive damages are only compensated in West Virginia if defendant's actions were reckless. The settlement eliminated Stern's task of proving that the defendants' actions exhibited gross misconduct. Plaintiffs' success hinges on influencing the jury's emotional reaction to victims' suffering.[20]

LOCKERBIE

On December 21, 1988, Pan Am Flight 103 from Frankfurt to Detroit via London and New York was destroyed by a bomb killing all 243 passengers, 16 crew, and 11 on the ground in Lockerbie, Scotland. After a 3-year joint investigation by Dumfries & Galloway Constabulary and the U.S. FBI, warrants were issued for two Libyan nationals in November 1991. In 1999, Libyan leader Muammar Gaddafi handed two men over for trial at Camp Zeist, Netherlands, after protracted negotiations and UN sanctions. In 2003, Gaddafi accepted responsibility and paid compensation to the victims' families, but he continually maintained that he never gave the order to bomb Pan Am 103. He offered $2.7 billion to the families of the 270 that were killed: $10 million per person; 40 percent released after UN lifted sanctions; 40 percent when U.S. trade sanctions are lifted; and 20 percent after the U.S. State Department removed Libya from its list of states sponsoring terrorism. A U.S. federal court found Pan Am guilty of willful misconduct due to lax security. Contingency fees were allowed for lawyers who successfully negotiated the settlement with Libya.[21]

Airplane crashes are different than most mass tort lawsuits. For example, "[a]irplane crashes immediately mobilize teams of inspectors from the Federal Aviation Agency."[22] "When a plane falls from the sky the passengers are not at fault; they or their families deserve full and swift compensation for their injuries. Unfortunately, the legal system seemingly aggravates their trauma."[23] "The present aviation tort system creates inflated transaction costs and strains judicial resources."[24] "The system is unpredictable with a wide range of compensation available, but airline accident victims usually must wait for years before the court finally awards damages."[25]

> Large-scale, complex litigation invariably results from a commercial air crash. Modern commercial aircraft carry hundreds of individuals, and each person on board represents a potential plaintiff if an accident occurs. Moreover, an aviation disaster commonly involves numerous defendants. Plaintiffs almost always name the airline as a defendant, citing pilot error or faulty maintenance, and plaintiffs typically sue the plane's manufacturer regarding the aircraft's design. These two defendants, in turn, frequently join the manufacturers of myriad component parts, such as altimeters, warning devices, landing gear, or engine bolts, any of which might contribute to a crash. Other potential defendants include airports and the United States government. The multiple parties and multiple actions which usually accompany air disasters produce massive litigation efforts in numerous federal and state courts.[26]

KATRINA AND HARVEY

In a hurricane, "[t]he winds blow so hard the ocean gets up on its hind legs and walks right across the land" (*Key Largo*, Warner Bros., 1948). A hurricane, without more, does not lend itself to recovery for damages. However, attorneys will always search for other sources of remuneration. For example, in *Turner v. Murphy Oil USA, Inc.*,[27] there was a settlement of a class-action suit brought about by the rupture of a large oil refinery tank during Hurricane Katrina.

> On August 29, 2005, Hurricane Katrina made landfall on the Louisiana/ Mississippi border resulting in one of the most devasting natural disasters ever to occur in the United States. As the storm passed over southeastern Louisiana, twenty-foot storm surges rolled into the Mississippi River-Gulf Outlet and swept over and breached some fourteen miles of a levee system intended to protect St. Bernard Parish, inundating nearly all the homes and businesses with massive flood waters. The proposed class-action settlement of $195 million was fair and reasonable, with appropriate attorney fees of $33,150,000, plus

previously escrowed $596,241.88, when the common fund was $195 million with none of it to be used for attorney fees.[28]

In re Katrina Canal Breaches Consolidated Litigation is a class-action for those residents of the New Orleans area that were harmed by breaches that occurred after Hurricanes Katrina and Rita destroyed the levee system that was created by the Army Corps of Engineers. This class-action was filed against the Corps of Engineers, levee districts and their respective boards of commissioners, sewerage and Water Board of New Orleans, Port of New Orleans, railroad, shipping company, insurers, and private contractors and engineers. The certification of the proposed class was warranted and the settlement of $17 million was deemed to be fair, adequate, and reasonable.[29]

Hurricane Harvey is tied with Hurricane Katrina as the costliest tropical cyclone on record, inflicting $125 billion in damages, primarily from catastrophic rainfall-triggered flooding in the Houston metropolitan area. It was the 5,000-year storm which may now come every five years because of global warming. It was formed on August 17, 2017, and dissipated September 2, 2017. There were 69 direct fatalities and 39 indirect fatalities. Throughout Texas, approximately 336,000 people were left without electricity and tens of thousands required rescue. More than 48,700 homes were affected by Harvey throughout Texas. Many locations in the Houston Metropolitan area observed at least 30" of precipitation with a maximum of 60.58" in Nederland. On August 28, 2017, the U.S. Army Corps of Engineer mistakenly began controlled water releases from Addicks and Barker Reservoirs in the Buffalo Bayou watershed to manage flood levels in the immediate area.[30]

The Harvey lawsuits sought compensation for damages to homes when the Army Corps of Engineers released water from the two dams. There are an estimated 10,000 homes that were affected by the release of reservoir water, with potential awards easily reaching billions of dollars. The lawyers must convince judges that the controlled release counts as an improper "taking" of private property under eminent domain law; however, the pay-out is not a sure thing. A federal judge blasted government lawyers for seeking unreasonable and insulting delays.[31]

Mass disasters and the lawsuits that they generate are reexamined in the light of Hurricane Harvey and its aftermath of devastating floods. The thrust of these lawsuits is to prevent these wanton, unprecedented damages from reoccurring. The City of Houston has developed flood prevention rules for construction as a response, which will establish a standard of care for future lawsuits. Unfortunately, only one in six American homes have flood insurance. Also, during Harvey, more than 70 toxic sites flooded; according to industry estimates, more than two million pounds of harmful cancer-causing chemicals were released into the atmosphere.[32]

NOTES

1. Judge Jack B. Weinstein, *Preliminary Reflections on the Law's Reactions to Disasters*, 11 Colum. J. Envtl. L. 11 (1986) (footnote omitted).

2. Robert Rabin, *Dealing with Disasters: Some Thoughts on the Adequacy of the Legal System*, 30 Stan. L. Rev. 281, 281–82 (Jan. 1978). See also Desmond Barry, *A Practice Guide to the Ins and Outs of Multidistrict Litigation*, 64 Def. Counsel J. 58 (Jan. 1997).

3. *Corburn v. 4-R Corp.*, 77 F.R.D. 43 (E.D. Ky. 1997); *In re Beverly Hills Fire Litig., Kiser v. Bryant Elec.*, 695 F.2d 207 (6th Cir. 1982). See also Deborah Hensler and Mark Peterson, *Understanding Mass Personal Injury Litigation: A Socio-Legal Analysis*, 59 Brook. L. Rev. 961, 970–71 (Fall 1983); and Robert Lawson, *Beverly Hills: The Anatomy of a Night Club Fire (Athens*, OH: Ohio Univ. Press 1984).

4. *In re Federal Skywalk Cases*, 77 F.R.D. 43 (E.D. Ky. 1997); *In re Federal Skywalk Cases*, 93 F.R.D. 4:15 (W.D. Mo. 1982). See also Hensler and Peterson, *Understanding Mass Personal Injury Litigation*, 59 Brook. L. Rev. at 972–74.

5. *In re MGM Grand Hotel Fire Litig.*, 570 F. Supp. 913 (Dist. Nev. 1983). See also Hensler and Peterson, *Understanding Mass Personal Injury Litigation*, 59 Brook. L. Rev. at 974–75.

6. *In re Fire Disaster at Dupont Plaza Hotel*, San Juan, Puerto Rico, on Dec. 31, 1986, 660 F. Supp. 982 (J.P.M.L. 1983); *In re San Juan Dupont Plaza Hotel Fire Litig.*, 129 F.R.D. 409 (D.P.R. 1989). See also Hensler and Peterson, *Understanding Mass Personal Injury Litigation*, 59 Brook. L. Rev. at 976–77.

7. Rabin, *Dealing with Disasters*, 30 Stan. L. Rev. 281, 284. See also Gerald Stern, *The Buffalo Creek Disaster: How the Survivors of One of the Worst Disasters in Coal-Mining History Sued the Coal Company and Won* (New York: Vintage Books, 1976).

8. Kai T. Erikson, *Everything in Its Path of Destruction: A Community in the Buffalo Creek Flood*, 26, n. 7 (New York: Simon & Schuster, 1976).

9. *Id.* at 30. See also Rabin, *Dealing with Disasters*, 30 Stan. L. Rev. 281, 284–85.

10. *Id.* at 286 (footnotes omitted).

11. See Stern, *Buffalo Creek Disaster* at 136–37, 145–52, 169–71.

12. Rabin, *Dealing with Disasters*, 30 Stan. L. Rev. 281, 287–88.

13. Stern, *Buffalo Creek Disaster* at 56–57, 200–205. See also Rabin, *Dealing with Disasters*, 30 Stan. L. Rev. 281–89, and Stern, *Buffalo Creek Disaster* at 131–33.

14. *Id.* at 245.

15. Stern, *Buffalo Creek Disaster* at ix.

16. Rabin, *Dealing with Disasters*, 30 Stan. L. Rev. 281, 291.

17. Erikson, *Everything in Its Path*, 153–54. See also Rabin, *Dealing with Disasters*, 30 Stan. L. Rev. 281, 291–92.

18. *Id.* at 293–94 (footnote omitted). See Erikson, *Everything in Its Path*, 220.

19. Rabin, *Dealing with Disasters*, 30 Stan. L. Rev. 281, 294. See Stern, *Buffalo Creek Disaster*, 62.

20. Rabin, *Dealing with Disasters*, 30 Stan. L. Rev. 281, 296–97. See Stern, *Buffalo Creek Disaster*, 51–53, 77, 88, 176.

21. See Kyle Brackin, *Salvaging the Wreckage: Multidistrict Litigation and Aviation*, 57 J. Air. L. & Com. 655 (Spr. 1992). See generally John Kennelly, *Litigation and Trial of Air Crash Cases* (2 vols.) (Mundelin, IL: Callaglian & Co. 1968); George Farrell, *Multidistrict Litigation in Aviation Accident Cases*, 38 J. Air L. & Com. 159 (1972); John Lawrie, *Air Crash Litigation and 28 U.S.C. Section 1407: Experience Suggests a Solution*, 1981 U. Ill. L. Rev. 927 (1981); Randall Craft, *Factors Influencing Settlement of Personal Injury and Death Claims in Aircraft Accident Litigation*, 46 J. Air L. & Com. 895 (1981); and Jack B. Weinstein, *Preliminary Reflections on the Law's Reaction to Disasters*, 11 Columbia J. Envt'l. L. 1 (1986).

22. Rabin, *Dealing with Disasters*, 30 Stan. L. Rev., 281, 285.

23. Brackin, *Salvaging the Wreckage*, 575, Air L. Com. 655, 656 (Spr. 1992).

24. *Id.* (footnote omitted).

25. *Id.* at 656–57.

26. Lowrie, *Air Crash Litigation*, 1981 U. Ill. L. Rev. 927, 921 (footnotes omitted).

27. *Turner v. Murphy Oil USA, Inc.*, 472 F. Supp. 2d 830 (E.D. La. 2007).

28. *Id.*

29. *In re Katrina Canal Breaches Consolidated Litigation*, 263 F.R.D. 340 (E.D. La. 2009).

30. See Sara Randazzo, *After Harvey, a Rush to the Courthouse*, Wall St. J. at A2 (Oct. 24, 2017); Gabrielle Banks, *Lawyers Vie for Top Spots in Flood Suits: Tens of Thousands of Victims Are Likely to Join Legal Fight, Federal Judges Told*, Houston Chronicle at A4 (Nov. 3, 2017); and Lise Olsen, *Judge Blasts Fed Effort to Delay Dam Suits. Move by Government Lawyers Handling Harvey Civil Cases Is Called Insulting*, Houston Chronicle at A1 (Dec. 22, 2017).

31. *Id.*

32. See Editorials, Sylvester Turner and Marvin Odum, *Better Protection Will be Key to City's Economic Future*; J. Eric Smith, *Insurance Industry Ready to Step Up On Disaster Coverage*; Bakeyah Nelson and Jennifer Powis, *For Fairness Sake, Give More People a Say in This Recovery*; and Loren Raun and Deborah January-Beverage, *Mother Nature Knows How to Keep High Water at Bay*, Houston Chronicle at A31 (Mar. 11, 2018).

Chapter 12

Big Pharma Generally

The pharmaceutical industry, or Big Pharma, is an enormous and hugely profitable enterprise that has a dominating presence in American life. It can be said that Big Pharma only cares about the bottom line of profitability. It has cut research and development, repackaged old drugs, marketed drugs of dubious value through direct-to-consumer advertising, and saved money after tort reform by designating certain sums for the inevitable litigation. It uses its great influence and wealth to orchestrate favorable government policies. Big Pharma with the acquiescence of the medical profession that depends on drug company soft bribes, assumed roles in medical treatment, clinical research, and physician education, which is totally inappropriate for a profit-driven industry that allegedly is in a fiduciary relationship with its clients. Big Pharma is compelled primarily by the financial aspirations of their investors and executives which is an incorrect analysis since prescription drugs are not like ordinary goods and the market for drugs is not like any other market.[1]

The key problem is the rising cost of prescription drugs. Big Pharma, not unlike the NRA in its disposition and approach, fights effectively against all efforts to control prices or limit the market for its brand-name drugs. "It channels these efforts and most of its public relations and lobbying activities through its trade association, the Pharmaceutical Research and Manufacturers of America (PhRMA), PhRMA's membership includes virtually all American manufacturers of brand-name drugs, and many foreign manufacturers as well."[2] "PhRMA contends that high profits are a necessary incentive for undertaking the risky and arduous business of discovering innovative drugs. [Since] [t]hese drugs are vital to the health of Americans . . . and it would be disastrously shortsighted to lessen the incentives to find them."[3]

RESEARCH AND DEVELOPMENT (R&D)

Pharmaceutical giant Pfizer's motto is "Life is our life's work." But the inspirational message of fair incentives for accomplishing world health does not hold up. In reality, the R&D budget is a relatively small part of the budgets for large pharmaceutical companies. The marketing and advertising expenditures are much larger. Big Pharma makes more in profits than their R&D investment. Their profits are much higher than those of any other American industry. Also, the pharmaceutical industry is not particularly innovative, and grows less each year. Most of the "new" drugs are not new at all, but patented drugs recycled for a different use; these are called "me too" drugs which attempt to capitalize on the success of "blockbuster" drugs (it's like sequels in the movie industry). "The few drugs that are truly innovative have usually been based on taxpayer-supported research done in nonprofit academic medical centers or at the National Institute of Health. In fact, many drugs now sold by drug companies were licensed to them by academic medical centers or small biotechnology companies."[4] Many marketed drugs add little or no medical value. The lifeblood of the industry is governmental monopolies, in the form of patents and FDA-approved exclusive marketing rights.

Drug candidates are usually the result of research into the molecular basis of the disease, which is primarily done in academic or governmental laboratories. The next step is pre-clinical R&D. "This involves biological screening and pharmacological testing in laboratory animals to determine how the drug is absorbed, metabolized, and excreted, to learn about its toxicity."[5] The next step is the clinical phase where testing is on human subjects. Finally, if all goes well, Phase III clinical trials are undertaken. These trials "evaluate the safety and the effectiveness of the drug in much larger numbers of patients (hundreds or thousands of them), with the expectation of gaining FDA approval if the trials are successful. No more than one in five drug candidates entering clinical testing make it through to FDA approval and reach the market."[6] "After approval of the drug the FDA requires that the manufacturer continues surveillance of the drug and report unanticipated side effects."[7]

THREE CASE STUDIES

The blockbuster Claritin is an antihistamine said to cause less drowsiness than cheaper over-the-counter-drugs such as Benadryl. Claritin was patented by Schering-Plough in 1981 but not approved by the FDA until 1993. In 2001, Claritin had sales of about $2.7 billion and brought in about one-third of Schering-Plough's revenues. The 17-year-old patent should have expired in 1998, but Hatch-Waxman added two years, GATT added 22 months, and pediatric testing added another six months. These three extensions added four-and-a-half-years to the drug's exclusivity—worth billions of dollars. Back in 1987, Schering-Plough patented the active metabolite of Claritin that is the molecule into which the body converts Claritin, which accounts entirely for the action of the drug. In December 2001, it received FDA approval to market the Claritin metabolite under the name Clarinex and began a massive promotional campaign to switch Claritin users to the new drug before Claritin was scheduled to lose its exclusivity in December 2002. In 2002, Schering-Plough petitioned the FDA to change Claritin from a prescription drug to an over-the-counter product. By law, the same drug at the same dose cannot be sold both ways, so the move stops generic companies from competing in the prescription market when the patent expires.

Next, Prozac, which was made by Eli Lilly, was the first of a new type of antidepressant called SSRIs. It was developed mainly from research conducted outside the company. In 1987, the FDA approved Prozac for the treatment of depression; in 1994, for the treatment of obsessive-compulsive disorder; in 1996, for bulimia; and in 1999, for geriatric depression. It rapidly replaced other types of antidepressants because of its milder side effects. Prozac soon accounted for one-quarter of Lilly's revenues, with annual sales reaching $2.6 billion.

Lilly sued generic makers who hoped to enter the market. In June 1999, Lilly patented Prozac Weekly, a new formulation that can be taken less often. It was approved by the FDA six months before the Prozac patent expired, and Lilly had exclusive marketing rights until 2004. The most ingenious move to extend the life of Prozac was the creation of Sarafem, which is the identical drug in the identical dose but colored pink and lavender instead of green, and taken for a new indication. In 1997, Lilly, faced with the imminent loss of Prozac's exclusivity, decided to license its use for premenstrual syndrome from Interneuron reportedly for $2 million plus a percentage of sales. Sarafem was approved by the FDA for "premenstrual dysphoric disorder," which is not yet officially recognized as a distinct disorder in the psychiatric diagnostic manual.

Prilosec, a heartburn drug made by British pharmaceutical firm AstraZeneca, was the number-one drug in the world, with sales of about $6 billion per year, until its patent expired in October 2001 after a six-month extension for pediatric testing. It sued generic companies for infringement of its eleven layers of patents. The company patented the active form, named it Nexium, and got FDA approval to market it just in time to switch people over to it before Prilosec's exclusivity ran out. AstraZeneca launched a massive advertising campaign to persuade Prilosec users and their doctors that Nexium was somehow better, even though there is every scientific reason to expect that a double dose of Prilosec would be equivalent to Nexium.[8]

CASE STUDY-HALCION

Halcion is used to treat insomnia, but also causes mental impairment with deadly results including hallucinations, rage, violent and bizarre behavior, aggressiveness, paranoia, psychosis, and homicide. In the United States, some scientists were concerned about the drug's safety and efficacy but have not convinced the FDA to withdraw it. Neither proponents nor critics of the drug are completely satisfied with the present status, partly due to the awareness that scientific reviews and determinations may have been subject to political and other external influences.[9]

CASE STUDY-FEN PHEN

This litigation involves claims regarding the health effects of two related prescription drugs—fenfluramine and dexfenfluramine. This regimen popular became known as "FenPhen," which was withdrawn from the market in 1997, since there was considerable information that these drugs caused heart damage. The FDA issued a public health advisory, so that there would be no further sales which cause a wave of litigation. Ultimately, there was a "global resolution" of the Diet Drug Litigation.[10]

The next case study involves addictive behavior and prescription drugs. A patient had restless legs syndrome and was given Mirapex; he had never gambled or shopped excessively before starting this medication. He has since gambled away his entire savings and lost his marriage.

The truth is that some medications have been linked to compulsive behavior, such as gambling, binge drinking, shopping, and even hypersexuality. Such behaviors are associated with the antipsychotic drug aripiprazole, Abilify, and drugs used to treat Parkinson's disease. These drugs affect the brain chemical dopamine.[11]

Pathological gamblers have a difficult time walking away from slot machines, blackjack tables, casinos, poker tournaments, and sports betting, even if they don't have the money to lose. One result is that they gamble on credit and drive themselves into serious debt. All addictive behaviors—drug use, sex, and gambling—are wired into this central dopamine reward pathway, and none stimulate it better than amphetamines.[12]

THE OPIOID EPIDEMIC

In a quest to increase their profits, drug makers began marketing new formulations of opioid narcotics in the mid-1990s as safe even though they were essentially the same as heroin. These drugs were effective in relieving pain, but also highly addictive. But Big Pharma claimed to have found a way to make them nonaddictive—they were less than candid. Doctors accepted Big Pharma's marketing at face value and began prescribing the drugs for almost any kind of pain. Unfortunately, these new formulations were not safe and acted as a catalyst for America's opioid crisis. The overdose rate has jumped over 1400 percent from 1998, and 60,000 Americans died from opioid overdose in 2016. The DEA tried to control the problem by freezing sales at suspected pill mills. After years of paying DEA fines for selling pills to illegal outlets, Big Pharma spent $106 million to lobby Congress for more industry-friendly laws. Now, 41 state attorneys and hundreds of cities and counties are suing opioid manufacturers for negligence and contributing to a multibillion-dollar health crisis that cost the American economy $504 billion in 2016, the equivalent of 2.8 percent of U.S. gross domestic product that year. On October 27, 2017, President Donald Trump announced "he was directing his Department of Health and Human Services to declare the opioid crisis a public health emergency. . . . [I]t would allow some grant money to be used for an array of efforts to combat opioid abuse and would ease certain laws and regulations to address it."[13] Also, on October 27, 2017, U.S. prosecutors brought a fraud and racketeering case against the founder of an opioid medication maker who pushes painkiller prescriptions amid an opioid epidemic. The indictment also alleges that they conspired to mislead and defraud insurance providers who were reluctant to approve payment for the drug when it was prescribed for patients without cancer.[14]

"While pill mills and rogue doctors have handed out millions of pills for no real medical purpose, well-meaning physicians that are trained to aggressively treat pain are [also] part of the problem."[15] Tragically, some patients can become addicted to opioids after just three days of taking pills. "About 97.5 million people across the nation used prescription pain relievers in 2015, according to the 2015 National Survey on Drug Use and Health. Of those, 87 percent used them as directed, and 13 percent misused the medication. About 2 million people have a substance use disorder involving pain pills."[16] Ironically, addictive opioid painkillers are actually less effective than common over-the-counter remedies such as Tylenol and prescription-strength analgesics. But, after Big Pharma's enormous marketing push for opioid painkillers they were prescribed "for anything that hurt."[17] However, developing countries do not give opioids for sprained ankles or wisdom tooth extractions.[18]

Tribes of Native Americans are ravaged by opioid abuse. The Cherokee Nation has sued big opioid distributors.

> Attorney generals from 41 states recently joined forces to investigate similar options. . . . The Cherokee suit argues that the pharmacy chains Walmart, Walgreens and CVS Health, as well as the giant drug distributors McKesson, Cardinal Health and AmerisourceBergen, flouted federal drug-monitoring laws and allowed prescription opioids to pour into the Cherokee territory at some of the highest rates in the country.[19]

The Department of Justice on February 27, 2018, announced plans to file a statement of interest in a multidistrict legal action, a massive case that bundles together hundreds of lawsuits against the giant pharmaceutical companies responsible for making the addictive drugs that are fueling the growing overdose epidemic. Attorney General Jeff Sessions promised to hold accountable those whose illegality has cost billions of taxpayer dollars.[20]

> February 13, 2018, the number of lawsuits continues to grow in a combined federal challenge of drug companies' role in the opioid crisis. Judge Dan Polster is overseeing the consolidated lawsuits in a case in federal court in Cleveland. The complaints allege drug manufacturers and drug distributors bear responsibility for the deadly overdose epidemic and for not doing enough to stop it.[21]

On December 13, 2017, Harris County Texas jumped into the legal fight against the opioid crisis, joining dozens of cities and counties in filing suit against the giant pharmaceutical companies responsible for making the painkillers that fuel the growing opioid epidemic. The Harris County complaint alleges that 21 companies and a handful of individual doctors and one pharmacist of conspiracy, neglect, and creating a public nuisance in a case that draws comparisons to the multibillion-dollar Big Tobacco litigation filed by state attorneys general in the 1990s. The county is seeking actual and punitive damages, penalties, and fines, which could easily stretch into the millions of dollars.[22] Big Pharma struck back against the Harris County lawsuit; the pharmaceutical industry say they are no longer willing to be scapegoats. One defendant responds "[w]e believe these copycat lawsuits filed against us are misguided and do nothing to stem the crisis."[23] "Purdue Pharma is credited with helping develop many modern tactics of aggressive pharmaceutical promotion. Its efforts to push OxyContin included OxyContin music, fishing hats and stuffed plush toys. . . . Purdue and other opioid makers and distributors face dozens of lawsuits in which they're accused of creating a public health crisis through their marketing of the painkillers."[24]

The opioid crisis has been described as the worst health epidemic in American history. But it was one that was entirely manufactured by Big Pharma. One response was that municipalities sued the opioid industry for the expenses that were used to provide health care, but municipalities have a difficult time to prove injury and causation. The Sackler family owns Purdue Pharma which helped fuel the epidemic. Lawsuits against Purdue Pharma must prove that the market for chronic use of opioids only occurred as a result of a relentless campaign of deception.[25]

An Oklahoma judge ordered Johnson & Johnson to pay $572 million for the sale of two prescription opioids and a fentanyl skin patch on the basis that it constituted a public nuisance.[26] In 2015 "over 326 million opioid pills were dispensed to Oklahoma residents, enough for every adult to have 110 pills." "In 2017 4.2% of babies born covered by Sooner Care were born with Neonatal Abstinence Syndrome (also called NAS), a group of conditions caused when a baby withdraws from certain drugs."[27] Oklahoma settled with Purdue Pharma for $270 million for the sale of Oxycontin in March 2019 and settled for $85 million with Teva Pharmaceuticals for the sale of generic drugs in May 2019. Johnson and Johnson predictably blamed the FDA by presenting an argument based on the preliminary supposition that the products were sold with FDA approval.[28] Millions of Americans, due to Big Pharma's unethical marketing, now believe that they are afflicted with dubious or exaggerated ailments.[29]

"The Vioxx tragedy is yet another example of misconduct by the pharmaceutical industry."[30] The opioid epidemic is a self-fulfilling prophecy orchestrated by Big Pharma, solely to maximize profits. State attorney generals and local district attorneys have sued Big Pharma to recoup the billions of dollars that Medicare spent to treat addicted citizens. Big Pharma's unprecedented profits are fueled and maintained by direct-to-consumer advertising.

NOTES

1. Arnold Relman and Marcia Angell, *America's Other Drug Problem: How the Drug Industry Distorts Medicine and Politics,* The New Republic 27 (Dec. 16, 2002). See also Marcia Angell, *The Truth about Drug Companies,* 45 Jurimetrics J. 465 (2005); and Harry F. Dowling, *Medicines for Man: The Development, Regulation, and Use of Prescription Drugs* (New York: Knopf, 1970).

2. Relman and Angell, *America's Other Drug Problem,* The New Republic 27 (Dec. 16, 2002).

3. *Id.* at 28.

4. *Id.* See also Marcia Angell, *The Truth about the Drug Companies: How They Deceive Us and What to Do about It* (New York: Random House, 2004).

5. Relman and Angell, *America's Other Drug Problem,* The New Republic 27, 28 (Dec. 16, 2002).

6. *Id.*

7. *Id.*

8. *Id.,* at 37–38 (all three case studies are from this article). See generally Bruce Kuhlik and Richard Kingham, *The Adverse Effects of Standard Less Punitive Damage Awards on Pharmaceutical Development and Availability,* 45 Food Drug Cosm. L. J. 693 (1990); Margaret Gilhooley, *Innovative Drugs, Product Liability, Regulatory Compliance, and Patent Choice,* 24 Seton Hall L. Rev. 1481 (1994); Rebecca Eisenberg, *The Problem of New Uses,* 5 Yale J. Health Pol'y, L. & Ethics 717 (Sum. 2005); Richard Davidson, *Source of Funding and Outcome of Clinical Trials, 1 J. Central Internal Medicine 155* (May/June 1986); Marcia Angell, *The Truth about the Drug Companies,* 45 Jurimetrics J. 465 (Sum. 2005); and *A Prescription for Better Drug Trials,* 41 Trial 54 (March 2005).

9. Committee on *Halcion: An Assessment of Data Adequacy and Confidence,* Div. of Health Sciences Policy, Institute of Medicine, Halcion; An Assessment of Safety and Efficacy Data (Washington, DC: Nat'l Academy Press 1997).

10. *Brown v. Am. Home Prods. Corp. (In re Diet Drugs)* (Phentermine, Fenfluramine, Dex-Fenfluramine) (Prods. Liab. Litig.), 2000 U.S. Dist. LEXIS 12275 *4-*17 (E.D. Pa.), *aff'd w/o opin.* 275 F. 3d 34 (3d Cir 2001).

11. Joe and Teresa Graedon, *The People's Pharmacy, Compulsive Behavior Reported as Side Effect for Some Medications,* Houston Chronicle at D6 (Dec. 11, 2007).

12. Walter Champion and I. Nelson Rose, *Gaming Law in a Nutshell,* 500 (St. Paul, MN: West Academic, 2d ed. 2018).

13. Julie Hirschfield Davis, New York Times, *Trump Declares Opioid Crisis a "Public Health Emergency,"* Houston Chronicle at A9 (Oct. 27, 2017).

14. AP, *Fraud Case Targets Opioid Maker,* Houston Chronicle at A9 (Oct. 27, 2017).

15. Carrie Teegardin, Atlanta Journal Constitution, *Doctors Forced to Rethink Pain Treatment, Unintended Effects of the Opioid Crisis Worry Physicians,* Houston Chronicle at Al5 (Dec. 24, 2017).

16. *Id.*

17. Jenny Dean, *Study Questions Opioid Efficacy. Research Finds "No Benefit" from Patient Pain-killers,* Houston Chronicle at A1 (Mar. 12, 2018).

18. *"Opiophobia" and Agony: Many African Nations, Fearing an Opioid Epidemic, Have Restricted Drugs That Could Bring Relief to Millions Who Are Suffering from Devastating Pain,* New York Times at D1 (Dec. 15, 2017).

19. Jan Huffman, *Ravaged by Opioids, Tribe Fights Big Pharmacies,* New York Times 1 (Dec. 17, 2017).

20. Keri Blakinger, *DOJ Wades into Fight Over Opioid Epidemic,* Houston Chronicle at A3 (Feb. 28, 2018).

21. *Lawsuits Growing Opioid Crisis,* Houston Chronicle at B2 (Feb. 15, 2018).

22. Keri Blakinger, *County Sues Over Opioid Epidemic*, Houston Chronicle at A1 (Dec. 14, 2017). See Blakinger, *County Opioid Lawsuit Riles Pharmaceutical Companies*, Deer Park Broadcaster at 2A (Jan. 13, 2018).

23. Blakinger, *Pharm Companies Plan to Fight Opioid Suit. Drug Distribution Says "Copy-Cat" Lawsuits . . . Are Misguided and Do Nothing to Stem the Crisis*, Houston Chronicle at A4 (Dec. 19, 2017).

24. See *Commonwealth of Pennsylvania v. Purdue Pharma L.P.*, Complaint, Civ. Action 257 MD 19 (Pa. Com. Ct., filed May 2, 2019); and Nino C. Monea, *Cities v. Big Pharma: Municipal Affirmative Litigation and the Opioid Crisis*, 50 Urban L. Rev. 87 (Spr. 2019). See also Beth Macy, *Dope-Sick: Dealers, Doctors, and the Drug Companies that Addicted America* (Little, Brown & Co., 2018); Roni Caryn Rabin, *Opioid Barons Stashed Assets: N.Y. Suit Says Subterfuge as Scrutiny of Oxycontin Grew*, New York Times A1 (Mar. 29, 2019); Danny Hakim, Roni Caryn Rabin, and William K. Rashbaum, New York Times, *Lawsuits Reveal Family's Role in Opioid Crisis*, Houston Chronicle B8 (Apr. 2, 2019); Geoff Mulvihill and Alanna Durkin Ricker, AP, *Family Behind Oxycontin Calls Opioid Lawsuit False*, Houston Chronicle B3 (Apr. 3, 2009); and Jordan Heller and Lenny Bernstein, Washington Post, *Biggest Civil Trial in U.S. History to Start in Ohio*, Houston Chronicle at A12 (July 22, 2019).

25. *State of Oklahoma v. Purdue Pharma*, Case No. CJ-2017-816 (Cleveland Cnty. Okla. Dist. Ct., Judge Thad Balkman, Aug. 26, 2019). See Sara Randazzo and Jared S. Hopkins, *Judge Rules Johnson & Johnson Helped Fuel Opioid Epidemic*, Wall St. J. A1 (Aug. 27, 2019); and Jan Hoffman, *Judge Requires Maker of Opioids Pay $572 Million: A Landmark Judgment Ruling against Johnson & Johnson Set Tone for Two Thousand Cases*, New York Times A1 (Aug. 27, 2019) (Wall Street Journal's Review & Outlook lambasted the Oklahoma decision as "opening a vast new arena for product-liability suits.").

26. *Oklahoma v. Purdue Pharma* at 2; Hoffman, *Judge Requires Maker of Opioids*, New York Times A1 (Aug. 27, 2019).

27. Jared Hopkins, *Pain Pill Giant Purdue to Stop Its Promotion of Opioid to Doctors*, Houston Chronicle at B4 (Feb. 10, 2018).

28. Rochelle Chodock, David Yolkut, and Dennis Connolly, *Insuring the Continued Solvency of Pharmaceutical Companies in the Face of Product Liability Class Actions*, 40 Tort Trial & Ins. Prac. L.J. 997 (Spr. 2005); Janet Fairchild, annot., *Promotional Efforts Directed toward Prescribing Physician as Affecting Prescription Drug Manufacturer's Liability for Product-Caused Injury*, 94 A.LR. 3d 1080 (originally published in 1979); Howard Denmark, *Improving Litigation Against Drug Manufacturers for Failure to Warn against Possible Side Effects: Keeping Dubious Lawsuits from Driving Good Drugs off the Market*, 40 Case W. Res. L. Rev. 413 (1989); Richard Ausness, *Unavoidably Unsafe Products and Strict Products Liability: What Liability Rule Should be Applied to the Seller of Pharmaceutical Products?*, 78 Ky. L.J. 705 (Sum. 1989/1990); Teresa Moran Schwartz, *Prescription Products and the Proposed Restatement (Third)*, 61 Tenn. L. Rev. 1357 (Sum. 1994); and James A. Henderson, *Prescription Drug Design Liability under the Proposed Restatement (Third) of Torts: A Reporter's Perspective*, 48 Rutgers L. Rev. 471 (1996).

29. Walter Champion, *A Tale of Two Cities: A Commentary on the Media's Response to Personal Injury "Feeding Frenzies" as a Result of the Vioxx and Silicosis Litigation,* 31 Whittier L. Rev. 47, 47–53 (2009).

30. *Id.,* at 48.

Chapter 13

Direct-to-Consumer Advertising

In the movie *Get Out*, Jordan Peele created a metaphor for our times, the beautiful people at his garden party are at best hypnotized, maybe even lobotomized. Those same perfect people and Betty Gabriel as Georgina with her wet, glassy eyes, banging to Get Out from the traps for black people in American life, are easily recognizable as the perfect people in Big Pharma's Direct-to-Consumer Advertising (DTCA). These impossibly perfect actors gladly swap a litany of often fatal side effects for better skin! In the DTCA universe, pharmaceutical companies directly target laypersons, without the buffer of medical advice and counsel. Those ads are like marketing-sirens whose sweet-singing voices lure American consumers to their death on the rocky shores of misguided and unnecessary medication. These lies are the basis of fraudulent advertising lawsuits. Big Pharma's DTCA is connected to its shell game of withholding clinical results.

Merck Co. and its Vioxx painkillers came under fire in the summer of 2004 for failure to disclose poor results from clinical studies. Although "20 million Americans took Vioxx between 1999 and 2004 when Merck stopped selling it after a clinical trial linked the drug to heart attacks and strokes in patients who used it for 18 months or longer. Company documents suggest Merck scientists were worried about Vioxx's potential heart dangers as early as 1997."[1] Merck's document hiding was compounded by their direct-to-consumer advertising. Vioxx "entered the market with great *fanfare* in 1991," and was an "*instant* Blockbuster."[2] Between 1997 and 2001, DTCA spending increased from "$1.1 billion to $2.7 billion per year . . . [y]et, significant concerns with regard to DTCA . . . persist."[3] These advertisements "do not fairly convey the risks and benefits of the drug, patient misperception of the drug's effectiveness could lead to patient pressure to prescribe inappropriate drugs. Patient misperception of DTCA could also lead to patient pressure to prescribe new drugs that have no significant benefit over similar, cheaper, older medications."[4]

"Vioxx (generic name rofecoxib) was marketed as a panacea for acute pain in adults, including women suffering from menstrual pain. . . . Vioxx's phenomenal success was absolutely connected to DTCA, which allowed the pharmaceutical companies to directly target lay persons in their marketing campaigns."[5] "Critics of DTCA advertising argue that it leads to inappropriate patient demands on providers, overuse of prescription drugs and in some instances, the increased demand for expensive me-too medicines when less expensive and equally effective alternatives are available."[6] "DTCA ads have become the subject of criticism from Capitol Hill, doctors and consumers who say they seem only to promote the benefits of drugs without fully explaining the risks."[7] Pope Francis is *not* a fan of fake news, and DTCA is a form of fake news; "the serpent in the Garden of Eden hissed the first fake news to Eve and it all went downhill from there." The Pope said that "[w]e need to unmask what could he called the 'snake-tactics' used by those who disguise themselves in order to strike at any time and place." "I would like to contribute to our shared commitment to stemming the spread of fake news." [8]

Similarly, CVS is striking a blow for honest marketing, and will no longer utilize significant touch ups of images used in its advertising for beauty products. "The company said it has a responsibility to think about sending messages of unrealistic body images to girls and young women." [9] This urge to make their models unnaturally beautiful is similar to DTCA's use of perfect actors as representative of sick people who desperately need, whether they know it or not, that next miracle drug.

THE DRUG CULTURE

DTCA feeds on and is nurtured by the drug culture. As Tiger Woods admitted, he sought a drug cocktail for composure. He was on the "other side" of too many years relying on pain medication to cope with his back surgeries,

> which led to his arrest on a DUI charge that he attributed to a bad mix of prescription drugs. Toxicology reports revealed that Woods had two painkillers (Vicodin and Dilaudid), a sleep drug (Ambien), an anti-anxiety drug (Xanax) and the active ingredient for marijuana in his system. He went through an in-patient treatment program to deal with prescription medication, and . . . pleaded guilty to a reckless driving charge that allowed him to avoid jail time.[10]

An alternative to DTCA, but still a cousin, is that doctors are now allowed to prescribe addiction medicine, without ever seeing the patient in person. Using media for DTCA or virtual doctor visits is counter to the customary doctor-patient relationship: "The face-to-face interaction establishes trust, allows him to pick up on body language. Plus, it's hard to do a urine drug test screen remotely and be sure that the sample belongs to the patient. A proper screen lets him know if his patients are taking their medication, instead of selling it."[11]

The plaintiff's lawyers have long solicited clients through television advertisements that warn of a drug's potentially harmful side effects. These ads offer wronged victims an opportunity to receive financial redress for defective drugs either through product liability and/or deceptive marketing. The allegedly deceptive marketing is usually supplied by Big Pharma's DTCA. Now, the pharmaceutical companies and doctors argue that the lawyer ads are to blame for patients suffering harm after dropping treatment. Rep. Bob Goodlatte (R. VA), chairman of the House Judiciary Committee, wants the legal ads to include a warning that patients should talk with their doctor before adjusting medicine. However, former ABA President Linda Klein said in a response to Mr. Goodlatte that while it is unfortunate if anyone suffered ill consequences by misunderstanding the ads, attorneys have a First Amendment right to advertise and the public benefits from knowing if drugs are potentially harmful.[12]

> The competing advertisements face different levels of scrutiny. All drug-company advertisements are subject to FDA rules, including a requirement that ads disclose a drug's risk of side effects, and the agency can stop broadcast of an ad and seek changes if it doesn't follow regulations. By contrast, the lawyer ads must conform to attorney ethics rules mandated by state bar associations requiring marketing to be honest and not fraudulent.[13]

> In a report by Health Affairs on patient encounters with DTCA, the report surveyed a national sample of 643 physicians . . . [where] patients discussed an advertised drug. Physicians thought that direct-to-consumer advertising (DTCA) led patients to seek unnecessary treatments.[14]

FDA'S ROLE IN DTCA

The Food and Drug Administration (FDA) requires that direct-to-consumer (DTC) advertisements be neither false nor misleading and that they provide a fair balance of risks and benefits, and indicate material facts, including a brief summary of risks.[15] These FDA requirements have been subject of debate as to their precise definitions, "leaving much latitude for how aggressively the FDA pursues consumer protection."[16] Marcia Angell, senior lecturer at the Department of Social Medicine at Harvard Medical School, believes that the drug companies "spend relatively little" on research and development.[17]

A change made in the legal community in 1997, "resulted in a 350 percent increase in expenditures for such advertising between 1996 and 2001."[18] Another marketing phenomenon is the so-called "me-too" drugs, where instead of promoting drugs to cure disease, pharmaceutical companies promote diseases to fit drugs.[19] The FDA's efforts to ensure that pharmaceutical ads are truthful are principally done through the FDA's Division of Drug Marketing, Advertising, and Communications (DDMAC).[20]

Even the Government Accountability Office raised concerns over misleading DTCA and FDA enforcement delays. Also, "the choice of enforcement sanctions was frequently weak."[21] Congressman Waxman opined that "[t] here simply is no incentive for drug manufacturers to tell the whole truth to consumers and there is no real penalty for them if they do not."[22]

> DTC ads have the promise of educating consumers about medical conditions, but that can only be fulfilled if the information is clear and accurate . . . is responsible for ensuring the accuracy of the DTC ads; however, the FDA's recent congressional investigations have indicated that the agency is failing at this task. . . . FDA enforcement actions against false and misleading ads have declined precipitously in recent years. . . . Although the FDA has the authority to take stronger actions with more deterrent effect, such as court actions or ultimately fines, the agency has not done so.[23]

In an essay entitled "Are Pharmaceutical Ads Deceptive?" (1994), Prof. Paul H. Rubin looked at an article in the annals of Internal Medicine that examined Big Pharma ads in medical journals, which found that these ads were "often misleading." Pharmaceutical ads in medical journals are a tamer version of DTCA. Although DTCA has been legal since 1985, it took off in 1997 when the FDA eased up on a rule obliging pharmaceutical companies to offer a detailed list of side effects in their infomercials (long format television commercials).[24]

DTCA ads in connection with the FDA's contrivance, create a perfect storm for Big Pharma abuse. It also guarantees the creation of feeding frenzies.

NOTES

1. Alex Berenson *Despite Vow, Drug Makers Still Withhold Data,* New York Times at A1 (May 31, 2005).

2. Richard Epstein, *Regulatory Paternalism in the Market for Drugs: Lessons from Vioxx and Celebrex,* 5 Yale J. Health Pol'y, L. & Ethics 741 (2005) (emphasis supplied).

3. Marshall Chin, *The Patient's Role in Choice of Medications: Direct-to-Consumer Advertising and Patient Decision Aids*, 5 Yale J. Health Pol'y, L & Ethics 771 (2005) (citations omitted).

4. *Id.*, at 776.

5. Walter T. Champion, *A Tale of Two Cities: A Commentary on the Media's Response to Personal Injury "Feeding Frenzies" as Result of the Vioxx and Silicosis Litigation*, 31 Whittier L. Rev. 47, 50–51 (2009). See also Walter Champion, *The Vioxx Litigation Paradigm: The Search for Smoking Guns*, 31 Thurgood Marshall L. Rev. 157 (2006).

6. James Jeffords, *Direct-to-Consumer Drug Advertising: You Get What You Pay For*, www.HealthAffairs@W4-253.com (2004), http//:DOI10.1377hlthaff.W4.253 (footnote omitted). See generally Lars Noah, *Death of a Salesman: To What Extent Can the FDA Regulate the Promotional Statements of Pharmaceutical Advertising in Leading Medical Journals*, 49 Food & Drug L.J. 21 (1994); and Charles Walsh and Alissa Pyrich, *FDA Efforts to Control the Flow of Information at Pharmaceutical Industry-Sponsored Medical Education Programs; A Regulatory Overdose*, 24 Seton Hall L. Rev. 1325 (1994).

7. Stephanie Saul, *Drug Makers to Police Consumer Campaigns*, New York Times at C7 (Aug. 3, 2005).

8. Jason Horowitz, New York Times, *For Francis, Fake News Goes Back to the Garden of Eden*, Houston Chronicle at A10 (Jan 25, 2018).

9. Anne D'Innocenzio, AP, *CVS Plans to End Touchups of its Beauty Images in Ads*, Houston Chronicle at B4 (Jan 16, 2018).

10. Doug Ferguson, AP, *Tiger "Loving Life" with Latest Setbacks behind Him. with Recent Arrest, Surgery in Rear View, Woods in Better Spot*, Houston Chronicle at C7 (Nov 29, 2017).

11. Emily Forman, *Telemedicine Still Fuzzy on Addiction Help. Few Physicians Opt to Prescribe Drugs via Virtual Visits*, Houston Chronicle at A19 (Dec 17, 2017).

12. Sara Randazzo and Johnathan Rockoff, *Lawmakers Are Critical of TV Commercials That Warn of Side Effects, Solicit Patients as Clients, Wall St. J. at B6 (Apr. 18, 2017).*

13. *Id.*

14. Joel Weissman et al., *Physicians Report on Patient Encounters Involving Direct-To-Consumer Advertising*, Health Affairs at W4-2 1 9 (2004) at DOI10.1377/hlthaff.W4.21 9 (footnote omitted).

15. 15 C.F.R §202.1(e) (2009).

16. Chin, *The Patient's Role*, 5 Yale J. Health & Pol'y L. & Ethics at 778.

17. Marcia Angell, *The Truth about the Drug Companies*, 45 Jurimetrics J. 465, 466 (2005).

18. Puneet Manchanda and Elizabeth Honda, *The Effects and Role of Direct-to-Physician Marketing in the Pharmaceutical Industry: An Integrative Review*, 5 Yale J. of Health Policy L. Ethics 785, 786 (2005) (citation omitted).

19. Angell, *The Truth about Drug Companies*, 45 Jurimetrics J. at 468.

20. Jeffords, *DTCA*, Health Affairs W4-253, 254.

21. Champion, *Vioxx Litigation Paradigm,* 31 T. Marshall L. Rev. 157, 159-62 (footnotes omitted).

22. Henry Waxman, *Ensuring That Consumers Receive Appropriate Information from Drug Ads: What Is the FDA's Role?,* www.Health Affairs @ W4-256.com (Apr. 28, 2004) at http://DOII0.1377hlthaff.W4.256.

23. *Id.*

24. Paul Rubin, *Are Pharmaceutical Ads Deceptive?,* 49 Food & Drug L. J. 7 (1994).

Chapter 14

FDA: A Wizard Should
Know Better!

Dr. Alexander Schmidt, former commissioner of the Food and Drug Administration (FDA), discusses the question of "pressure" on the FDA from, *inter alia.*, Big Pharma lobbyists. Dr. Schmidt continues—"A well-known orthopedic surgeon got rave notices in the press when he used the forum of a Congressional hearing to blast FDA, in colorful and thus widely reported language, for considering approval of a dangerous drug [chymopapain] that he said was nothing more than purified meat tenderizer."[1] The FDA is a federal agency of the U.S. Dept. of Health and Human Services.

The FDA is responsible for protecting and promoting public health through the control and supervision of food safety, tobacco products, dietary supplements, prescription and over-the-counter medications, vaccines, bio-pharmaceuticals, blood transfusions, medical devices, cosmetics, animal foods, and feed and veterinary products. As of 2017, three fourths of the FDA budget are funded by the pharmaceutical companies due to the Prescription Drug User Fee Act. The FDA regulates more than $1 trillion worth of consumer expenditures in the United States, which includes $466 billion in food sales, $275 billion in drugs, and $60 billion in vitamin supplements. The FDA's federal budget is generated by user fees, the majority of which are paid by pharmaceutical firms for drug reviews. New drugs receive extensive scrutiny before FDA approval in a "new drug application"; critics argue that FDA standards are not sufficiently rigorous, allowing unsafe or ineffective drugs to be approved.[2]

On March 15, 2018, federal officials began an initiative to slash levels of addictive nicotine in cigarettes; the FDA can regulate nicotine but cannot eliminate it completely. "[T]he FDA estimates the U.S. smoking rate could fall as low as 1.4 percent by 2060, down from the 15 percent of adults who smoke now. The greatest impact, though, would come from preventing young people from ever becoming addicted."[3]

The FDA has investigated supplements Opiate Detox Pro and Kratom, a botanical substance that is advertised as a safe opioid substitute. A public advisory warning was issued that it carries "deadly risks," and that Kratom imports can be seized. The FDA stated that, "unfortunately, unscrupulous vendors are trying to capitalize on the opioid epidemic by illegally marketing products as dietary supplements, with unproven claims about their ability to help in the treatment of opioid use disorder, or as all-natural alternatives to prescription opioids."[4]

DRUG APPROVAL

A drug manufacturer must demonstrate that the new drug is both safe and effective. The FDA then approves the drug for uses shown to be effective. The manufacturer must not promote the drug for any other unapproved uses. But medical doctors routinely prescribe drugs for "off-label" uses. An off-label use is described as a use other than the FDA-approved uses described on the drugs' official labeling. "However, off-label drug uses also create special risks that are not present when drugs are used in manners that the FDA has approved."[5]

In 1938, Congress passed the Food, Drug and Cosmetic Act which gave the FDA regulation authority. Under this Act, the FDA was given the authority to regulate all drugs and vaccines sold in interstate commerce. The Act also required drug manufacturers to submit a new drug application to the FDA before marketing any new drug and demonstrate that it was safe for the described uses. Although this regulation slowed down the entry of new drugs into the market somewhat, innovation in new drugs continued to flourish under these guidelines until 1962. In 1962, in response to the thalidomide tragedy, Congress passed the Kefauver-Harris Amendments to the Food, Drug and Cosmetics Act. These amendments broadened the definition of "new drugs" and repealed the 60-day automatic approval for new drug applications. Under these amendments, the FDA was required to decide on a new drug application within 180 days, but the amendments provided no sanctions if the FDA failed to do so. More importantly, however, two of the amendments provisions directly affected the FDA's drug approval process, and these provisions have had a tremendous impact on drug innovation in the United States. . . . The first of these provisions is the requirement that the drug manufacturer produce

> substantial evidence that the drug will have the effect it purports . . . to have under the conditions of the use prescribed, recommended or suggested in the proposed labeling. . . . The second of the 1962 provisions are the institution of

investigational new (IND) requirements for human testing. . . . Once an IND study has been approved, the FDA still had the authority to halt the test if the preliminary results are unsatisfactory.[6]

"The testing required of a new drug prior to approval for marketing in the United States . . . provides FDA with a reasonable basis upon which to determine efficiency and relative safety at the time of approval."[7] However, preapproval clinical trials at the time a drug is first approved for marketing usually provide little human information about rare events, late latent effects, drug interventions, or effects in specialized populations. Therefore, it is imperative to maintain post-marketing surveillance of the safety of products.[8] The FDA realizes the limitations of the clinical trial system. There is also bias and a lack of diversity in the clinical trials so that "racial and ethnic minorities [are] less likely than white men to participate in clinical trials."[9]

> FDA scientist Dr. David Graham hinted that the FDA has become too chummy with the industry it regulates. . . . The key to approval or withdrawal are the clinical studies, but the FDA is not immune from drug industry pressure. . . . Furthermore, the drug industry is not always honest with how it deals with negative studies. For example, Merck hid an "unpublished study showing an increased risk of cardiovascular problems with Vioxx. . . . The major incentive is the initial clinical trial that must favorably impress the FDA in its role as market gatekeeper.[10]

> [T]o begin the testing process a drug must be registered with the FDA, which approves all drugs for safety and effectiveness before sale. There are four phases of clinical testing. These trials evaluate hundreds or thousands of patients, with the expectation of gaining FDA approval if the trials are successful. . . . Even after approval, the FDA requires continued surveillance and the obligation to report unanticipated side effects. Clinical studies after initial approval are designated as Phase IV trials.[11]

However, before the FDA will consider approving a new drug, the company must present the results of at least one, and usually more, Phase III trials for FDA review as part of the new drug application. "Pre-clinical and clinical testing and the other tasks required before a drug can be brought to the FDA for approval can be long, difficult, and very expensive."[12]

A part of the problem may be the mission of the FDA itself as recounted after the Vioxx withdrawal.

> Modern drugs provide unmistakable and significant health benefits. It is well recognized that FDA's drug review is the gold standard. Indeed, we believe that FDA maintains the highest worldwide standards of drug approval. FDA grants approval to drugs after a sponsor demonstrates that they are safe and effective.

Experience has shown that the full magnitude of some potential risks does not always emerge during the mandatory clinical trials conducted before approval to evaluate these products for safety and effectiveness.[13]

In a hearing before the Health, Education, Labor and Pensions Committee, it was asked what is the FDA's drug approval process:

> We expect the FDA to approve a new drug only if it's safe, effective, and the known benefits of the drug outweigh the known risks, if it's used as intended. We expect the FDA to ensure that companies are communicating the benefits and the risks of their drugs to patients and physicians in a clear and consistent manner. We expect the FDA to keep tabs on the drugs on the market, to ensure their continued safety, and to take appropriate actions if new information demonstrates new risks that were not apparent when a drug was initially approved. . . . When patients go to their medicine cabinets to open a prescription bottle, they deserve an assurance that the medicines that they take are safe and effective.[14]

FDA OVERSIGHT

The FDA's regulation of Avandia appeared to mimic their botched Vioxx protocol. Avandia's boss, the CEO of GlaxoKlineSmith indicated that a large clinical study was at risk, but this admission did not create a "feeding frenzy." The FDA was lampooned as a "feckless watchdog unable to protect consumers from unsafe medicines."[15]

Case Study-Mer/29—Triparanol, marketed as Mer/29, was the first synthetic cholesterol lowering drug. Respondent used Mer/29 and developed cataracts and ichthyosis; conditions that can be caused by too much cholesterol in the blood. The alleged purpose of Mer/29 was to inhibit the body's ability of produce cholesterol, thus aiding in the prevention of heart attacks and strokes. However, in Merrell's testing, all the rats died, and their results with monkeys were falsified.

> After more lies and false marketing, the FDA in April 1960, granted Merrell's application to market MER/29. Merrell was obligated under §355(b) of the Federal Food, Drug, and Cosmetic Act to submit full reports of investigations sharing the drug's safety; however, the reports to the FDA were falsified. Strict liability of manufacturer to injured drug user was justified on grounds that product was marketed without proper warning of its known dangerous effects.[16]

DRUG REGULATION

"[T]he prescription drug industry is the most heavily regulated industry (for safety purposes) in this country today."[17] "[T]he vast majority of products liability litigation concern the provision of warnings and information about safe use of drugs, a major area of FDA regulation."[18] FDA regulation is "the strongest case for accepting governmental safety standards as conducive when an injured plaintiff sues a pharmaceutical manufacturer for iatrogenic injuries allegedly caused" by a prescription drug.[19] "The FDA's regulatory power touches upon every stage of a product's life cycle. In addition to deciding whether to approve new drugs, biologics and medical devices for marketing, the FDA requires the initial laboratory and clinical testing, reviews proposed product labeling, sets manufacturing practices, monitors marketed products for adverse reactions and takes enforcement actions when companies fail to comply with agency requirements."[20]

The Supreme Court of New Jersey in *Feldman v. Lederle Laboratories*[21] and the Supreme Court of Kansas in *Wooderson v. Orthro Pharmaceutical Corp.*[22] held that the FDA's specific scientific judgment may be "revealed" by the courts in civil actions for damages. This affords redress against Big Pharma for breaching the state's common law duty to warn of potential side-effects based on scientific evidence that FDA finds insufficient to compel warning labels. In *MacDonald v. Ortho Pharmaceutical Corp.*, the Supreme Judicial Court of Massachusetts held that drug companies may be required to directly warn patients of risks where the FDA itself requires direct patient warnings, in language that is different from specifically approved FDA warnings.[23]

Even with the neediest of victims, the FDA shows little compassion. Desperate AIDS victims sought use of ganciclovir to combat CMV, a viral eye infection, but has the side effect of not tolerating AZT, the only drug approved to extend the lives of AIDS patients. However, there is a new drug on the block, Foscarnet, that both alleviates CMV retinitis and tolerates AZT. This conundrum should fall precisely within the FDA's compassionate Investigative New Drug (IND) protocol, but the perverse result is that only wealthy or well-connected patients can afford the treatment.[24]

The sleeping pill Halcion also causes deadly psychotic episodes, as in the case of Ilo Grunberg, who inexplicably killed her 86-year-old grandmother with eight shots from a handgun while holding a cheerful birthday card. Ms. Grundberg sued on the grounds that Halcion is a defective drug with misleading and inadequate labeling; she settled with Upjohn for a confidential, but reputed, multi-million-dollar amount.[25]

Case Study-Clegene—The Celgene pharmaceutical company settle claims of $280 million for the off-label marketing of their cancer drugs. Thalomid and Relmid, for unapproved uses. Celgene was greedy and imagined that their drugs could be a magic, and lucrative cure for cancer, autoimmune diseases, and AIDS. However, Celgene did not properly gain FDA approval.[26]

In an article in *The Economist* entitled "From Bad to Awful; The Pharmaceuticals Industry," it was argued that the FDA's compliance with Big Pharma's faulty testing and marketing is a primary source of litigation. But, now the regular itself, the FDA is under attack and has lost public confidence. David Graham, an FDA scientist before the Senate's Finance Committee, testified that the FDA overvalues the benefits of drugs and "seriously undervalues, discards and disrespects drug safety."[27]

The FDA is too chummy with Big Pharma. FDA's reliance on Big Pharma to self-report problems is a huge error. Merck's defense of Vioxx was that it kept no information from the FDA. However, that defense is less effective when most Americans believe that the FDA is in collusion with the shackled Big Pharma bosses that parade in newspapers and on the evening news as convicted criminals.[28]

The FDA did not detect the irregularities in the approval of Vioxx nor penalize Merck for their voluntary withdrawal. Vioxx had the potential to be the quintessential feeding frenzy but was neutralized by Merck's aggressive legal tactics.

NOTES

1. Alexander M. Schmidt, *The FDA Today: Critics, Congress and Consumerism*, 29 Food Drug Cosm. L. J. 575, 581 (1974).

2. See generally Matthew Perrone, AP, *FDA Begins Push to Cut Nicotine Levels in Cigarettes in Effort to Halt Addition*, Houston Chronicle at A12 (Mar. 16, 2018); Sheila Kaplan, *Anger Over Supplements Claim of Helping Addicts*, NY.Times at B3 (Dec. 9, 2017); Note, *A Question of Competence: The Judicial Role in the Regulation of Pharmaceuticals*, 103 Harv. L. Rev. 773 (Jan. 1990); Richard Cooper, *Drug Labeling and Products Liability: The Role of the food and Drug Administration*, 41 Food Drug Cosm. L. J. 233 (1986); and Harvey Dowling, *Medicines for Man, the Development, and Regulation, of Prescription Drugs* (New York: Alfred A. Knopf, 1970).

3. Perrone, AP, *FDA Begins Push to Cut Nicotine Levels*, Houston Chronicle at A12 (March 16, 2018).

4. Kaplan, *Anger Over Supplements Claim*, New York Times at B3 (Dec., 2017).

5. Kaspar Stoffelmayr, *Products Liability and Off Label Uses of Prescription Drugs*, 63 U. Chi. L. Rev. 275, 275 (Wntr.,1996). See also Lars Noah, *Constraints on*

the Off-Label Uses of Prescription Drug Products, 16 J. of Products & Toxic Liability 139 (1994).

6. Beth Myers, *The Food and Drug Administration's Experimental Drug Approval System: Is It Good for Your Health?,* 28 Houston L. Rev. 309, 312-18 (Jan. 1991) (footnotes omitted).

7. Gerald Faich, *Adverse Drug Experience Reporting and Product Liability,* 41 Food, Drugs, and Cosmetics L. J. 444 (1986).

8. *Id.,* at 444–55.

9. Glantz (interview*), A Prescription for Better Drug Trials,* 41 Trial 54 (Mar. 2005).

10. Walter Champion, *The Vioxx Litigation Paradigm: The Search for Smoking Guns,* 31 T. Marshall L. Rev. 157, 165 (Spr. 2006) (footnotes omitted).

11. *Id.,* at 168 (footnotes omitted).

12. Arnold Relman and Marcia Angell, *America's Other Drug Problem: How the Drug Industry Distorts Medicine and Politics,* New Republic at 527 (Dec. 16, 2002).

13. Sandra Kweder, *Deputy Director, Office of New Drugs, FDA, Merck and Vioxx: Pulling Patient Safety First?,* Hearings before Sen. Comm. on Finance, 108th Cong. (Nov. 18, 2004), https://www.finance.senate.gov/imo/media/doc/111804sktest.pdf. See also Richard Epstein, *Regulatory Paternalism in the Market for Drugs: Lessons from Vioxx and Celebrex,* 5 Yale J. Health Pol'y. L. & Ethics 741, 754 (2005).

14. U.S. Senator Michael Enzi (R-WY) Holds a Hearing on the FDA's Drug Approval Process before the U.S. Senate Health, Education, Labor and Pensions Committee, 2005 WL 481528, verbatim transcript, 2005 WL 481528 (March 1, 2005).

15. Walter Champion, *A Tale of Two Cities: A Commentary on the Media's Response to Personal Injury & Feeding Frenzies as a Result of the Vioxx and Silicosis Litigation,* 31 Whittier L. Rev. 47, 75–78 (2009) (footnotes omitted).

16. *Toole v. Richardson-Merrell, Inc.,* 251 Cal. App.2d 689, 760 Cal. Rptr. 398, 29 A.L.R. 3d 988 (Cal. App. 1st Dist. 1967).

17. Michael Green, *Statutory Complaints and Tort Liability: Examining the Strongest Case,* 30 U. Mich. J. L. Reform 461, 463 (Spr. 1997).

18. *Id.* at 464.

19. *Id.* See generally Paul Sabatier, *Social Movements and Regulatory Agencies: Toward a More Adequate—And Less Pessimistic Theory of "Clientele Capture,"* 6 Policy Sciences 301 (1975); Sidney Shapiro, *Limiting Physician Freedom to Prescribe a Drug for Any Purpose: The Need for FDA Regulation,* 73 N.W U. L. Rev. 801 (1978, 1979); Richard Cooper, *Drug Labeling and Products Liability: The Role of the Food and Drug Administration,* 41 Food, Drugs, and Cosmetics. L. J. 233 (1986); Teresa Moran Schwartz, *The Role of Federal Safety Regulations in Products Liability Actions,* 41 Vand. L. Rev. 1121 (Nov. 1988); and note, *A Question of Competence: The Judicial Role in the Regulation of Pharmaceuticals,* 103 Harv. L. Rev. 773 (Jan. 1990).

20. Jeffrey Griggs and Bruce Mackler, *Food & Drug Administration Regulation and Products Liability: Strong Sword, Weak Shield,* 22 Tort & Ins. L. J. 194, 196 (1987) (footnotes omitted).

21. *Feldman v. Lederle Laboratories,* 97 N.J. 429, 479 A.2d 374 (1984).

22. *Wooderson v. Ortho Pharmaceutical Corp.*, 235 Kan. 387, 681 P.2d 1038, *cert. denied*, 105 S. Ct. 365 (1984).

23. *MacDonald v. Ortho Pharmaceutical Corp.*, 394 Mass. 131,475 N. E.2d 65, *cert. denied*, 106 S. Ct. 250 (1985). See Charles Walsh and Marc Klein, *The Conflicting Objectives of Federal and State Tort Law Drug Regulation*, 41 Food, Drugs, Cosmetics L. J. 171 (1986).

24. Beth E. Myers, *The Food and Drug Administration's Experimental Drug Approval System: Is It Good for Your Health*, 28 Houston L. Rev. 309, 310-18 (Jan. 1991).

25. Gregory Jackson, *Pharmaceutical Product Liability May be Hazardous to Your Health: A No-Fault Alternative to Concurrent Regulations*, 42 Am. U. L. Rev. 199, 199–202 (Fall 1992) (footnotes omitted).

26. Katie Thomas, *Celgene, a Drug Maker, Will Pay $280 Million to Settle a Fraud Suit*, New York Times at B4 (July 26, 2017).

27. *From Bad to Awful: The Pharmaceuticals Industry*, The Economist at 64 (Nov. 27, 2004).

28. *Id.*

Chapter 15

The Vioxx Moment

Drug manufacturer Merck and Company voluntarily withdrew its popular arthritis and pain medication, Vioxx, on September 30, 2004.[1] This unprecedented withdrawal led to a so-called "feeding frenzy" as attorneys sought clients allegedly harmed by the drug.[2] In early 2006, less than two years after Vioxx was withdrawn from the market, the ensuing litigation settled "into something of a groove."[3]

In each case, Merck attorneys repeatedly insisted that Vioxx's potential dangers were fully disclosed to regulators and the public.[4] However, plaintiffs' attorneys cited e-mails and other documents that purported to show that Merck scientists "were concerned about Vioxx's risks long before Merck withdrew the drug."[5] The plaintiff's lawyers found their "smoking gun."

In the summer of 2004, the drug industry came under fire for its failure to disclose poor results from clinical studies.[6] The *New York Times* reported that "About 20 million Americans took Vioxx between 1999 and 2004," before "a clinical trial linked the drug to heart attacks and strokes in patients who used it for 18 months or longer."[7] The plaintiffs' bar alleged that the insurance industry blamed trial lawyers for creating a health care "crisis," driving doctors out of business as a result.[8]

"Trial lawyers claim that only they battle pharmaceutical giants. . . . The highest-profile example involves Vioxx . . . that contributed to tens of thousands of deaths from heart attacks, strokes, and blood clots. Merck's own memos prove the company knew Vioxx posed heart risks as early as 1997, but Merck ignored its own facts and made billions through aggressive marketing."[9]

The Vioxx tragedy is yet another example of misconduct by the pharmaceutical industry.[10]

VIOXX AND DRUG CULTURE

Vioxx (generic name rofecoxib)[11] "entered the market with great fanfare in 1999" and was an "instant blockbuster" as a panacea for acute pain in adults, including women suffering from menstrual pain.[12] Vioxx is known as a COX-2 inhibitor, which is a drug that can effectively treat pain and inflammation without the uncomfortable gastrointestinal side effects sometimes present in ibuprofen (Motrin) and naproxen (Naprosyn).[13]

A large contributor to Vioxx's success was direct-to-consumer advertising (DTCA),[14] which allowed the pharmaceutical companies to directly target laypersons in their marketing campaigns.[15] DTCA spending rose to $2.7 billion in 2007, up from $1.1 billion in 1997.[16] Those that criticize DTCA aver that advertisements do not fairly convey the risks and benefits of prescription drugs.[17] It is possible that a patient's misperceptions of the effectiveness of a drug could lead to that patient's request for newer, inappropriate drugs, drugs that might "have no significant benefit over similar, cheaper, older medications."[18] The FDA requires that these advertisements be neither false nor misleading.[19]

These FDA requirements have been subject of debate as to their precise definitions, "leaving much latitude for how aggressively the FDA pursues consumer protection."[20] Congressman Henry Waxman of California remarked that "there simply is no incentive for drug manufacturers to tell the whole truth to consumers, and there is no real penalty for them if they do not."[21] Accordingly, the FDA reacted by issuing recommendations for more consumer-friendly language.[22] The pharmaceutical industry then issued guidelines attempting to ameliorate some of the most egregious DTCA concerns.[23] The new guidelines "were developed to fend off stricter government regulation" and "improve the industry's public relations." These guidelines would make Super Bowl erectile dysfunction ads, and 15-second TV teaser ads that give little more than the drug's name without explaining the benefits or risks, a thing of the past.[24]

Capitol Hill critics aver that such advertising leads to increased use of "[COX]-2 inhibitors by patients who would have done just as well with more traditional painkillers."[25] Senator Charles Grassley of Iowa was one such critic who advocated closer monitoring of pharmaceuticals by the FDA.[26] The FDA made plans to hold a public hearing on drug advertising, but a hearing "would not necessarily mean that the [FDA] would draft new rules."[27]

Drug companies "spend relatively little" on research and development.[28] DTCA was allowed in 1997, which resulted in a 350 percent increase in expenditures for such advertising between 1996 and 2001.[29] "Me-too" drugs marketing promoted diseases to fit drugs.[30] Since there is a larger market for healthy people,[31] millions now believe they have dubious ailments.[32]

The pharmaceutical industry is an "enormous and hugely profitable enterprise [that] has become a dominating presence in American life."[33] The industry has a hand in "directing medical treatment, clinical research, and physician education."[34] The Vioxx phenomenon is the primary example of the inherent failure of the "drug culture"; indeed, the drug's success is attributable to Merck's "apparent ability to satisfy the best of both possible worlds by relieving pain without provoking the risk of stomach or intestinal bleeding."[35]

Because Merck had a great deal of confidence regarding Vioxx, the company sought "to expand the portfolio of permissible uses"; it was during these trials that "Merck discovered . . . an apparent increase in the number of negative cardiovascular occurrences."[36] Many read Merck's decision to withdraw Vioxx "as a fatal admission of dangerous conduct by a firm that should never have made the launch in the first place."[37] As a result of Merck's withdrawal of Vioxx, the company was forced to forgo any future profits from a recorded $2.5 billion in sales in 2003, and erasing $26.8 billion from its market capitalization.[38]

The Vioxx "feeding frenzy" was initiated by Merck itself when it voluntarily withdrew the drug from the market.[39] The plaintiff's bar smelled blood in the water. Merck's trial strategy was clear: the company admitted no liability unless there was a sustained history of usage of at least 18 months.[40] However, a study by McGill University[41] revealed that out of the patients who suffered a heart attack, a quarter of them did so within the first two weeks of taking Vioxx;[42] the risk of heart attack decreased thereafter.[43] On May 11, 2006, "Merck announced that an APPROVE[44] follow-up study . . . did not show a statistically significant difference in risk between those who had been taking Vioxx and those who had been taking a placebo."[45] But there was an immediate reaction from some who interpreted a graph in the follow-up study as suggesting an increased risk after only four months of use.[46]

Although Merck admitted that there was a statistical error in the follow-up study, the company claimed the error did not alter the study results.[47] Commentators were unsure whether these studies would impact upcoming Vioxx litigation.[48] Of the six cases that went to trial by May 2006, Merck had been successful half the time.[49] One plaintiff used Vioxx for seven months and won.[50] But two others who had used it for less than two months lost.[51]

The first jury trial, *Ernst v. Merck*, took place before a jury in a state district court in Angleton, Texas, and concerned the death of a 59-year-old triathlete who died in 2001 after taking the drug for less than seven months.[52] Merck claimed that he died not from a heart attack but as a result of cardiac arrhythmia.[53] It also argued that multiple clinical studies proved the drug had no harmful side effects before introducing the drug in 1999,[54] and that the company continued research for years before immediately withdrawing it when a study showed that it had heart risks.[55] After deliberating for a day-and-a-half, a Texas jury found Merck liable and awarded $253.5 million.[56] The award consisted of $24.5 million for mental anguish and economic losses, and an additional $229 million in punitive damages due to Merck's recklessness in selling Vioxx despite knowing of the risks associated with it.[57] However, under the Texas law that caps punitive damages, part of the award was automatically limited to $1.6 million, meaning the overall award could not exceed $26.1 million.[58]

Humeston v. Merck was the second state jury trial and took place in New Jersey in the fall of 2005.[59] Just as in Texas, the defense focused on whether Vioxx was the actual cause of Frederick Humeston's heart attack.[60] Mr. Humeston, a 60-year-old postal worker from Idaho, had other risk factors including stress and obesity and took Vioxx for only two months before his heart attack, which he survived.[61] Merck won decisively in this case: A nine-member jury found by an eight-to-one vote that Vioxx was not the cause of Mr. Humeston's heart attack.[62] The jury also concluded that Merck acted properly in the marketing of the drug.[63]

The first federal jury trial took place in Houston and began in late 2005.[64] Richard Irvin's widow contended that her husband died from a heart attack at age 53 after taking Vioxx for one month.[65] Merck claimed that their clinical studies showed that short-term use did not cause heart attacks, and that it was heart disease that led to Mr. Irvin's death, not Vioxx.[66] This case was declared a mistrial.[67] Another trial was set in a New Jersey state court where the jury found for John McDarby, age 77, holding that Merck did not properly warn patients of the dangers of Vioxx, and that the drug had caused plaintiff's heart attack.[68]

The jury awarded McDarby, who had taken Vioxx for four years, $3 million in compensatory damages and an additional $1.5 million to his wife.[69] The jury also found that Merck had committed consumer fraud against McDarby and Thomas Cona, age 60, a second plaintiff, who suffered a heart attack in 2003.[70] The jury did not award compensatory damages to Mr. Cona, who claimed to have taken Vioxx for almost two years, but only had three prescriptions covering a few months.[71] Merck unsuccessfully argued that McDarby's history as a former smoker, along with his diabetes and clogged arteries, would have contributed to his heart attack even if he never used Vioxx.[72]

On April 21, 2006, a state court jury in Rio Grande City, Texas awarded $32 million in damages to the family of Leonel Garza, who died at the age of 71 in 2001 after briefly taking Vioxx.[73] Merck argued that Mr. Garza, who took Vioxx for less than one month, had a lengthy history of heart disease that included a previous heart attack.[74] The $32 million jury award was later reduced to $7.75 million under a Texas law that caps punitive damages.[75] New Jersey jurors felt differently on July 13, 2006, when they concluded that Vioxx was not the cause of a 68 year-old woman's heart attack.[76] Although the court found that Merck had warned Elaine Doherty's doctor of Vioxx's risks, the drug company lost on one issue—when jurors held that Merck did not warn plaintiff herself about the drug.[77] Merck successfully argued that Doherty was an overweight diabetic whose age, weight, diabetes, cholesterol, blood pressure, and clogged arteries contributed to her heart attack.[78]

Therefore, as of August 2006, the tide seemed to be turning in Vioxx's favor. Merck gained ground in the Vioxx litigation—at least for the moment. A California jury ruled that Merck's painkiller Vioxx did not cause the heart attack that Stewart Grossberg, 66, had in September 2001. The case was Merck's second consecutive victory, following a win for the company in New Jersey in July 2006.

Lawyers on both sides agree that Merck's victories, and its stated strategy of trying every case rather than settling any, are discouraging plaintiffs with weaker claims. Lawyers for plaintiffs have withdrawn more than 300 federal suits, mainly after finding that their clients could not produce adequate evidence that they took the drug. Merck, however, still faced 14,000 federal and state suits over Vioxx, covering about 27,000 plaintiffs.[79] After Merck withdrew Vioxx in September 2004, the company insisted its behavior was legal, and that it would contest every suit brought by a plaintiff claiming that Vioxx caused injuries.[80] Out of the seven cases that went to a jury since the *Ernst* decision in 2005, Merck won five—the two exceptions are a New Jersey trial won by the plaintiff's attorney in *Ernst*, and a case in a south Texas jurisdiction that has been considered plaintiff-friendly.[81] As a result, some anticipated that by the time the two-year statute of limitations passed, Merck would likely take on far fewer plaintiffs than many analysts and lawyers expected.[82] In fact, by August 2006, plaintiffs began to withdraw cases in both state and federal courts.[83] Even so, Merck still had to face an additional eight trials before the end of 2006.[84]

On August 17, 2006, a New Orleans federal jury awarded a retired FBI agent $51 million for a mild heart attack he suffered after taking Vioxx for almost three years.[85] A unanimous jury found Merck responsible for Gerald Barnett's heart attack, as the company failed to warn doctors about the risks associated with Vioxx.[86] After deliberating for less than a day, the jury awarded Barnett $50 million in compensatory damages and $1 million in punitive damages.[87] However, on August 30, 2006, a District Court judge overturned the compensatory award of $50 million on the grounds that it was excessive, which warranted a new trial as to damages.[88]

Although there was evidence to suggest that the plaintiff might have lost nine or ten years of life expectancy as a result of using Vioxx, that did not alter the fact that he was retired and therefore, could not recover for lost wages or lost earning capacity.[89] And although he may have experienced a decrease in energy, the plaintiff was able to return to many of his daily activities.[90] Although the District Court was "not troubled" by the $1 million punitive damage award, a new trial was ordered on the issues of compensatory and punitive damages, as "no reasonable jury could have found that the Plaintiff was entitled to $50 million in compensatory damages."[91]

On September 26, 2006, another federal jury in New Orleans ruled for Merck, finding insufficient evidence to link Vioxx to the heart attack of Robert Garry Smith, who had used the drug for about four-and-a-half months.[92] Merck's lawyer could not identify any medical testimony that indicated Vioxx had anything to do with his heart attack, and commented that due to Mr. Smith's body type and vigorous physical activity that day, he would have suffered a heart attack regardless of whether he had taken Vioxx.[93] Therefore, as of September 26, 2006, Merck had won five cases and lost four in state and federal courts.[94]

On November 15, 2006, federal jurors in New Orleans again found for Merck, rejecting the claims of Charles Mason, 64, who alleged Vioxx caused his heart attack in 2003.[95] Merck contended, and ultimately convinced the jury, that plaintiff's clogged arteries were the cause of his heart attack, not his ten months of Vioxx use.[96] One commentator noted that Merck's apparent strategy of litigating each Vioxx claim had "resulted in more victories than losses."[97]

On December 13, 2006, another New Orleans federal jury determined that Anthony Dedrick's heart attack was not primarily caused by Vioxx, as the plaintiff had other risk factors, including high blood pressure, high cholesterol, diabetes, and the buildup of plaque in his arteries.[98] On December 15, 2006, an Alabama state jury took less than two hours to find for Merck, agreeing with Merck's lawyer, who argued that plaintiff Gary Albright's "small heart attack did not cause permanent damages to his lifestyle."[99] Merck's lawyers successfully argued that the plaintiff had a high risk of heart trouble due to his diabetes, weight, high blood pressure, and high cholesterol.[100]

On January 18, 2007, a mistrial was declared in a California Superior Court when a jury split on whether two men's heart attacks were caused by Vioxx.[101] The jury deadlocked as to whether the plaintiffs' doctors would have recognized the drug's potential risks or side effects.[102]

On March 2, 2007, a New Jersey state jury ruled that Merck had failed to provide adequate warnings about the risks of Vioxx before an Atlantic City man suffered a heart attack in 2001.[103] But in a second connected case, the jury ruled that the death of the plaintiff had occurred after the company had provided adequate warning, having strengthened the drug's label on its risks in 2002.[104] In both cases, however, the "jury ruled unanimously that Merck had committed consumer fraud by misleading doctors and patients and by intentionally suppressing, concealing or omitting information about" Vioxx's risks.[105] In the initial trial's first phase, the jury ruled on Merck's behavior, while in the second phase, the jury heard testimony specifically related to the heart attack suffered by the plaintiff, Frederick Humeston, and the damages to be awarded.[106]

In the second trial, the jury ruled that Merck had given adequate warnings before the other plaintiff, Brian Hermans, died of a heart attack in September 2002 at the age of 44.[107] The differences between the two verdicts likely result from Merck's revision of the Vioxx label in April 2002, which added information regarding the heart risks associated with the drug.[108] The first plaintiff, Mr. Humeston, was initially unsuccessful.[109] But on March 12, 2007, a New Jersey jury awarded Fred Humeston $47.5 million on the basis that Merck's handling of Vioxx was "oppressive, outrageous, or malicious."[110] The jury awarded $18 million to Mr. Humeston and $2 million to his wife Mary in compensatory damages and $27.5 million in punitive damages.[111] As to the second plaintiff, Mr. Hermans' request to overturn the jury verdict in favor of Merck was denied.[112]

On March 27, 2007, jurors in an Illinois state court found that Vioxx was not responsible for the 2003 death of 52-year-old Patricia Schwaller.[113] The jury held that Vioxx was not the proximate cause of her death, even though she had taken the drug for twenty months.[114] Her other risk factors for heart disease included obesity, diabetes, high blood pressure, and a sedentary lifestyle.[115] This victory was Merck's tenth in 15 cases.[116]

In a decision which surely supported Merck's decision to try every case, Texas State District Judge Randy Wilson, who oversaw all Texas Vioxx cases,[117] held on April 19, 2007, that Ruby Ledbetter could not sue on the basis that Merck failed to properly warn her of the risks of taking Vioxx.[118] If this ruling had been upheld on appeal, it would have effectively gutted all Texas Vioxx cases.[119] But the issue was rendered moot by the Supreme Court's decision in *Wyeth v. Levine*,[120] on March 4, 2009, which held that state law failure-to-warn claims against a pharmaceutical manufacturer were not preempted by FDA approval.[121] Another indication of the demise of the "feeding frenzy" was *In re Vioxx Products Liability Litigation*, in which the Eastern District of Louisiana denied the plaintiffs' steering committee's request for certification as a nationwide class of all those Vioxx users who claimed either personal injury or wrongful death.[122] Similarly, on September 6, 2007, the Supreme Court of New Jersey rejected a class action lawsuit against Merck over Vioxx.[123] The ruling is a huge legal victory for the company, which faced nearly 27,000 individual lawsuits from people claiming that Vioxx caused heart attacks and strokes. The state's highest court, reversing two lower court decisions, ruled that a nationwide class was not appropriate for the lawsuit.

The suit had been brought by a union health plan on behalf of all insurance plans that paid for Vioxx prescriptions, or about 80 percent of all Vioxx sold.

Had the class action been allowed to proceed, it also would have been a major setback to the company's strategy of fighting the Vioxx lawsuits individually. Of the cases that have reached verdicts, Merck has won nine and lost five. A new trial was ordered in one case, and two others ended in mistrials.[124] As a result, in the two years of Vioxx litigation, Merck's financial status remained robust, with the company reporting strong second-quarter results on July 24, 2007.[125] Investors moved Merck's stock to $52.33, up 7 percent.[126] Over a year period, Merck's shares gained over 40 percent, "well ahead of the Standard & Poor's 500 stock index and other big drug companies."[127] Of the 45,000 people who sued Merck, none of them received money from the company as of August 21, 2007.[128] The company continued to appeal guilty verdicts, which avoided any payments to successful claimants.[129] This led to a recovery of Merck's stock and a decrease in the company's ultimate liability for Vioxx.[130]

Around the time of Merck's victory in *Ernst v. Merck*,[131] the plaintiff's bar appeared to be taking greater interest in other potential mass tort issues. One such example concerns the use of stents, "the tiny metal devices that prop open heart arteries," which allegedly kill 2,000 patients per year, according to a study described in a 2006 *New York Times* article.[132] Dr. Sanjay Kaul stated that the drug-coated stents "were being used far too frequently in cases where clinical data suggests that bare-metal stents or long-term drug therapy would be safer."[133] So far, the plaintiff's bar has not rallied around the alleged unnecessary use of drug-coated stents, or the associated risks of fatal blood clotting and serious heart attacks.

Another potential mass tort involves Gardasil, a drug from Merck that inoculates young women against the human papillomavirus (HPV), which can cause cervical cancer.[134] A backlash against proposed mandatory vaccinations ensued, perhaps "undermining eventual prospects for the broadest possible immunization."[135] However, the controversy over Gardasil has also not ignited a "litigation crisis."

A potentially more dangerous concern to Merck involved problems associated with Arcoxia, a drug that was once anointed as the successor to Vioxx.[136] A study showed that Arcoxia's risks are in combination to the painkiller diclofenac, which, although widely used in Europe, has raised concerns in the United States over potential liver problems.[137] Some claim that Merck was less than forthcoming about releasing the study's full details, noting that the company's reputation was already damaged after it failed to inform doctors of the risks associated with Vioxx.[138] As such, Merck was under pressure to persuade skeptical regulators and doctors that it had fully disclosed Arcoxia's potential risks.[139]

THE VIOXX SETTLEMENTS

Merck's strategy was bold: No settlements—take every case to trial. By October 1, 2007, some two years after the *Ernst* decision, no plaintiff had received as much as one penny from Merck,[140] but they eventually reached a mass settlement in November 2007.[141]

The Merck attorneys assumed that their strategy of forcing plaintiffs to trial would reduce the number of Vioxx lawsuits and automatically reduce liability. Merck's position simply remained that the company had done nothing wrong. Prior to the voluntary withdrawal of Vioxx on September 30, 2004, Merck and its CEO, Ray Gilmartin, were known as the advocates of "corporate social responsibility."[142] In fact, Merck received a triple-A ethical rating, one of only two in a ranking of America's 25 biggest firms by the consulting firm Management & Excellence.[143] Upon his arrival as Merck CEO in 1994, Ray Gilmartin "established the position of chief ethics officer. The company created a global code of conduct . . . [with] ongoing training and workshops."[144] Even after Merck's withdrawal of Vioxx, the British medical journal, *The Lancet*, complimented the company for acting "promptly in the face of [their] most recent safety concerns [which] is commendable and should serve as an example of responsible pharmaceutical industry practice."[145]

Merck's attitude and legal strategy appears to be working, as the company accomplished an "impressive two-year-long turnaround."[146] On July 23, 2007, Merck reported strong second-quarter results and said, "its profits for all of 2007 would easily beat analysts' expectations."[147] This news resulted in investors bidding up Merck's stock almost 7 percent.[148]

Merck's defense to the Vioxx crisis essentially neutralized the threat of a "feeding frenzy," but the threat alone created a push to strengthen the FDA's power to police and regulate the drug industry. The need for more effective regulations led to the introduction of the FDA Revitalization Act,[149] which was to fundamentally change the agency's operations by giving it more power to ensure that drugs are as safe as advertised.[150] Essentially, this helped to guarantee that the FDA, and not the drug companies, would be liable for the defective drugs that slipped through the FDA regulatory process. Thus, the FDA now has the "power to police drug safety, order changes in drug labels, regulate advertising and restrict the use and distribution of medicines found to pose serious risks to consumers."[151]

When Congress started debating the Revitalization Act, pharmaceutical companies worried that it would restrict their drug ads; however, in the final version, such marketing was largely spared.[152] The FDA received the power to require pharmaceutical companies to submit television ads for review, but it could only recommend, not require, changes.[153] The Revitalization Act allowed the FDA to levy fines for false and misleading ads,[154] and although it strengthened the FDA's drug-safety oversight capacity, "its impact on the pharmaceutical industry . . . depended largely on how the agency opted to use its new powers."[155] The Act also increased the fees that drug makers paid the FDA to review their drugs, a portion of which went towards monitoring the safety of drugs after being released on the market.[156]

After the Vioxx withdrawal, lawmakers and consumer groups accused the FDA of allowing drug makers to delay making label changes.[157] The now-strengthened FDA could lean on the Act's provisions to require such label changes and other measures--bolstered by civil monetary penalties for noncompliance--without having to secure cooperation via a quid-pro-quo with the pharmaceutical industry.[158] But of course, the FDA could just as well rely on its past practices, and seek from the pharmaceutical industry "mutually acceptable ways" to resolve safety concerns.[159]

Vioxx did not initiate the ultimate feeding frenzy, but it did spur the plaintiff's bar to look for other mass tort class actions. Although breast implants were an established mass tort with many plaintiffs and defendants, hip and knee implants became a convenient and profitable alternative to the loss of Vioxx.

NOTES

1. Rochelle Chodock, David Yokult, and Dennis R. Connolly, *Insuring the Continued Solvency of Pharmaceutical Companies in the Face of Product Liability Class Actions,* 40 Tort Tr. & Ins. Prac. L. J. 997, 997 (2005). See generally Walter T. Champion, Jr., *A Tale of Two Cities: A Commentary on The Media's Response to Personal Injury "Feeding Frenzies" as a Result of the Vioxx And Silicosis Litigation,* 31 Whittier L. Rev. 47 (2009).

2. Mary Alice Robbins, *Texas Vioxx Litigation to Test H.B. 4 Reforms,* 20 Tex. Law. 11 (Nov. 1, 2004).

3. Alex Berenson, *Jury to Start Deliberation in Two Vioxx Injury Cases,* New York Times C4 (Apr. 4, 2006).

4. *Id.*

5. *Id.*

6. Alex Berenson, *Despite Vow, Drug Makers Still Withhold Data,* New York Times A1 (May 31, 2005).

7. Mark A. Stein, *Detroit Gets Its October Sales Numbers and Winces,* New York Times C2 (Nov. 5, 2005).

8. Bill Straub, *The Gloves Are Off,* 42 Tr. 24, 26 (July 2006) (quotation omitted); "The federal government in recent years has all but abandoned its duty to protect the American public from unsafe pharmaceuticals." *Id.*

9. *Id.* at 28.

10. *Id.*

11. Marshall H. Chin, *The Patient's Role in Choice of Medications: Direct-to-Consumer Advertising and Patient Decision Aids,* 5 Yale J. Health Policy, L. & Ethics 771, 781 (2005).

12. Walter T. Champion, *The Vioxx Litigation Paradigm: The Search for Smoking Guns,* 31 Thurgood Marshall L. Rev 157, 195 n. 7 (2006); Richard A. Epstein, *Regulatory Paternalism in the Market for Drugs: Lessons from Vioxx and Celebrex,* 5 Yale J. Health Policy, L. & Ethics 741 (2005).

13. *Id.*

14. See Straub, *supra* n. 8, at 28.

15. Chin, *supra* n. 11, at 775.

16. *Id.* at 772.

17. *Id.* at 776; *accord* Joel S. Weissman et al., *Physicians Report on Patient Encounters Involving Direct-to-Consumer Advertising W4-220,* http://dx.doi.org/10.1377/hlthaf.W4.219 (Apr. 28, 2004).

18. Chin, *supra* n. 11, at 776; Weissman, *supra* n. 17.

19. 21 C.F.R. § 202.1(e) (2009); Champion, *supra* n. 1, at 159; James M. Jeffords, *Direct-to-Consumer Drug Advertising: You Get What You Pay For,* http://dx.doi.org/10.1377/hlthaff.W4.253 (Apr. 28, 2004).

20. Chin, *supra* n. 11, at 778.

21. Henry A. Waxman, *Ensuring That Consumers Receive Appropriate Information from Drug Ads: What Is the FDA's Role?,* http://content.healthaffairs.org/cgi/content/full.hlthaff.W4.256vll0c (Apr. 28, 2004).

22. *Id.*; Chin, *supra* n. 11, at 778.

23. Stephanie Saul, *Drug Makers to Police Consumer Campaigns,* New York Times C7 (Aug. 3, 2005), *Id.*

24. *Id.*

25. *Id.*

26. *Id.*

27. *Id.*

28. Marcia Angell, *The Truth About the Drug Companies,* 45 Jurimetrics J. 465, 466 (2005).

29. Puneet Manchanda and Elisabeth Honka, *The Effects and Role of Direct-to-Physician Marketing in the Pharmaceutical Industry: An Integrative Review,* 5 Yale J. of Health Policy, L. & Ethics 785, 786 (2005) (citation omitted). See also Sen. Comm. on Health, Educ., Lab., & Pen., *What's Driving Health Care Costs and the Uninsured?,* Sen. Hrg. 424, 108th Cong. 4 (Jan. 28, 2004); Families USA, *Off the Charts: Pay, Profits and Spending by Drug Companies,* 3, http://www.familiesusa.org/assets/pdfs/offthecharts6475.pdf (July 2001); Dick R. Wittink, *Analysis of ROI for Pharmaceutical Promotion* (AARP) 7 http://www.rxpromoroi.org/ arpp/media/arpphandout0927.pdf (Sept. 18, 2002).

30. Angell, *supra* n. 28, at 468.

31. *Id.*

32. *Id.*

33. Arnold S. Relman and Marcia Angell, *America's Other Drug Problem: How the Drug Industry Distorts Medicine and Politics,* The New Republic 27 (Dec. 16, 2002) (available at http://www.commercialalert.org/relmanagel1.pdf).

34. *Id.*

35. Epstein, *supra* n. 12, at 742; *accord* Alex Berenson, *Merck's Board Appoints Panel to Investigate Handling of Vioxx,* New York Times C6 (Dec. 8, 2004); Barnaby J. Feder, *Pfizer and Celebrex: The Company; Criticism of Drug May Leave Pfizer Awash in Lawsuits,* New York Times C1 (Dec. 18, 2004); Barnaby J. Feder, *Merck's Actions on Vioxx Face New Scrutiny,* New York Times C1 (Feb. 15, 2005) (examples of the gravity of the Vioxx phenomenon in popular media coverage); Bruce Japsen, *Merck Withdraws Arthritis Drug: Vioxx Increased Danger to Heart,* Chicago Tribune 1 (Oct. 1, 2004); Andrew Leckey, *Prognosis Is Cautious for Merck Shares,* Analysts Say, Chicago Tribune 8 (Nov. 7, 2004); Anahad O'Connor & Denise Grady, *Pfizer and Celebrex: The Patients*: *Problems May Send Many Patients Back to Age-Old Aspirin,* New York Times C1 (Dec. 18, 2004); Andrew Pollack, *New Scrutiny of Drugs in Vioxx's Family,* New York Times C1 (Oct. 4, 2004); FDA, *Vioxx (Rofecoxib) Questions and Answers,* 9, http://www.fda. gov/Drugs/DrugSafetyPostmarketDrugSafetyInformationforPatientsandProviders/ucm106290.htm; (updated June 18, 2009).

36. Epstein, *supra, n.* 12, at 742.

37. *Id.* Reactions included "ordinary tort actions for personal injuries buttressed by congressional investigations, inquiries by the Securities and Exchange Commission, derivative actions, suits for refunds, [and] internal inquiries," *Id.,* at 742–43.

38. Barbara Martinez et al., *Merck Pulls Vioxx from Market After Link to Heart Problems,* Wall St. J. A1 (Oct. 1, 2004).

39. See Chodock et al., *supra* n. 1.

40. Stein, *supra* n. 7; Alex Berenson, *Merck Admits a Data Error on Vioxx,* New York Times C1 (May 31, 2006).

41. Allison Torres Burtka, *Vioxx Studies Question Timing of Heart Attack Risk,* 42 Tr. 98 (July 2006).

42. *Id.*

43. *Id.*

44. *Id.,* The acronym "APPROVE" stood for "*Adenomatous Polyp Prevention on Vioxx,*" *Id.*

45. *Id.; Accord* Alex Berenson, *Follow-Up Study on Vioxx Safety Is Disputed,* New York Times C3 (May 13, 2006).

46. Heather Won Tesoriero and Ron Winslow, *New Merck Data Suggests Risks from Vioxx Begin Earlier in Use,* Wall St. J. A2 (May 18, 2006).

47. Burtka, *supra* n. 41; Berenson, *Merck Admits a Data Error, supra* n. 40.

48. See *Id.*

49. *Id.*

50. *Id.*

51. Burtka, *supra* n. 41.

52. Richard Stewart, *Widow's Suit against Vioxx Maker to Set the Tone for Rest,* Houston Chronicle A1 (July 4, 2005).

53. Id.; Richard Stewart, *The Vioxx Trial; Motion Challenges Plaintiffs Experts, Jury Selection Is Expected to Start Today in Lawsuit against Drug Firm,* Houston Chronicle B1 (July 11, 2005).

54. Stewart, *Widow's Suit, supra* n. 52.

55. Associated Press, *Judge Will Not Delay Vioxx Trial in Texas,* New York Times C1 (July 6, 2005); Alex Berenson, *In First of Many Vioxx Cases, a Texas Widow Prepares to Take the Stand,* New York Times C3 (July 13, 2005).

56. Alex Berenson, *Jury Calls Merck Liable in Death of Man on Vioxx,* New York Times A1 (Aug. 20, 2005).

57. *Id.*

58. *Id.*

59. Alex Berenson, *Second Trial for Merck on Vioxx Begins,* New York Times C1 (Sept. 15, 2005).

60. *Id.*

61. Alex Berenson, *Merck Is Winner in Vioxx Lawsuit on Heart Attack,* New York Times A1 (Nov. 4, 2005).

62. *Id.*

63. Alex Berenson, *Doctor Links Merck Trial to His Demotion,* New York Times C3 (Dec. 10, 2005).

64. Reuters, *Jurors in Vioxx Trial are Told to Press On,* New York Times, 147 (Dec. 11, 2005).

65. Associated Press, *Lawyer Tells Third Vioxx Trial That a Month's Use Was Fatal,* New York Times C9 (Nov. 30, 2005).

66. Alex Berenson, *A Mistrial Is Declared in Third Suit Over Vioxx,* New York Times C1 (Dec. 13, 2005).

67. Alex Berenson, *A Second Loss for Merck over Vioxx,* New York Times C1 (Apr. 6, 2006).

68. *Id.*

69. *Id.*

70. *Id.*

71. *Id.*; Alex Berenson, *Jury to Start Deliberation in Two Vioxx Injury Cases,* New York Times C4 (Apr. 4, 2006).

72. Alex Berenson, *Merck Loses Vioxx Suit in Texas,* New York Times C1 (Apr. 22, 2006).

73. *Id.*

74. Associated Press, *Judge Cuts Amount of Vioxx Award,* New York Times C2 (Dec. 22, 2006); Associated Press, *Judge Lets $7.75 Million Vioxx Award Stand,* Wall St. J. A12 (Mar. 9, 2007).

75. Bloomberg News, *Merck Wins Vioxx Case in New Jersey,* New York Times C4 (July 14, 2006).

76. *Id.*

77. *Id.*

78. Alex Berenson, *Legal Stance May Pay off for Merck,* New York Times C1 (Aug. 4, 2006).

79. *Id.*

80. *Id.*

81. *Id.*

82. *Id.*

83. *Id.* Alex Berenson, *Merck Suffers a Pair of Setbacks over Vioxx,* New York Times C1 (Aug. 18, 2006).

84. *Id.*

85. *Id.*

86. *In re Vioxx Prod. Liab, Litig.,* 448 F. Supp. 2d 737, 740 (E.D. La. 2006).

87. *Id.*

88. *Id.*

89. *Id.,* at 741; Bloomberg News, *Judge Rules Damage Award in Vioxx Case Is Excessive,* New York Times C-11 (Aug. 31, 2006). Tiffany Farr, *Verdict Win for Merck in Vioxx Trial,* http//:Houston.injuryboard.com/fda-andprescriptiondrugs/ verdict-wn-for-merck-in-vioxx-trial.aspx?googleid206860 (Sept. 29, 2006).

90. Tiffany Farr, *Verdict Win for Merck in Vioxx Trial,* http://houston. injuryboard.com/fda-andprescriptiondrugs/verdict-win-for-merck-in-vioxx-trial.asp x?googleid=206860 (Sept. 29, 2006).

91. Business Wire, *Merck Wins Federal Vioxx Product Liability Case: Smith v. Merck & Co., Inc.,* http://findarticles.comlp/atticles/mimoEIN/is_2006_Sept_26/ ain1683723 (Sept. 26, 2006).

92. Associated Press, *Jury Backs Merck in Vioxx Lawsuit,* New York Times C6 (Sept. 27, 2006).

93. Bloomberg News, *Merck Is Winner in a Vioxx Lawsuit,* New York Times C4 (Nov. 16, 2006).

94. *Id.; cf. In re Vioxx Prod. Liab. Litig.* 239 F.R.D. 450, 462-63 (E.D. La. 2006); (Judge Fallon denied class action status for Vioxx plaintiffs on Nov. 22, 2006); Associated Press, *Judge Denies Class Status for Lawsuits over Vioxx,* New York Times C2 (Nov. 23, 2006).

95. Mike Tolson, *Vioxx Maker Notches Gains with Strategy: Merck Fights Each Lawsuit, but the Costs Run $1 Million a Day,* Houston Chronicle 1 (Nov. 28, 2006).

96. Reuters, *Vioxx Suit Is Won Quickly by Merck,* New York Times C2 (Dec. 14, 2006).

97. Associated Press, *Merck Wins Suit in Alabama Over the Painkiller Vioxx,* New York Times C2 (Dec. 16, 2006) (quotations omitted).

98. *Id.;* Associated Press, *Merck Scores Win in Alabama Over the Painkiller Vioxx Drug,* Wall St. J. A5 (Dec. 16, 2006).

99. Associated Press, *Mistrial Declared Over Vioxx Risks,* New York Times C6 (Jan. 19, 2007).

100. *Id.*

101. David Voreacos, *Merck Failed to Warn of Vioxx Heart Risk, Jury Finds,* http://www.bloomberg.com/apps/news?pid=20601103&sid=a20EULq55XVM (Mar. 2, 2007).

102. *Id.*

103. Andrew Pollack, *Mixed Verdicts for Merck in Vioxx Cases,* New York Times C8 (Mar. 3, 2007).

104. *Id.*

105. *Id.*

106. *Id.*

107. *Id.*

108. Globe News wire, *$47.5 Million Total Rendered Against Merck & Co.,* http://www.globenewswire.com/newsroom.html/d=115365 (Mar. 12, 2007).

109. Heather Won Tesoriero, *Jury Awards $47.5 Million to Man in Vioxx Retrial,* Wall St. J. A3 (Mar. 13, 2007); Associated Press, *In Big Penalty, Jury Reverses a Vioxx Verdict,* New York Times C8 (Mar. 13, 2007).

110. Associated Press, *Vioxx Plaintiff is Denied a Second Chance,* New York Times C11 (Mar. 6, 2007).

111. Steve Gonzalez, *Jury Finds Merck Not Liable for Schwaller's Death,* http://www.madisonrecord.com/printer/article.asp?c=192528 (Mar. 27, 2007).

112. Steve Gonzalez, *Plaintiff Who Lost Madison County's Only Vioxx Trial Wants Piece of Settlement Pie,* http://www.madisonrecord.com/printer/article.asp?c=204364 (Nov. 21, 2007).

113. Associated Press, *Illinois Jury Sides with Merck in 10th Trial over Painkiller,* New York Times C7 (Mar. 28, 2007).

114. Heather Won Tesoriero, *Merck Prevails in Vioxx Case Brought by Illinois Widower,* Wall St. J. A11 (Mar. 28, 2007).

115. Heather Won Tesoriero, *Merck's Vioxx Troubles May Ebb with Rulings Poised to Aid Defense—Expected Case Dismissal Could Weaken Legal Basis for All 1,000 Texas Suits,* Wall St. J. A3 (Apr. 13, 2007).

116. Mary Flood, *Judge Tosses Major Part of Vioxx Case,* Houston Chronicle B-3 (Apr. 21, 2007); Judge Wilson based his rulings on a 2003 Texas reform law and a related U.S. Supreme Court case, *Buckman Co. v. Plaintiffs' Leg. Comm.,* 531 U.S. 341 (2001). The Texas law states that "when the [FDA] has approved a drug, it is presumed the warnings are adequate. The person suing would have to rebut that presumption. In this case Ledbetter alleges Merck lied to the FDA . . . but the judge found that the U.S. Supreme Court has ruled that only the FDA can determine if it has been defrauded, thus barring the argument [that] Merck lied to the FDA," Mary Flood, *Harris County (TX) Judge Nixes Vioxx Lawsuit,* Houston Chronicle (Apr. 21, 2007). See *Ledbetter v. Merck & Co., Inc.,* 2007 WL 1181991 (Tex. Dist.) (Tr. Order, Apr. 19, 2007).

117. See Mary Flood, *Judge Casts Doubt on Vioxx Point; Plans to Toss Part of Arguments Could Raise Bar for all Pharmaceutical Cases,* Houston Chronicle B1 (Apr. 17, 2007); Flood, *Judge Tosses, supra* n. 116; Won Tesoriero, *Troubles May Ebb, supra* n. 115.

118. *Wyeth v. Levine,* 129 S. Ct. 1187 (2009).

119. *Id.* at 1196–98.

120. *In re Vioxx Prod. Liab. Litig.,* 239 F.R.D. 450, 452 (E.D. La. 2006); Associated Press, *Judge Denies Class Status for Lawsuits over Vioxx,* New York Times C2 (Nov. 23, 2006).

121. Associated Press, *Court Denies Class Status for Plaintiffs Against Merck,* New York Times C2 (Sept. 7, 2007).

122. *Id.*

123. Alex Berenson, *Another Quarter of Strong Results by Merck,* New York Times C3 (July 24, 2007); Peter A. McKay, *Blue Chips Bounce Back a Bit, Paced by Merck's Legal Win,* Wall St. J. C-l (Sept. 7, 2007); Heather Won Tesoriero, *Vioxx Ruling Eases Threat to Merck—New Jersey Court Bars Class-Action Status for Health Insurers' Suits,* Wall St. J. A3 (Sept. 7, 2007); *Class in New Jersey,* Wall. St. J. A14 (Sept. 10, 2007).

124. *Id.*

125. *Today in Business,* New York Times C2 (Aug. 21, 2007).

126. *Id.*

127. *Id.*

128. *Id.*

129. *Merck v. Ernst,* 2009 WL 1677857; Mike Tolson, *Vioxx Maker Notches Gains with Strategy: Merck Fights Each Lawsuit, but the Costs Run $1 Million a Day,* Houston Chronicle B1 (Nov. 28, 2006).

130. Barnaby J. Feder, *Newer Stents Pose Dangers, Two Doctors Say,* New York Times A22 (Oct. 12, 2006).

131. *Id.*

132. Stephanie Saul and Andrew Pollack, *Furor on Rush to Require Cervical Cancer Vaccine,* New York Times A1 (Feb. 17, 2007).

133. *Id.*

134. Alex Berenson, *Merck Sees Successor to Vioxx,* New York Times C1 (Aug. 24, 2006).

135. *Id.*

136. *Id.*

137. *Id.*

138. Alex Berenson, *Plaintiffs Find Payday Elusive in Vioxx Cases,* New York Times A1 (Aug. 21, 2007).

139. Carrie Johnson, *Merck Agrees to Blanket Settlement on Vioxx,* Wash. Post D10 (Nov. 10, 2007).

140. *The Acceptable Face of Capitalism? Ray Gilmartin of Merck May be a New Role Model for Post-Celebrity Client Executives,* 365 The Economist 61 (Dec. 14, 2002) (quotations omitted).

141. *Id.* "Merck has donated $100 [million] worth of vaccines against such scourges as hepatitis to the Global Alliance for Vaccines and Immunisation. More recently, it committed $50 [million] to Botswana, working with the Gates Foundation and the government to build a better health-care delivery system to combat AIDS." Id.

142. Kim Norris, *Merck CEO Says Its Voluntary Recall of Vioxx Drug Was Ethical Choice,* Detroit Free Press (Nov. 11, 2004).

143. *Vioxx: An Unequal Partnership between Safety and Efficacy,* 634 The Lancet 1287, 1287 (Oct. 9, 2004).

144. Berenson, *Another Quarter, supra* n. 123.

145. *Id.*

146. *Id.*, see Bloomberg News, *Cholesterol Pill Sales Bolster Two Drug Makers,* New York Times C9 (Oct. 21, 2006); and Peter Loftus, *Merck's Revival Helps Enhance Schering's Net,* Wall St. J. A2 (Jul. 24, 2007).

147. Pub. L. No. 110–85, 121 Stat. 823 (2007). The FDA Revitalization Act was enacted as the "Food and Drug Administration Amendments Act of 2007," *Id.* at §1 (Italics added).

148. Leg. Not. S. 1082, The FDA Revitalization Act (Apr. 30, 2007); see also Gardiner Harris, *Senate Takes up Bill to Change Drug Agency Operators*, New York Times A18 (May 10, 2007); Robert Pear, *Senate Approves Tighter Policing of Drug Makers*, New York Times A1 (May 10, 2007).

149. *Id.* See accord Harris, *Senate Takes Up Bill, supra* n. 148; Sen. 1082, 100th Cong. (May 8, 2007); Gardiner Harris, *House Passes Bill, Giving More Power to the F.D.A.,* New York Times A18 (Sept. 20, 2007); Bloomberg News, *Drug Safety Bill Sent to Bush,* New York Times A15 (Sept. 21, 2007).

150. Anna Wilde Matthews and Stephanie Kang, *Media Industry Helped Drug Firms Fight Ad Restraints,* Wall. St. J. B1 (Sept. 21, 2007).

151. *Id.*

152. *Id.*

153. Sarah Rubenstein, Heather Won Tesoriero, and Anna Wilde Matthews, *Congress Expands FDA's Oversight on Drug Safety,* Wall St. J. A12 (Sept. 21, 2007).

154. *Id.*

155. *Id.*

156. *Id.*

157. *Id.*

158. *Id.*

159. *Id.*

Chapter 16

Hip, Knee, and Breast Implants

"I told you not to put metal in the science oven . . ." [Irving Rosenfeld, as played by Christian Bale in *American Hustle*, Atlas Entertainment, 2013]. Implants might be rejected since they are alien to the body and are not biodegradable. "More than one million U.S. women have received breast implants. For these women, local complications that require additional surgical procedures are an important problem . . . complications occurred in 24% of the women, the most frequent problems were capsular contraction, implant rupture, hematoma, and wound infection."[1]

There is disagreement among scientists over the toxicity of silicone breast implants. Generally, as regards mass exposure litigation—"Scientific research into causation is a slow, arduous process, often barely begun when litigation commences."[2] "Whether intact or ruptured, silicone implants interfere with mammography and therefore may impede the early detection and prompt treatment of breast cancer. More controversial are the links between medical problems such as connective tissue disorders and autoimmune diseases and exposure to silicone leaked from intact implants or escaped from ruptured ones."[3]

Hip and knee replacements have also generated class actions and been subject to recalls. For example, "Sulzer Orthopedics, Inc., has offered to settle some 1,300 hip and knee implant lawsuits by compensating patients who received the defective implants up to $97,500 in cash and stock . . . after the company discovered that an oily residue left on the shell of the implant . . . prevented it from bonding with patients' pelvic bones."[4]

The problem with all implants is that there is always the possibility that alien pathogens can infect the immune system.

While most antigens exist outside the body, some natural antigens exist within our own cell structure. An important function of a healthy immune system is to recognize those antigens as 'self' and not attack them. If the immune system loses this ability to separate friendly antigens from foreign ones, the body will

151

then produce antibodies that in effect attack its own tissue (autoantibodies) which can produce autoimmune diseases. As it turns out, silicone is not entirely inert but, like other foreign invaders, triggers a defensive body reaction.[5]

In *Pick v. American Medical Systems, Inc.*, a recipient of a silicone elastomer penile implant brought a products liability suit against the implant manufacturer alleging that the implant causes autoimmune disorder and systemic coccal diseases. In these scenarios, the success of the case relies on the admission of scientific evidence, and then it is a battle of scientists. The plaintiff, Laura Pick, contends that AMS failed to warn of the immune related connective tissue disorders and silicone-associated health risks and that the implant was unreasonably dangerous because of the silicone content. The plaintiff further alleges that Barry Pick suffered from various disorders that were caused or aggravated by the silicone and/or coca bacteria from the implant. The implant was removed in 1993 but Barry Pick died after the litigation was filed.[6]

The legal standard for the admissibility of scientific evidence is established in *Daubert v. Merrell Dow Pharmaceuticals, Inc.*,[7] which obliges the trial judge to act as a "gatekeeper" and screen scientific evidence for reliability and relevance. Barry claims that silicone in his implant caused him to develop "siliconosis" and a "systematic inflammatory illnesses caused by the silicone devices." Epidemiological studies assess general causation via statistical probability, comparing the incidence of disease in people exposed to a substance as opposed to people not exposed to a substance. The court held that plaintiff's epidemiological study finding some statistical connection between silicone gel and autoimmune diseases was admissible under *Daubert*. The court also held that plaintiff's case studies involving gel implants were similarly admissible.[8]

BREAST IMPLANTS

In specific breast implant trials, scientific expert testimony admissible under *Daubert* will reveal this state of the science to the legal factfinder whether the factfinder is presented simply with rival conclusions or with a more detailed picture of the scientific basis for those conclusions. Presented with testimony that attests to the uncertainty among scientists, a reasonable legal factfinder would, it seems, have to conclude that the causal powers of silicone implants are unknown.[9]

FDA Commissioner David Kessler in 1992 banned silicone-gel-filled breast implants, which affected about 2 million American women. "Most women with implants had simply wanted to enlarge their breasts, but about 20% had obtained them for reconstruction after mastectomy for breast cancer."[10] "[M]any people were jubilant about the FDA ban—including advocates of tough government regulation, women who believed breast implants had caused them to become ill, and feminists who thought it was about time someone put a stop to women being pressured to conform to male fantasies."[11] "[B]reast implants . . . cause devastating effects on the rest of the body . . . [such that] the immune system that turns the body's protective defenses against itself. The result is an autoimmune defense—that is, a prolonged civil war within the body that can produce profound weakness and fatigue along with variable damage to the joints, skin, and internal organs."[12]

"After the FDA ban, when the manufacturers were clearly on the ropes, the plaintiffs' attorneys moved in to capture the profits of the manufacturers."[13] "[S]ometimes a lawyer can win just by getting the game in play."[14] "[Aggravated] implant recipient Maria Stern sued Dow Corning in 1982. Stern's implants had ruptured and were removed in 1981. She suffered from chronic fatigue and joint pains before and after the implants were removed. Her doctors speculated that leakage of silicone gel into her body from the ruptured implants might be the cause of her problems."[15]

Hersh & Hersh, a small plaintiffs' firm in San Francisco that specialized in women's health issues, represented Stern in her suit against Dow Corning. . . . During discovery proceedings, Dan Bolton, an associate at Hersh & Hersh, found thousands of internal Dow Corning memos relating to breast implants, several of which made the company look extremely irresponsible. . . . Bolton used these documents to great effect at the trial in July 1984.[16]

December 1990 . . . episode of *Face to Face with Connie Chung* which focused on implants. Chung's show frightened and outraged thousands of implant recipients. Chung referred to silicone gel as "an ooze of slimy gelatin that could be poisoning women." One interviewed woman, Sybil Goldrich, revealed her chest, disfigured by operations to remove implants. Goldrich and other witnesses . . . discussed the possibility that . . . implants promote cancer and cause immune reactions leading to serious illnesses, including lupus and rheumatoid arthritis.[17]

Silicone breast implants were an improvement over liquid silicone injections when they were first introduced by Dow Corning in 1963. The FDA in 1963 lacked authority to regulate medical devices, however Congress fixed that loophole in the Food, Drug and Cosmetic Safety Act in 1976 that excluded medical devices from FDA regulation. In December 1991, a San Francisco jury awarded $7.3 million to a woman who claimed that her leaked implants caused permanent autoimmune disorder. The jury based their award on internal Dow Corning memoranda indicating that, by the early 1970s, Dow knew the implants were associated with health problems; the jury found that Dow acted with fraud, oppression, and malice including faking quality control records.[18]

The FDA had documented that Dow improperly withheld data about the implant's safety problems. Under FDA pressure in March 1992, Dow announced that it would no longer manufacture the implants. A Texas state jury in Spring 1993 awarded $5 million in compensatory damages and $20 million in punitive damages, including $2 million in attorney fees and $1 million in prejudgment interest, totaling $28 million. In September 1993, Dow Corning proposed a $4.75 billion settlement of all pending and future breast implant cases. The agreed to amount ultimately rounded out to about $4.25 billion, which was the largest class action settlement to date.[19]

Case Study-Sharon Evans—This is a medical malpractice informed consent case. Sharon Evans alleged that Dr. Jack Conlee

> failed to inform and misrepresented . . . [to] Evans the risks and results of reconstructive breast implant surgery. The trial court granted summary judgment in Conlee's favor. We reverse the summary judgment and remand the cause to the trial court . . . but for Conlee's advice and consultation she would not have consented to either the mastectomies or the consequent implant surgery.[20]

HIP AND KNEE IMPLANTS

The settlement in *In re Sulzer Hip and Knee Implant Plaintiffs* set the stage for the class action litigation for defective and injurious hip and knee replacements. There were also individual lawsuits and bellwether settlements that were a part of the overall litigation. Sulzer agreed to a $1 billion settlement after withdrawing 25,000 hip replacements.[21]

There are many different manufacturers of joint replacements, which necessitate different litigation strategies. There is always the risk of metal-on-metal (MoM) contact where metallic components abrade against each other, including degradation and wearing down of the component materials. One of the results is metallosis which is a putative medical condition involving deposition and build-up of metal debris. Metallosis can cause dislocation of noncemented implants as the healthy tissue that would normally hold the implant in place is weakened or destroyed; it has also been demonstrated to cause osteolysis (wearing down of the bones).[22]

The De Puy knee replacement lawsuit dealt with the De Puy Altune Knee Replacement System which is a medical device designed by De Puy Synthes to improve range of motion. The lawsuit alleged liability for patients who undergo knee replacement surgery. Knee replacement is supposed to improve the quality of life, but complaints by recipients include device failure, loosening of device, pain, swelling, difficulty walking, and constructive surgery. "In the *Sulzer* Medica settlement, there were 4,000 lawsuits that were filed over faulty devices, revision surgery and loosening of devices. . . The manufacturer either knew or should have known of the device's defects; and the manufacturer failed to warn patients of the defects and their potential consequences."[23]

Products liability claims against manufacturers of hip replacement components were transferred by the Judicial Panel on Multidistrict Litigation in the case titled *In re Inter-Op Hip Prosthesis Liability Litigation*—the class was provisionally certified and the settlement agreement preliminarily approved: "Sulzer Orthopedics, Inc. is a designer, manufacturer and distributor of orthopedic implants for hips, knees, shoulders, and elbows. One of its products is known as the 'Inter-Op acetabular shell,' which is one component of a system used for complete hip replacements. . . . Sulzer voluntarily recalled specific lots of hip replacement devices, which again initiated a feeding frenzy among lawyers."[24]

The American Association for Justice (AAJ) is the group that represents plaintiffs' lawyers; they have prepared a litigation packet for MoM hip implant cases—AAJ members across the nation are investigating and litigating cases involving defective MoM artificial hip implants. Problems with the implants were first identified in devices with metal cups and femoral heads, but other components have also been linked to serious complications, including osteolysis, metallosis, neurological problems, loosening, and premature failure. Revision surgery is often required, and it may provide only partial relief for patients.[25] The AAJ has prepared a litigation packet on Toxic Hip Replacements. Hundreds of lawsuits have been filed against the makers of so-called MoM artificial hips alleging that the implants fail prematurely and cause other medical problems. "If you are considering representing someone who has been injured by a MoM implant, you need to understand how the implants work, the problems that patients have encountered, potential cause of those problems, and what to look for in your client's case."[26]

LITIGATION TIPS

When you take a hip replacement case, you must first definitively confirm what the device is. Obtain a copy of the device labels from the surgical implant record that describe each implanted component. . . . These are approved by the FDA and are the equivalent of the package insert for prescription medications. Once in discovery, obtain the manufacturer's published marketing and promotional materials.[27]

The FDA in January 2013 issued a proposal calling on companies that manufacture all-metal hip replacements to provide additional information proving that they are safe and effective before being allowed to continue to sell them. "With wear, all-metal implants can shed metal where two components connect, potentially damaging bone and soft tissue surrounding the implant."[28]

CASE STUDIES: INDIVIDUAL LAWSUITS

Rupp v. Sulzer Orthopedics—A Texas jury has returned a verdict of $15.5 million in the first Sulzer hip implant case to go to trial. The suit was brought by three elderly women whose hips were replaced with defective Sulzer products. *Rupp, et al. v. Sulzer Orthopedics Inc.*, No. 01-60581-4, verdict rendered (Tex. Dist. Ct., Nueces County, Aug. 30, 2001). . . . The six-person jury in Nueces County, Texas, took only 10 hours to deliberate before returning a verdict for each of the Corpus Christi plaintiffs.[29]

Agoglia v. Stryker Howmedica Osteonics—A Brooklyn, New York, couple has filed a lawsuit seeking $17.5 million in damages for injuries from an allegedly defective hip implant manufactured by Stryker *Howmedica Osteonics. Agoglia, et al. v. Stryker Howmedica Osteonics, et al.*, No. 02–5210, complaint filed (E.D.N.Y., Sept. 24, 2002). The complaint alleges that Ralph Agoglia underwent hip replacement surgery in December 1998 and that the hip implant fractured in October 1999 causing him to have to undergo revision surgery to replace the device. "The fracture was not the result of natural 'wear and tear,' but rather was caused by the negligent and improper design, manufacture, testing, and marketing of the device. . . . The suit alleges strict liability and breach of express and implied warranties."[30]

Scroggins v. Zimmer Holdings—A Louisiana woman has filed a $1 million lawsuit in a New Orleans federal court against five medical device companies alleging that they manufactured a defective hip implant that caused her to undergo a second replacement. *Scroggins v. Zimmer Holdings, Inc., et al.*, No. 03-CV-1496, complaint filed (E.D. La., May 15, 2002). "The suit seeks $1 million in damages and interest. Certain ceramic hip implants manufactured by Zimmer, Depuy, and Stryker were recalled by the U.S. Food and Drug Administration on Sept. 14, 2001. According to the agency, the ceramic zirconia femoral head part of the implant has a higher than acceptable fracture rate."[31]

Some observers feel that breast implant litigation was based entirely on junk science. This is incorrect; the leakage of a possible toxic chemical into the body *will* have some effect on the autoimmune system. As regards hip and knee implants, the lubricating chemical, silicone, and the joint replacement system based on metal-on-metal technology is an inherent design defect.

Although litigation has appeared to be successful, none of the companies "lost" money; even though the settlement numbers appeared to be astronomical, the companies in some cases were sold—at a profit. At the time, when it seems like the numbers of knee and hip replacement cases were dwindling, the plaintiff's bar discovered that football concussions caused brain damage. Much of the mass litigation protocols can be used to sign and evaluate potential clients, where the plaintiffs were an identifiable subgroup that played football.

NOTES

1. *Local Complications from Breast Implants,* 6 Medical-Legal Watch 46 (n. 8, Aug. 1997). See generally Daniel Penolsky, *Cosmetic Silicone Breast Implant Litigation,* 55 Am. J. Trials 1 (originally publ'd 1995, Feb. 2018 update); Marcia Angell, *Science on Trial: The Clash of Medical Evidence and the Law in the Breast Implant Case* (New York: W.W. Norton & Co., 1996); and Heidi L. Feldman, *Science and Uncertainty in Mass Exposure Litigation,* 74 Tex. L. Rev. 1 (Nov. 1995).

2. *Id.* at 17 (footnote omitted).

3. *Id.* at 19–20 (footnotes omitted).

4. *Sulzer Offers $700 Million Settlement of Hip and Knee Implant Suits,* 4 Andrews Drug Recall Litig. Rptr. 6 (n. 12, Sept. 2001).

5. *Pick v. American Medical Systems, Inc.,* 958 F. Supp. 1151, 1156 (E.D. La. 1997) (footnotes omitted).

6. *Id.* at 1154–55.

7. *Daubert,* 509 U.S. 579, 113 S.Ct. 2786 (1993).

8. *Pick,* 958 F. Supp. 1151, 1157–63.

9. Feldman, *Science and Uncertainty,* 74 Tex. L. Rev. 1

10. Angell, *Science on Trial,* 19 (footnote omitted).

11. *Id.* at 19–20.

12. *Id.* at 21–22.

13. *Id.* at 30.

14. David Bernstein, Review Essay, *The Breast Implant Fiasco, Science on Trial,* 87 Cal. L. Rev. 457, 461 (March 1999).

15. *Id.*

16. *Id.* at 463–64 (footnotes omitted).

17. *Id.* at 467–68 (footnotes omitted). See also Rebecca Weisman, *Reforms in Medical Device Regulation: An Examination of the Silicone Gel Breast Implant Debacle,* 23 Golden Gate U. L. Rev. 973 (Sum. 1993); Kathy King-Cameron, *Carving Another Exception to the Learned Intermediary Doctrine: Application of the Learned Intermediary Doctrine in Silicone Breast Implant Litigation,* 68 Tul. L. Rev. 937 (Mar. 1994); Kerith Cohen, *Truth & Beauty, Deception & Disfigurement: A Feminist Analysis of Breast Implant Litigation,* 1 Wm. & Mary J. Women & L. 149 (Fall 1994); Jack Snyder, *Silicone Breast Implants: Can Emerging Medical, Legal, and Scientific*

Concepts Be Reconciled?, 18 J. Legal Med. 133 (Jun. 1997); Sherine Gabriel et al., *Complications Leading to Surgery after Breast Implantation*, 336 N.E. J. Med. 677 (1997); Julie Spanbauer, *Breast Implants as Beauty Ritual: Woman's Scepter and Prison*, 9 Yale J. L. & Feminism 157 (1997); Anne Bloom, *Rupture, Leakage, and Reconstruction: The Body as a Site for the Enforcement and Reproduction of Sex-Based Legal Norms in the Breast Implant Controversy*, 14 Colum. J. Gender & L. 85 (2005); Eric Handelman, *Proof of Defective Breast Implants*, 129 Am. Jun. P.O. F.3d 457 (originally published, 2012; Feb. 2018 update); and *Breast Implant-Plaintiff to Defendant Manufacturer*, I Trial Practice Check lists § 6: 109 (2d ed.) (April 2017 update).

18. Deborah Hensler and Mark Peterson, *Understanding Mass Personal Injury Litigation: A Socio-Legal Analysis*, 59 Brook. L. Rev. 961. 992–94 (Fall 1993).

19. *Id.* at 994–98.

20. *Evans v. Conlee*, 787 S.W.2d 570 (Tex. App.—Corpus Christi-Edinburg, 1990).

21. *Sulzer Medica Accepts $1 Billion Settlement Deal with Hip and Knee Implant Plaintiffs*; In re Sulzer Hip and Knee Prostheses Prods. Liab. Litig., 9 No. 6 Andrews Med. Devices Litig. Rptr. 11 (Jun. 14, 2002); See *In re Sulzer Hip and Knee Prostheses Prods. Liab. Litig.*, 2002 WL 32156882 (Judgment & Order), Verdict and Settlement (May 31, 2020).

22. *Id.* See also *Sulzer Medica Accepts $1 Billion Settlement Deal with Hip and Knee Implant Plaintiffs; In re Sulzer Hip and Knee Prostheses Prods. Liab. Litig.*, 9 No. 6 Andrews Medical Devices Litig. Rptr. No. 11 (June 14, 2002); *Knee Replacement Litigation-Settlements and Notable Cases*, https://www.drugwatch.com>litigation; *Metallosis (Knee or Hip or Poisoning)*, https://cnmwikipcdiaorg>wiki>metal. See generally Oliver Hahn, *Liability of Manufacturer or Distributor for Injuries Arising from Allegedly Defective Artificial Knee Devices or Prostheses*, 89 A.L.R. 337 (originally published in 2013).

23. See *Sulzer Denies Liability in Answers to Two Complaints*, 7 No. 21 Andrews Med. Devices Litig. Rptr. 4 (March 23, 2001); *Sulzer Offers $700 Million Settlement of Hip and Knee Implant Suits*, 8 No. 8 Andrews Med. Devices Litig. Rptr. 3 (Aug. 24, 2001); *Judge Grants Preliminary Approval to Sulzer Settlement Plan; "Objectors Appeal,"* 8 No. 9 Andrews Med. Devices Litig. Rptr. 3 (Sept. 7, 2001); *Sulzer Medica Accepts $1 Billion Settlement Deal with Hip and Knee Implant Plaintiffs; In re Sulzer Hip and Knee Prostheses Prods. Liab. Litig.*, 9 No. 5 Andrew Mass Tort Litig. Rptr. 10 (Jul. 2002); and Adam Zimmerman, *The Bellwether Settlement*, 85 Fordham L. Rev. 2275 (Apr. 2017).

24. *In re Inter-Op Hip Prosthesis Liability Litigation*, 204 F.R.D. 330, 335 (N.D. Ohio. 2001).

25. *Metal-on-Metal Hip Implant Resources*, 45 SEP Trial 55 (Sept. 2013).

26. *Id.*

27. George McLaughlin, *Toxic Hip Replacements. Hip Replacement Implants Made with Metal-on-Metal–Components Have Been Causing Problems for Patients Worldwide, Forcing Many to Undergo Further Surgery, Here's a Look at This Issue and the Landscape of the Resulting Litigation*, 48-FEB Trial 40 (Feb. 2012) (footnotes omitted).

28. *FDA Moves to Tighten Controls on All Metal Hip Implants,* 19 No. 24 Westlaw Journal Medical Devices 2 (Jan. 28, 2013).

29. *Texas Jury Returns $15 Million Verdict in Hip Implant Cases.* Rupp v. Sulzer Orthopedics, Inc., 21 No. 7 Andrews Med. Devices Litig. Rptr. 22 (Dec. 11, 2001).

30. *Brooklyn Couple Seeks $17.5 Million in Damages over Defective Hip Implant.* Agoglia v. Stryker Corp., 9 No. 16 Andrews Med. Devices Litig. Rptr. 9 (Oct. 18, 2002).

31. *Louisiana Woman Sues Hip Implant Makers for $1 Million.* Scruggins v. Zimmer Holdings, 9 No. 6 Andrews Med. Devices Litig. Rptr. 9 (June 14, 2002).

Chapter 17

Football Concussions

Concussion in sports, mostly football, will cause Chronic Traumatic Encephalopathy (CTE). "The routine tackle, sack, . . . are typically accompanied by violent blows to the players' heads. . . . In a recent settlement agreement, the NFL agreed to compensate former players with a qualifying diagnosis. . . . CTE is the only disease that cannot be diagnosed while a person is alive, preventing NFL players from being compensated for the disease during their lifetime."[1]

Dr. Bennett Omalu (as played by Will Smith in *Concussion*) examined the brain tissue of deceased NFL players including "Iron Mike" Webster who had suffered multiple concussions in their careers and discovered CTE. Prior to their premature deaths, they presented deteriorated cognitive functions and psychiatric symptoms. "CTE is a neurological disorder first discovered in athletes (such as boxers) who sustained multiple blows to the head. . . . [T]he disorder may progress into dementia or Parkinsonism, with symptoms such as a general slowing in muscle movement, hesitancy in speech, and hand tremors."[2]

Professional hockey players sued the NHL and the Chubb Insurance Co. for workers' compensation claims, seeking documents concerning comp claims by hockey players for head trauma or brain disease. Chubb objected to the subpoena as illegal on the basis that it sought disclosure of personal information. The plaintiffs amended their request to seek only the medical examinations submitted in connection with concussion injury claims by retired NHL players. "The court concludes that requiring the IMEs [independent medical exams] be produced pursuant to a . . . Protective Order and requiring that they be anonymized, sufficiently addresses Chubb's concerns about any privacy rights a retiree may assert in this information."[3]

In *Breland v. Arena Football One, LLC*, a professional arena football player sued for concussive injuries suffered while employed with the New Orleans Voodoo. Lorenzo Breland alleges misrepresentation, fraud, negligence, and breach of contract. He sustained a concussion, but he argues that the team encouraged him to return, starting the following game. The plaintiff sustained a severe blow to his head in the next game which caused a second concussion. He avers that he received inadequate medical care and was pressured to return before he was fully rehabilitated. The plaintiff seeks damages, past and future medical expenses related to the concussions, and medical monitoring to facilitate the diagnosis and treatment of future disorders caused by the injuries. Here, the plaintiff was obligated to prove that his injuries were a result of an intentional act.[4] In *Oliver v. Riddell, Inc.*, former NFL football player Paul Oliver committed suicide; his estate sued the NFL after it was discovered that Paul suffered from CTE. His estate claims that the basis of Paul Oliver's suicide was Riddell's unsafe helmet and a conspiracy between the NFL and Riddell aimed at hiding the dangers that those helmets presented to players. In these cases, defendants will argue that plaintiff's state claims are preempted by federal law. However, here, defendants have not shown that any of the plaintiff's claims require interpreting the Collective Bargaining Agreements, which means that they have not carried their burden of showing that a federal question exists.[5]

Case Study-Youth Football—"A Boston University study found that athletes who began playing tackle football before the age of 12 had more behavioral and cognitive problems later in life than those who started playing after age 12." Safety concerns have driven parents to urge their children to concentrate on other safer sports such as flag football, soccer, baseball, and lacrosse. "Pop Warner, the most established youth football organization in the country, has reduced the amount of contact in practice . . . and changed game rules. . . . Pop Warner is facing a class-action lawsuit asserting that it knowingly put players in danger by ignoring the risks of head trauma."[6]

High Schools and Universities—All football organizations, from youth football to high schools to colleges to professional football have initiated concussion protocols for players who are concussed while playing football.

High Schools—In high schools, these protocols were promulgated by state statutes. These statutes created a standard of care, which can be used in individual lawsuits or class actions. The coaches must follow these protocols or risk liability when players are injured as a result of violating the law; for example, not having a trainer evaluate a player who appears concussed before sending him back into the game. Some of these laws are categorized as "Return to Play" statutes.

In Texas, Chapter 38, Sub-Chapter D of the Texas Education Code, amended by H. B. 2038, promulgates concussion management guidelines. The statute stipulates a return to play form that must be completed and submitted to the athletic trainer, or other person, not a coach, who is responsible for compliance with the Return to Play Protocol established by the Concussion Oversight Team, as determined by the district superintendent (See § 38.157(c)

TEC)). The Return to Play Guidelines requires parents' consent for their child to return to participation following a concussion and that they understand the state's sovereign immunity protection. There is also a Concussion Acknowledgement Form, which is required for all student-athletes in grades 7–12.[7] "Texas House Bill 2038 established a three-step process for dealing with concussions in student-athletes. The bill, dubbed Natasha's Law, became effective on September 1, 2011. The Act calls for state-mandated education for all parties, removal from play of athletes suspected with a concussion, and guidelines for return to activity."[8]

In *Serell v. Connetquot Cent. Sch. Dist. of Islip,* the plaintiff sustained a serious injury as a result of a series of head injuries incurred while playing football at a public high school. In this case, the plaintiffs alleged that the New York State Public High School Athletic Organization breached its duty to promulgate rules concerning head injuries and return to play protocol. The breach of this duty was alleged to be a proximate cause of the plaintiff's injuries. However, the court held that plaintiff failed to raise a triable issue of fact that the athletic association breached a duty to promulgate rules concerning injuries and return to play after a head injury.[9] Football participation causes concussions; therefore, most states have enacted legislation and injury protocols to avoid concussive-type injuries. For example, Georgia's Return to Play Act provided for concussion-related recognition information, education, and established a return-to-play policy for youth athletes suffering from concussions.[10]

Before concussion protocols, an injured high school football player who suffered a subdural hematoma from a caved helmet successfully sued the helmet manufacturer on the grounds that its failure to warn that the helmet would not protect against subdural hematomas was gross negligence entitling the player to an award of $750,000 in exemplary damages.[11]

Universities—"The long-term effects of traumatic brain injuries and suicides of former collegiate football players, highlights the NCAA's lack of adequate regulations and protections, . . . [which] leaves the National Collegiate Athletic Association (NCAA) vulnerable to mass tort concussion litigation."[12] "[T]he cognitive decline and diseases that can manifest later in life from concussions sustained as a student-athlete are analogous to the injuries sustained in the mass tort claims stemming from asbestos and Agent Orange exposure."[13]

The NCAA requires that student-athletes self-report concussion-like symptoms, but also acknowledges that athletes will undoubtedly underreport concussions. In 2010, the NCAA initiated regulations to ensure that member schools have a concussions management plan in place.[14] Plaintiffs were certified as a class in *In re NCAA Student-Athlete Concussion Injury Litig.* but were subject to a number of modifications. The settling plaintiffs are a putative class of current and former collegiate student-athletes who have sued the NCAA, asserting contractual and common law claims relating to the way in which the NCAA has addressed concussions and concussion-related risks. Among other things, the settling plaintiffs seek medical monitoring for the class, because they contend that the class is at risk for developing future symptoms related to concussions and/or the accumulation of subconcussive hits.[15]

"Those modifications included: (1) creating subclasses for student-athletes in Contact and Non-Contact sports; (2) requiring notification to class members via the NCAA's website . . . (3) deleting provisions that require a class member to submit a claim to his or her health insurance company . . . (4) extending the Medical Monitoring Period . . . (5) requiring that the $5 million contribution from the NCAA for concussion research go to research . . . (6) implementing publicity campaigns during the Medical Monitoring Program on the ten-year, twenty-year, thirty-year, and forty-year anniversaries of the commencement of the Medical Monitoring Program . . . (7) enabling the Court to require reports . . .as needed; and (8) excluding Class Counsel from the waiver of future claims."[16]

The estate of a former university football player who was diagnosed with CTE caused by repetitive head impacts and his wife, individually and as fiduciary of his estate, brought action against NCAA for negligence, fraud by concealment, breach of express and implied contract, and loss of consortium. The court held that the estate and wife stated claims for negligence and fraudulent concealment. Plaintiff's complaint alleges a scenario where NCAA voluntarily oversaw and promulgated rules and regulations for college football for the purpose of providing a competitive environment that was safe and ensured fair play but that it knew of the risks of concussive and subconcussive impacts yet failed to warn or disclose such risks to player, that it failed to promulgate rules to protect against such risks, and that it placed its economic interests over plaintiff's safety, who in turn developed the latent brain disease of CTE.[17] The NCAA has a duty to protect its student-athletes from concussions.

National Football League (NFL)—The NFL has paid disability benefits for "totally and permanently disabled" players, including those who suffer from CTE. "The proposed settlement of lawsuits against the NFL has prevented the courts from determining the NFL's liability for concussions."[18] NFL players are employed under a collective bargaining agreement. The NFL has negotiated a settlement for a class action lawsuit brought by over 4,500 players and their families. This initial settlement agreement for $765 million was rejected by Judge Anita Brody of the United States District Court for the Eastern District of Pennsylvania since the amount was insufficient to cover all future claimants. The settlement agreement allows the NFL to avoid a lengthy discovery process that would have uncovered the medical histories of retired players from the 1940s to the present, something they did not want as an open record. The pool of money will top a billion dollars.[19] "This class action suit is largely based on a theory of negligence. In alleging that the NFL owed a duty of care of plaintiffs, the retired NFL players alleged that the NFL breached its duty by failing to warn players of the unreasonable harm that results from repeated concussions."[20]

Retired professional football players brought various separate actions, including a putative class action against the NFL alleging failure to take reasonable actions to protect players from chronic risks created by head injuries and concealment of those risks. After consolidation as a multidistrict litigation, players moved for class certification and final approval of settlement. The motion for class certification and final approval of the settlement was granted.[21]

The concussion settlement caused a mini-feeding frenzy of sales pitches filled with urgency and emphasized familiarity. "Act now or risk missing out on millions of dollars. Trust us because we are part of the N.F.L. brotherhood." This slick marketing pitch is aimed at former NFL players who stand to receive remuneration from the billion-dollar settlement. "Now lawyers, lenders and would-be advisers are circling the retired players trying to get a cut of the money."[22]

Judge Anita Brody, who is overseeing the settlement worth an estimated $1 billion, voided all contracts with lenders who were supposed to be repaid when the players receive cash awards for their severe neurological and cognitive problems. "Sometimes the retired players' cognitive conditions impair their ability to fully understand the consequence of borrowing from these lenders." This process can be daunting: "the players and their lawyers said they have had their claims rejected and bogged down by requests of additional paperwork."[23]

Aaron Hernandez, a former NFL player, who murdered people and hung himself in jail, was found to have CTE after an autopsy. His estate sued the NFL and his former team, the New England Patriots, for concealing the true dangers of football and failing to protect the safety of Aaron Hernandez. It's a difficult lawsuit. The CTE must be connected to suicide and violence. The autopsy showed that he had the raisin-size brain of a 70-year-old, even though he was only 27. The Hernandez family can join the settlement but they would give up their right to sue the NFL. The suit hopes to recover the remainder of his $40 million contract extension.[24] Football concussion litigation is an unlikely source of a feeding frenzy. The epidemic of sexual abuse in college football, which may also be related to CTE, is yet another mass tort. The sexual abuse scandals associated with USA Gymnastics and profligate studio executives and billionaire financiers are similarly situated as mass tort class actions.

NOTES

1. Sarah James, *Ringing the Bell for the Last Time: How the NFL's Settlement Agreement Overwhelmingly Disfavors NFL Players Living with Chronic Traumatic Encephalopathy (CTE),* 11 J. Health & Biomedical L. 391, 391–93 (2016) (footnotes omitted).

2. Joseph Hanna, *Concussions May Prove to be a Major Headache for the NFL,* 84 N.Y. St. B.J. 10, 12 (Oct. 2012) (footnotes omitted). See generally Dionne Koller, *Putting Public Law into "Private" Sport,* 43 Pepp. L. Rev. 681 (2016).

3. *In re National Hockey League Players' Concussion Injury Litigation,* 2016 WL 3815132, *5 (D. Minn.).

4. *Breland v. Arena Football One, LLC,* 2017 WL I954240 (E.D. La.).

5. *Oliver v. Riddell, Inc.,* 2016 WL 7336412 (N.D. Ill.)

6. Ken Belson, New York Times, *Youth Tackle Football Blamed for Brain Issues. Study Shows Problem Likelier for Athletes Who Play Before Twelve,* Houston Chronicle at C6 (Sept. 20, 2017). See also AP, *Former Booster Seeks Youth Football Ban,* New York Times at S8 (Sept. 24, 2017). ("[C]hildren playing football, continually hitting their heads, whether it is concussive or repetitive hitting, is detrimental to your health.")

7. *See* Mark Anderson, *Texas' New Football Helmet Law,* 75 Tex. B.J. 924 (Dec. 2012); and Taylor Adams, *The Repercussions of Concussions in Youth Football Leagues: An Analysis of Texas's Concussion Law and Why Reform is Necessary,* 18 Scholar: St. Mary's L. Rev. & Soc. Just. 285 (2016).

8. Jason McDaniel, *New Law Increases Focus on Concussions, High Annual Rate of Injury Spurs Safety Calls,* Houston Chronicle at C5 (July 17, 2011). See Walter T. Champion, *Fundamentals of Sports Law* §14.3 at 294 (West: 2d ed. 2014–15 Supp.)

9. *Serell v. Connetquot Cent. School Dist. Islip,* 19 A.D. 3d 683, 798 N.Y.S. 2d. 493 (N.Y. Supr. Ct., App. Div. 2005). See generally Walter T. Champion, *Recreational Injuries, Cases, Documents, and Materials,* 26–27 (Aspen, 2016).

10. *Georgia's Return to Play Act of 2012,* HB 673 (Ga. 2011).

11. *Rawlings Sporting Goods Co., Inc. v. Daniels,* 619 S.W. 2d 435 (Tex. Civ. App-Waco 1981).

12. Ashley Adams, *Intercollegiate Concussions: What the NCAA Can Do to Ease the Pain from an Inevitable Headache,* 87 Temp. L. Rev. 193, 193 (Fall 2014).

13. *Id.* at 194 (footnote omitted).

14. *Id.* at 206–8 (footnotes omitted). See also Bryant Lee, *Knocked Unconscionable: College Football Scholarships and Traumatic Brain Injury,* 85 Geo. Wash. L Rev. 613 (March 2017).

15. *In re NCAA Student-Athlete Concussion Injury Litigation,* 2016 WL 3854603, * 1 (N.D. Ill.).

16. *Id.* (footnote omitted).

17. *Schmitz v. NCAA,* 67 N.E. 3d 852 (Ohio App. 2016).

18. Ashley Adams, *Intercollegiate Concussions: What the NCAA Can Do to Ease the Pain from an Inevitable Headache,* 87 Temp. L. Rev. 193, 208–9 (Fall 2014) (footnote omitted).

19. *Id.*

20. *Id.* at 210 (footnotes omitted). See generally Joseph Hanna, *Concussions May Prove to be a Major Headache for the NFL,* 84 N.Y. St. B.J. 10 (Oct. 2012); Sarah James, *Ringing the Bell for the Last Time: How the NFL's Settlement Agreement Overwhelmingly Disfavors the NFL Players Living with Chronic Traumatic Encephalopathy (CTE),* 11 J. Health & Biomedical L. 391 (2016); Christopher Daubert, I. Glenn Cohen, and Holly Fernandez Lynch, *Protecting and Promoting the Health of NFL Players: Legal and Ethical Analysis and Recommendations,* 7 Harv. J. Sports & Ent. L. 1 (Nov. 2016); Daubert, Cohen, and Lynch, *Company Health-Related Policies and Practices in Sports: The NFL and Other Professional Leagues,* 8 Harv. J. Sports & Ent. L. 1 (May 2017); and Mason Byrd, *Concussions and Contracts: Can Concern over Long-Term Player Health Pave the Way to Greater Guarantees in NFL Contracts,* 59 Ariz. L. Rev. 511 (Sum. 2017).

21. See *In re National Football League Players' Concussion Injury Litigation,* 307 F.R.D. 351 (E.D. Pa. 2015) aff'd, 821 F.3d 410 (3d Cir: 2016). See generally Mitch Koczerginstki, *Who Is at Fault When a Concussed Athlete Returns to Action,* 47 Valparaiso Univ. L. Rev. 63 (Fall 2012); and Rodney Smith, *Solving the Concussion Problem and Saving Professional Football,* 35 T. Jefferson L. Rev. 127 (Spr. 2017).

22. Ken Belson, *Fear of Preying on Ex-Athletes Owed by N.F.L. Concussion Deal Spurs Flurry of Legal Offers,* New York Times at A1 (July 17, 2017); and *Football Destroyed My Husband's Mind. He Chose the Sport, but He Did Not Choose Brain Damage,* New York Times at SR1 (Feb. 4, 2018).

23. Ken Belson, *Impaired N.F.L. Players May Not Have to Repay Loans, Judge Rules,* New York Times at B9 (Dec. 9, 2017).

24. *Hernandez Had Advanced CTE,* Houston Chronicle at C6 (Sept. 22, 2017).

Chapter 18

College Football Players, Larry Nassar, and the Culture of Rape

It seems that the year 2017 was ground zero for exposing endemic sexual abuse and the ongoing culture of rape. A line is drawn in the sand which has generated class action lawsuits against Hollywood moguls, politicians, clerics, universities, professional athletes, football programs, athletic organizations, and sports doctors. The defendants, however, *should* have a fiduciary relationship with their victims. Many of those defendants acquiesced to, at the very least, a sexually abusive environment and a culture of rape. Additionally, in a legal sense, many of our leaders have exhibited "smoking guns" that might be used in class action suits.

> President Trump thrust himself into the national debate over sexual misconduct
> . . . , asserting that a "mere allegation" could destroy the lives of those accused,
> even as his own White House was engulfed by charges of abusive behavior. .
> . . At a time when charges of sexual harassment and abuse are bringing down
> famous and powerful men from Hollywood to Washington, Mr. Trump's defiant
> stance put him at odds with much of the country. . . .[1]

Former Vice President Joe Biden said he'd like to beat the hell out of Trump over his mistreatment of women.[2]

Will Things Really Change in America's Workplaces?—In an article in the *New York Times*, Pulitzer prize winner Jodi Kantor asks whether American workplaces are really making progress in curbing sexual harassment. Unfortunately, sexual harassment is universally pervasive because "structures intended to address it are broken: weak laws that fail to protect women, corporate policies that are narrowly drawn and secret settlements that silence women about abuses."[3] Unfortunately, the time is ticking for sexual abuse victims to file lawsuits; usually the statute of limitations gives you two years to file. "Statutes of limitations are devised to protect people from false allegations that are impossible to defend because evidence is stale, witnesses are dead, and documents have been lost. But as schools increasingly confront sexual abuse carried out against children in their care, sometimes decades ago, the statutes have also become a way for them to avoid paying victims."[4]

Trump gives Moore his Support in Senate Race.—"President Donald Trump . . . offered a strong endorsement of Roy Moore, the Republican Senate candidate in Alabama embroiled in accusations that he had inappropriate sexual relations with underage girls.*"[5]* However, Moore lost.

"It was revealed that House offices shelled out nearly $175,000 in taxpayer money to settle with employees over sexual harassment or sex discrimination claims from 2008–2012. The Office of Compliance (OCC) paid out $359,450 since fiscal 2013 to address six claims made against House member-led offices, $84,000 of which was for a sexual harassment claim against Texas Rep. Blake Farenthold."[6] However, Tim Robbins of *Shawshank Redemption* fame said, "People losing their careers based on an innuendo or accusation is troubling for me. There is a process for this: a legal system. Convicting someone on an accusation is really dangerous territory to be living in."[7]

"Attorney General Eric Schneiderman launched a civil rights probe into the New York City-based [Weinstein] company in October 2017, after the New York Times and the New Yorker exposed allegations of sexual assault and harassment spanning decades."[8]

Why Do They Do It? "A series of sexual-harassment accusations against well-known business leaders, celebrities and politicians has left people wondering why some successful men behave this way."[9]

Aspiring actress Kadian Noble files sex-trafficking lawsuit against Harvey Weinstein for groping and forced sex in a Cannes, France, motel room in federal court in Manhattan. "Her attorney Jill Greenfield says her client was seeking damages for 'personal injury' plus expenses and 'consequential loss' arising out of a series of sexual assaults by Weinstein. Civil claims for rape and sexual assault are uncommon in Britain."[10]

In an Associated Press-NORC Center for Public Research poll, most Americans say sexual misconduct is a major problem and that too little is being done to protect the victims.[11]

COLLEGE FOOTBALL PLAYERS

Jasmin Hernandez, a former Baylor University student, sued Baylor for being "deliberately indifferent" to rape allegations against former Baylor football player Tevin Elliott, who was later convicted of sexually assaulting her. Hernandez argues that Baylor's failure to act caused her emotional difficulties, failing grades, and losing her scholarship to study nursing. She sued the board of regents, former athletic director Ian McCaw, and former football coach Art Briles for, inter alia, recruiting a player without regard to the harm he may cause to fellow students and violating Title IX protections against sexual harassment.[12]

Baylor students wore black on Saturday November 5, 2016, not to protect the 17 victims of sexual assault by 19 football players, but to mourn the firing of football coach Art Briles, even though Baylor released a statement that coach Briles knew of at least one gang rape involving five football players.

A table sold the shirts before the TCU football game so more could have the opportunity to support the coach who condoned sexual assault. "$20 for a short sleeve and $25 for a long sleeve."[13] A year and 4 months later Art Briles received $15.1 million from Baylor.[14]

"Texas lawmakers have reinvigorated campus sexual assault reporting requirements in the wake of the Baylor football sexual assault scandal. More than a dozen women contend that Baylor officials ignored or suppressed their assault claims and fostered a rape culture within the football team."[15]

"In the latest fallout from a sexual assault scandal, the U.S. Department of Education is opening another investigation into Baylor University focused on the school's annual compiling of crimes reported on campus."[16]

A former female volleyball player at Baylor University filed a Title IX lawsuit on the basis that the university failed to properly handle her allegations of a gang rape by football players. The lawsuit shows that there was a prevailing "rape culture" which boasted a "'show 'em a good time' policy" to attract top recruits by underage high school players to strip clubs where female students were gang raped. These sexual brutalities were incorporated as a "bonding experience," with the players circulating photos and videos of the rapes among team members.[17]

A member of the Baylor University women's volleyball team filed a Title IX lawsuit against the school on Tuesday, alleging that the university improperly handled allegations that she was gang raped by school football players in February 2012. The lawsuit paints a detailed picture of a rape culture at the school that university officials failed to control, and allegedly fostered. This is the seventh Title IX lawsuit against the school in recent years. . . . "This case arises from Baylor's deliberately indifferent response to multiple events of student-on-student sexual assault and subsequent sex-based harassment," the complaint says. Doe claims that because the university didn't effectively handle past allegations of campus sexual assault, they created conditions that increased her chances of being assaulted and brought about increased sexual harassment on campus. The lawsuit alleges that the Baylor football program, led by Coach Art Briles, had a "Show 'em a good time" policy for their players, as a means of attracting top recruits. That allegedly included taking underage recruits to strip clubs and funding off-campus parties where players allegedly gang raped female students. The allegations specifically state that as a method of hazing freshman teammates, players would bring freshman girls to parties hosted at players' houses.[18]

A particular statement in the lawsuit revealed organized crime: "At the parties under investigation young girls would be drugged and gang raped; or in the words of the football players, 'trains' would be run on the girls. . . . These were allegedly 'bonding' experiences for the team. Players then allegedly circulated photos and videos of the rapes among themselves."[19]

"The NCAA conducted an investigation into the Baylor football sexual abuse scandal which led to the firing of coach Art Briles and the departure of the school president."[20] The Philadelphia law firm of Pepper Hamilton found that the football program operated as if it was "above the rules" and that staff members interfered with the investigation. The lawsuits allege several gang rapes and a "culture of violence" within the football program.[21]

Former student Jasmin Hernandez, who was raped by football player Tevin Elliot in an off-campus apartment, sued Baylor in 2016, two months before the results of their internal investigation was released which found that the University had mishandled rape cases. Baylor tried to settle with Hernandez, who was raped by a former football player in 2012, who was later sentenced to 20 years in prison.[22]

Baylor football players taught new recruits how to target female students, creating a "gang rape culture" and lived by the mantra "you weren't one person's woman, you were everybody's." Baylor University officials knew of the problem but looked at it as "locker room" behavior, one which tolerated gang rapes. The book *Violated: Exposing Rape at Baylor University Amid College Football's Sexual Assault Crisis* by Paula W. Lavigne and Mark Schlabach reveals the attempts that the school made to cover-up the scandal. "A lawsuit filed in January claims that between 2011 and 2014, 31 Baylor football players committed at least 52 rapes."[23]

In *Samuelson v. Oregon State University*, a female university student was drugged at an off-campus party and raped by a cousin of a football player. The university was not liable for sexual harassment, and claims based on the university's alleged deliberate indifference were time-banned.[24] In *Doe v. University of Tennessee*, female university students who were assaulted by male football and basketball players sued university for violations of Title IX and the Campus Save Act, alleging that the school's policies rendered female students vulnerable to sexual assault and that its inadequate response to students' reports of assaults subjected students to a further denial of access to educational benefits. The court held that the university was liable under Title IX since it had actual knowledge of prior incidents of sexual assaults that put it on notice of the risk to female students.[25]

USA GYMNASTICS SEXUAL ABUSE SCANDAL

Aly Raisman, Olympic gymnast who won in the 2012 and 2016 Olympic Games with a combined three medals, two silver and one bronze, was systematically sexually abused, along with 200 girls and women, by Dr. Larry Nassar, who was the USA Gymnastics team doctor; he was sentenced to a 60-year federal prison term for child pornography and a 125-year state sentence in Michigan for 10 sexual assault convictions.

Raisman is suing USA Gymnastics and U.S.O.C. (U.S. Olympic Committee) claiming that they should have prevented Nassar, the former team doctor. She seeks a jury trial for "serial molestation, sexual abuse, and harassment." "Thousands of young athletes continue to train and compete every day in this same broken system, Raisman said. I refuse to wait any longer for these organizations to do the right thing. It is my hope that the legal process will hold them accountable and enable the change that is so desperately needed."[26]

The U.S. Olympic Committee didn't intervene in USA Gymnastics' handling of sexual-abuse allegations against longtime national-team doctor Larry Nassar in 2015, even after USA Gymnastics' then-president told two top USOC executives that an internal investigation had uncovered possible criminal behavior by the doctor against Olympic athletes.

A July 2015 phone call and a September 2015 email shed new light on the Olympic Committee's knowledge of a scandal that has since engulfed American gymnastics. The interactions also raise questions about why officials at USOC, which oversees USA Gymnastics and has criticized that organization's response to the Nassar scandal, didn't reach out to athletes, law enforcement or Dr. Nassar's other employers in the year before allegations against him became public in September 2016.[27]

The House Oversight and Government Reform Committee investigating the Larry Nassar abuse case has asked former USA Gymnastics women's national team coordinators Bela and Martha Karolyi to produce documents and materials concerning their relationship with USA Gymnastics and Nassar dating back to 1996.[28]

The sexual-abuse scandal at Michigan State University widened when authorities charged a former dean [William Strampel] with failing to protect patients from sports doctor Larry Nassar, along with sexually harassing female students and pressuring them for nude selfies.[29]

Michigan State University Interim President John Engler says he wants to reach a legal settlement with more than 200 people who were allegedly abused by former MSU sports medicine doctor Larry Nassar "before the semester's over."[30]

The Maryland House of Delegates proposed a bill that would allow judges to admit evidence of other, earlier, similar sexual offenses. The sponsor of the bill, State Senator James Brochin, indicated that this bill was a direct response to the actions of Dr. Larry Nassar and Bill Cosby.[31]

Katherine T. Sullivan, the Principal Deputy Director of the Department of Justice Office on Violence Against Women (OVW) testified before the Senate Judiciary Committee on a hearing entitled

> The Need to Reauthorize the Violence Against Women Act (VAWA). She emphasized that the reauthorization of VAWA would ensure the continuation of government efforts to respond to sexual assault, domestic violence, date rape, and predatory stalking. One beneficiary of VAWA grant dollars is Michigan's Sexual Assault Unit, which successfully prosecuted Larry Nassar, the former doctor for USA Gymnastics who sexually assaulted over 150 young women and girls. The OVW grants also assisted in providing access to services for Nassar's victims.[32]

The *New York Times Magazine* compiled "Voices" in a "Conversation" entitled *"The Reckoning, On Power and Sex in the Workplace"* which asked questions such as "Can Workplace Culture Really be Changed?" "Brought Together Seven Women to Discuss Questions of Sex, Power, Ambition, and Fairness" including Amanda Hess, Emily Bazelon, Anita Hill, Laura Kipnis, Soledad O'Brien, Lynn Porich, and Danyel Smith.[33]

The conclusion is that the #MeToo movement comes on the shoulders of Anita Hill and others: "Sexual harassment has been clearly against the law since the 1980s." A part of "the struggle [was] for women's autonomy over their own bodies, meaning access to birth control, activism around rape, and the fight for abortion rights."[34]

The plaintiff's bar has incorporated the excesses of #MeToo, rape by college football players, and the sexual abuse of female gymnasts into mass tort class actions. These suits are necessary to dictate appropriate future behavior. It is imperative that misguided "tort reform" does not curtail this avenue of redress and redemption.

NOTES

1. Mark Lander, *Citing "Mere Allegation," Trump Appears to Doubt the #MeToo Movement,* New York Times at Sun. 16 (Feb. 11, 2018).

2. *President Boasts He'd Make Crazy Joe Cry as They Trade Jabs,* Houston Chronicle at A11 (Mar. 23, 2018).

3. Jodi Kantor, New York Times, *Will Things Really Change in American Workplaces,* Houston Chronicle at C3 (Mar. 26, 2018). See generally Andrew Taslitz, *Willfully Blinded: On Date Rape and Self-Deception,* 28 Harv. J. L. & Gender 381 (Sum. 2005); Bethany Withers, *The Integrity of the Game: Professional Athletes and Domestic Violence,* 1 Harv. J. Sports & Ent. L. 145 (Spr. 2010); Francis Shen, *How We Still Fail Rape Victims: Reflecting on Responsibility and Legal Reform,* 22 Colum. J. Gender & L. 1 (2011); and Nancy Cantalupo, *Jessica Lenaham (Gonzales) v. United States & Collective Entity Responsibility for Gender-Based Violence,* 21 Am. U.L. Gender Soc. Poly & L. 231 (2012).

4. Elizabeth A. Harris, *Sex Abuse Victims' Obstacle to Justice: The Clock. Time Limits on Cases Can Shield Schools,* New York Times at A1 (Dec. 5, 2017).

5. Eileen Sullivan, New York Times, *We Need His Vote: Trump Gives Moore His Support in Senate Race,* Houston Chronicle at A10 (Dec. 5, 2017).

6. Griffin Connolly, RollCall, *Three Settlements Revealed in Cases of Congressional Misconduct,* Houston Chronicle at A-10 (Dec. 20, 2017). See also Kevin Diaz, *Official Says He'll Pay Back $84,000. Farenthold Vows Personal Refund, in Harassment Case,* Houston Chronicle at A5 (Dec. 5, 2017).

7. Maureen Dowd, *Hollywood Is Changing, Says Its Veteran Activist, Tim Robbins,* New York Times at A1 (Feb. 4, 2018).

8. Tom McElroy, AP, *New York Attorney General Files Suit against Weinstein,* Houston Chronicle at A8 (Feb. 12, 2018).

9. Elizabeth Bernstein, *The Role "Power" Plays in Sexual Harassment; Psychologists Say High Powered Men Who Abuse Women Have Different Motivation but Often Share Certain Personality Traits; For Some, "Parallels to Alcohol,"* Wall St. J. at A13 (Feb. 6, 2018).

10. Colleen Lang, AP, *Actress Who Filed Suit against Weinstein, Details Allegations,* Houston Chronicle at A16 (Nov. 29, 2017). See generally Ryan Faughnder, *Surprise Bid for Movie Company, Former Obama Official Proposes Female-Majority Weinstein Board,* Houston Chronicle at B8 (Nov. 21, 2017); Rose McGowan, *Brave* (New York: Harper One, 2018); Nicholas Kristal, *Woody Allen Meets "#MeToo,"* New York Times at SR9 (Feb. 4, 2018); Maureen Dowd, *A Goddess, a Mogul, and a Mad Genius: Uma Thurman Is Ready to Talk About the Men Who Made Her Angry,* New York Times at SR1 (Feb. 4, 2018); and Cary Darling, *Anime Fest Draws #MeToo Boycott: Organizer of Convention Faces Claims of Sexual Harassment from Models,* Houston Chronicle at A1 (Mar. 29, 2018).

11. AP, *Most Americans See Sexual Misconduct as Big Problem, Poll Finds,* Houston Chronicle at A24 (Dec. 24, 2017).

12. AP, *Baylor Sued over Sex Assault Response. Woman Says the School Ignored Date-Rape Allegations Aimed at Football Players,* Houston Chronicle at A4 (Apr. 1, 2016). See generally Craig Anderson, *Political Correctness on College Campuses: Freedom of Speech Doing the Politically Correct Thing,* 46 SMU L. Rev. 171 (Sum. 1992); Deborah Brake, *The Struggle for Sex Equality in Sport and the Theory Behind Title IX,* 34 U. Mich. J. L. Ref. 13 (Fall & Wntr. 2000 & 2001); Ann Scales, *Student*

Graduations and Sexual Assault: A New Analysis of Liability for Injuries Inflicted by College Athletes, 15 Mich. J. Gender & L. 205 (2009); Amy Tracy, *Athletic Discipline for Non-Sport Player Misconduct: The Role of College Athletic Department and Professional Legal Discipline and the Legal System's Penalties and Remedies,* 9 Va, Sports & Ent. L. J. 254 (Spr. 2010); Grayson Song Walker, *The Evolution and Limits of Title IX Doctrine on Peer Sexual Assault,* 45 Harv. C.R.C. L. Rev. 95 (Wntr. 2010); Dan Subotnik, *The Duke Rape Case Five Years Later: Lessons for the Academy, the Media, and the Criminal Justice System,* 45 Akron L. Rev. 887 (2011–2012); *Penalty on the Field: Creating a NCAA Sexual Assault Policy,* 19 VIII. Sports & Ent. L. J. 463 (2012); Diane Rosenfeld, *Uncomfortable Conversations: Confronting the Reality of Target Rape on Campus,* 128 Harv. L. Rev. 359 (Jun. 2015); Lauren Yan Driessen, *The Campus Sexual Violence Elimination Act: Is It Enough to Combat Sexual Assault on Campuses?,* 68 Rutgers U. L. Rev. 1841 (Sum. 2016); Diane Heckman, *The Assembly Line of Title IX Mishandling Cases Concerning Sexual Violence on College Campuses,* 336 Ed. Law Rptr. 619 (Dec. 29, 2016); Joseph Storch and Andrea Stagg, *Missoula: Jon Krakauer's Story of College Sexual Violence That Is Both Complex and Entirely Common,* 42 J. C. & U. L. 451 (2016); Deborah Brake, *Lessons from the Gender Equality Movement: Using Title IX to Foster Inclusive Masculinities in Men's Sport,* 34 Law & Ineq. 285 (Sum., 2016); Jessica Luther, *Unsportsmanlike Conduct: College Football and the Politics of Rape* (Brooklyn: Edge of Sports, 2016); Deborah Brake, *Fighting the Rape Culture Wars through the Perponderance of the Evidence Standard,* 78 Mont. L. Rev. 109 (Wntr. 2017); Karen Tani, *An Administrative Right to Be Free from Sexual Violence? Title IX Enforcement in One Historical and Institutional Prospective,* 66 Duke L. J. 1847 (May 2017); Kelly Alison Behre, *Ensuring Choice and Voice for Campus Sexual Assault Victims: A Call for Victims' Attorneys,* 65 Drake L. Rev. 293 (2d Q. 2017); Bethany Corbin, *Riding the Wave or Drowning: An Analysis of Gender Bias and Twombly/Iqbal in Title IX Accused Student Lawsuits,* 85 Fordham L. Rev. 2665 (May 2017); Maureen Weston, *Tackling Abuse in Sport Through Dispute System Design,* 13 U. St. Thomas L. J. 434 (Wntr. 2017); Jayma Meyer, *It's on the NCAA: A Playbook for Eliminating Sexual Assault,* 67 Syracuse L. Rev. 357 (2017); Samantha Iannucci, *"Due" the Process: The Sufficiency of Due Process Protection Afforded by University Procedures in Handling Sexual Assault Allegations,* 95 Or. L. Rev. 609 (2017); and Hillary Hunter, *Strike Three: Calling Out College Officials for Sexual Assault on Campus,* 50 Tex. Tech. L. Rev. 277 (Wntr. 2018).

13. Sydney Mahl, *College Football and Rape Culture,* burntx at http://www.burntx.com/2016il1il6/a-conspiracy-of-silence/ (Nov. 16, 2016).

14. Jenny Dial Creech, *Adding Insult to Injury,* Houston Chronicle at C2 (Apr. 1, 2018).

15. *CFB: Baylor Scandal Inspires Raft of Texas Campus Assault Bills,* 4/5/17 Sports Network 14:17:32.

16. Philip Ericksen, *Baylor Faces Crime Report Investigation. New Federal Inquiry One of Several against University After Rape Scandal,* Houston Chronicle at A6 (May 3, 2017).

17. Ronn Blitzer, *Lawsuit Alleges Gang Rapes, Dog Fighting at Baylor University Football Team Parties,* 2017 WLNR 15340155 (May 17, 2017).

18. *Id.*

19. *Id.*

20. *CFB: Baylor Confirms NCAA Investigation after Sex Abuse Scandal,* 6/26/17 Sports Network 18:36:16.

21. Joseph Duarte, *Baylor Scandal: University Says It Now Is Target of NCAA Probe; School Also Will Release Information on All Sexual Assaults Dating to 2003,* Houston Chronicle, 2017 WLNR 19818287 (Jun. 27, 2017).

22. *Lawyer: Baylor Settles Lawsuit with Woman Raped by Player,* Houston Chronicle at C7 (Jul. 16, 2017).

23. Daniel Bates, *Baylor Football Players Taught New Recruits How to Target Female Students Creating a "Gang Rape Culture" and Lived by the Mantra,* Daily Mail Online, 2017 WLNR 2576–2632 (Aug. 21, 2017).

24. *Samuelson v. Oregon State University,* 162 F. Supp. 3d 1123 (Dec. 1, 2016).

25. *Doe v. University of Tennessee,* 186 F. Supp.3d 788 (M. D. Tenn. 2016).

26. Christine Hausen, New York Times, *Raisman Suing USOC, USA Gymnastics. Gold Medalist Claims Group Should Have Kept Nassar in Check,* Houston Chronicle at C6 (Mar. 2, 2018).

27. Rebecca Davis O'Brien, *USOC Failed to Act on Reports of Abuse. Olympic Committee Learned of Allegations Against Gymnastics Team Doctor in 2015,* Wall St. J. at A3 (Feb. 2, 2018).

28. David Barron, *House Committee Sends Letter to Karolyi. Nassar Investigation Requests Documents, Materials, and Records,* Houston Chronicle at C2 (Feb. 10, 2018).

29. David Eggert, AP, *Sports Doctor Scandal Snares Dean. Ex. Michigan State Educator Changed with Negligence, Sex Harassment in Nassar Case,* Houston Chronicle at A8 (Mar. 28, 2018).

30. Brian McVicar, *Engler Wants MSU Settlement with Nassar Victims before the Semester Is Over,* Flint J. at A1 (Mar. 17, 2018).

31. Michael Dresser, *Sex Offense Bill Gains: Disclosure of Suspect's Previous Offenses Expected to Pass Senate, House Panel,* Baltimore Sun at 2 (Mar. 15, 2018).

32. Principal Deputy Director Katharine T. Sullivan of the Justice Department's Office on Violence Against Women Delivers Testimony before the Senate Judiciary Committee. State New Service 00.00.00 (Mar. 20, 2018).

33. *The Reckoning, on Power and Sex in the Workplace,* New York Times Mag. at 40-C (Dec. 17, 2017).

34. *Id.*

Chapter 19

Tort Reform or Tort Retreat

Alleged "tort reform" in the United States proposes change in the civil justice's system aimed at reducing both the ability of victims to litigate and the damages they can receive if they choose to litigate. Tort reform measures might not be anything more than disguised attempts to protect and benefit businesses, hospitals, physician practices, and health systems that have injured innocent victims. Tort reform's aim is to reduce the ability of victims to bring tort litigation and/or reduce damages. Tort reform advocates propose procedural limits on the ability to file claims and capping the award of damage.[1]

Tort reform measures are highly variable from state to state. As of 2016, 33 states have imposed caps on damages sustained in medical malpractice lawsuits, including California, Colorado, Florida, Massachusetts, Michigan, New Jersey, North Carolina, Texas, and Wisconsin. Tort reform advocates focus on state personal injury Common Law rules. Tort reformers misstate the existence of real factual issues, such as in the McDonald's hot coffee case, and criticize the tort system as disguised corporate welfare. The tort reform zealots cite certain reasons for their advocacy: (1) litigation cost and compensation payouts by insurance companies—if there are less payouts, then there will be lower premiums in a trickle-down effect; (2) cost of tort system, and in particular medical malpractice suits, which raises the cost of health care; and (3) tort liability could stunt product liability cases since it would deter innovation and the manufacturer will be reluctant to test products for fear of subjecting themselves to massive tort claims.[2]

Tort reform advocates argue that too many of the 15,000,000 lawsuits filed each year are frivolous lawsuits. These advocates claim that the tort system is too expensive and clogs up the court system; and that trial attorneys make too much money in high profile cases. It's like a lottery, they say, trial lawyers seek the magical combination of plaintiff, defendant, judge, and jury. John Grisham's book *The Runaway Jury* (Doubleday, 1996) looked at the jury in a wrongful death lawsuit for lung cancer against a tobacco company, while the movie version (Regency Enterprise, 2003) dealt with jury tampering in a workplace shooting in New Orleans against a gun manufacturer, alleging gross negligence. The prospect of paying a relatively small damage award has little effect in correcting the wrongdoing behind the lawsuit. Consumer advocates argue that lawsuits encourage corporations to produce safe products and safe effective medical practices. Defendants automatically categorize litigation as a frivolous lawsuit which transforms this marketing ploy as a popular target of American humor. This is probably unnecessary given there are existing rules that are already available which regulate frivolous lawsuits, namely, throwing out flimsy cases and penalizing the offending attorneys with sanctions.[3]

THE FRIVOLOUS LAWSUIT ARGUMENT

Tort reform advocates will argue that "plaintiffs file frivolous lawsuits based upon dubious injuries" and seek to exploit the legal system for profit, rather than seek redress for severe and serious injuries; they are, succinctly put, "gold-diggers." The argument conjures a man wearing a neck brace in the courtroom for the benefit of the jury, who will remove it once a verdict is delivered, and then play scratch golf. The term "frivolous lawsuit" encompasses more than cases in which an alleged injury is questionable; it also includes cases where the injury is not physical, or even psychological, but where a litigant seeks vindication of a suspect claim against another party.[4]

THE LITIGATION EXPLOSION ARGUMENT

Another tort reform bromide is that plaintiff lawsuits have placed society in the throes of a litigation explosion. The observation that there are too many lawsuits is an assertion accepted as fact. The way it is couched—an "explosion"—creates an ambience of crisis, and the evident need to address the matter becomes a virtual imperative. "As a general proposition, proponents of tort reform tend to identify three sets of costs that result from the apparent proliferation of lawsuits: (1) those sustained by the courts; (2) costs from paying lawsuits; and (3) consequences of fearing the possibility of lawsuits."[5]

THE TORT REFORMER'S BLAME GAME

The discourse of the tort reformers invokes traditional values such as self-reliance, personal responsibility and property rights to castigate the contemporary civil justice system as unfairly redistributive social welfare and destructive of core American values. Reformers shift compassion from the injured claimant to the corporation as a victim. Their goal is to show that an American tort monster victimizes corporations. The imagery creates confusion and ambivalence about the American civil litigation system. Applying the word "victim" to corporate wrongdoers is as misleading as referring to nuclear weapons as "peacekeepers." Reformers misleadingly label tort limitations as reformers rather than retrenchment. "Tort reform" has become a code phrase . . . . to limit rights of women [and] minorities. . . .[6]

THE MCDONALD'S HOT COFFEE CASE

"It is a dangerous business, Frodo, going out your door. You step onto the road, and if you don't keep your feet, there's no knowing where you might be swept off to."[7] Stella Liebeck stepped onto the road and was burned by McDonald's super-heated coffee and became the unlikely poster child for tort reform.

Seventy-nine-year-old Stella Liebeck of Albuquerque, New Mexico, in 1992, was in the passenger seat of her grandson's car when she was severely burned by a cup of coffee purchased at a local McDonald's drive through window. Her grandson stopped so that she could add cream and sugar; she placed the cup between her legs and attempted to remove the lid but spilled the entire liquid contents into her lap. She suffered full thickness burns to her thighs, buttocks, groin, and genital area amounting to 6 percent of her total body surface area. Ms. Liebeck was hospitalized for 8 days. She had debridement, local wound care, and skin grafts. Ms. Liebeck was willing to settle for $20,000 but McDonald's made a strategic decision to fight the claim. McDonald's has faced over 700 claims by people who had suffered burns from the coffee from 1982 to 1992.[8]

McDonald's admitted coffee temperature was purposefully kept between 180- and 190-degrees Fahrenheit. A consultant advised that this temperature range was the best tasting. McDonalds knew that coffee was consumed while still in their car. The statement on the side of the cup was only a "reminder" that the coffee was hot. McDonalds' own quality assurance manager testified that restaurants were told to keep the coffee pot temperature at 185 degrees. The jury awarded Liebeck $200,000 in compensatory damages and $2.7 million in punitive damages, which was reduced to $160,000 since she was 20 percent at fault. The punitive damages award seemed high but only amounted to about two days' worth of national coffee sales for McDonald's at that time. The high punitive damages award got quite a lot of press. The trial court, probably believing the punitive damages award was too high, reduced that part of the award to $480,000, but said that McDonald's conduct was "reckless, callous, and willful."[9]

The press gravitated towards tales of allegedly frivolous lawsuits including a $3.4 billion verdict against CSX, a $4 million verdict against BMW for a bad paint job, and of course, the $2.9 million Liebeck verdict. The hot coffee was used to implement tort reform in Republicans' Contract with America. Comedians loved it, such as Jay Leno, David Letterman's Top Ten List, and Seinfeld, who put Kramer in a hot coffee lawsuit. This case became the darling of media attention.[10]

The goals of punitive damages are to punish guilty tortfeasors and teach defendants a lesson so that the tort will not be repeated. Tort reformers used punitive damages as the boogeyman behind the alleged "jackpot" excess of *Liebeck v. McDonalds' Restaurants*. Even if punitive damage awards are sufficiently large or frequent to warrant legal concern, tort reform damage caps are an ineffective answer.[11]

LEGISLATIVE INITIATIVES

"Tort reform has quickly become the battle cry for political candidates in both parties at every level of government."[12] "In early 2003, the public became alarmed when thousands of physicians protested against increasing medical malpractice insurance premiums by temporarily closing their practices. Some physicians complained that skyrocketing premiums were forcing them to leave their home states or to retire altogether."[13]

"The tort reform statutes of most states are based on the presumption that too many lawsuits are filed and that court awards—especially those for punitive damages or pain and suffering—tend to be excessive."[14]

"Tort reform became an important issue during the 1994 Congressional Campaign as part of the Republican Party's Contract with America. Since then, many federal and state laws have attempted to reduce both liability and recovery in tort actions."[15]

CONSTITUTIONAL LIMITATIONS ON TORT REFORM

"Tort Reform" is the offspring of the "medical malpractice" crisis of the early 1970s. The medical profession persuaded state legislatures to restrict liability in negligence suits which prompted the insurance industry to pursue similar changes in negligence and products liability law. But, in the 13 years since

California first enacted medical malpractice reform there have been many constitutional challenges.[16]

The Liebeck case has been frequently mentioned by Congressional proponents and opponents of federal tort reform. In 1996, Congress passed a product liability law, and established a fifteen-year statute of repose. President Clinton vetoed this federal legislation based upon his objection to the bill's selective preemption of state law, arbitrary ceilings on punitive damages, and elimination of joint and several liabilities for non-economic damages.[17]

STATES STRIKE DOWN TORT REFORM LIMITS

States have reconsidered tort reform legislation, eliminating some limits on liability, damages, and statutes of limitations. Oregon and Ohio revoked their alleged tort reform statutes by striking down damage caps, strict statutes of limitation, and other liability limits including preserving the right to trial by jury in civil cases.[18]

Tort reform advocates label all personal injury lawsuits as frivolous claims for dubious injuries. They call it roulette justice. But tort reform has emboldened tortfeasors such as Big Pharma to lessen R&D and embrace the profitability of the expected, but emasculated, personal injury onslaught. It's just another expense. Now, personal injury lawyers must reject legitimate lawsuits with horrific injuries based on purely economic reasons. It is especially difficult to enlist a competent medical malpractice attorney, since after tort reform, it is now a battle of the experts, where the plaintiffs invariably lose as the insurance company's pocket is much deeper.

The impetus for the zeal of the torts reformers is *Liebeck v. McDonald's Restaurants,* whose facts do not match the headlines; "$2.9 million for spilled coffee!!!" *Liebeck* was the impetus for the explosion of the anti–punitive damages movement. But, Stella Liebeck's treating physician testified that it was one of the worst liquid burns he had ever seen. Stella wrote to McDonald's and asked for reimbursement of her medical bills but was promptly rejected by the company. McDonald's had already settled several hundred similar complaints and paid out close to $1 million dollars in settlements. The original award for punitive damage was $2.7 million, reduced to $480,000 by the judge; she probably settled in the $100,000 range. The myth of the *Liebeck* case dominated public debate on punitive damages, but its reality illustrates the importance of punitives in convincing companies that safety comes before profits, and the tortfeasor has a duty to act on hazards that can easily be corrected.[19] The McDonald's hot coffee case clearly was not a frivolous lawsuit.

But it was used by big corporations as an example of the excesses of trial lawyers. Tort reform is used to eliminate "feeding frenzies," regardless of corporate guilt or plaintiffs' injuries. Mass torts continue unabated, and the trial bar must be ever vigilant to push the envelope as much as misguided tort reform allows. However, it is more important than ever, that lawyers choose wisely and harness their efforts on cases that demand justice.

NOTES

1. See generally Kenneth Abraham, *Individual Action and Collective Responsibility: The Dilemma of Mass Tort Reform*, 73 Va. L. Rev. 845 (Aug. 1987); Gary Moran, Brian Cutler, and Anthony DeLisa, *Attitudes toward Tort Reform, Scientific Jury Selection, and Jury Bias: Verdict Inclination in Criminal and Civil Trials*, 18 L. & Psychol. Rev. 309 (Spr. 1994); Michael Perino, *Class Action Chaos? The Theory of the Core and an Analysis of Opt-Out Rights in Mass Tort Class Actions*, 46 Emory L. J. 85 (Wntr. 1997); Andrew Popper, *A One-Term Tort Reform Tale: Victimizing the Vulnerable*, 35 Harv. J. on Legis. 123 (Wntr. 1998); Joanna Shepherd, *Tort Reforms' Winners and Losers: The Completing Effects of Care and Activity Levels*, 55 UCLA L. Rev. 905 (Apr. 2008); Georgene Vairo, *The Role of Influence in the Arc of Tort Reform*, 65 Emory L.J. 1741 (2016); Roland Christenson, *Behind the Curtain of Tort Reform*, 2016 B.Y.U L. Rev. 261 (2016); and Scott DeVito and Andrew Jurs, *An Overreaction to a Nonexistent Problem: Empirical Analysis of Tort Reform from the 1980s to 2000s*, 3 Stan. J. Complex Litig. 62 (Wntr. 2015).

2. Stephen Daniels and Joanne Martin, *The Strange Success of Tort Reform*, 53 Emory L. J. 1225 (Sum. 2004); Paul Rubin and Joanna Shepherd, *Tort Reform and Accidental Deaths*, 50 J. L. & Econ. 221 (May 2007); Ronen Avraham, *An Empirical Study of the Impact of Tort Reforms on Medical Malpractice Settlement Payments*, 36 J. Legal Stud. S183 (Jun. 2007); and Christopher Roederer, *Democracy and Tort Law in America: The Counter-Revolution*, 110 W. Va. L. Rev. 647 (Wntr. 2008).

3. See Joni Hersch and W. Kip Viscusi, *Punitive Damages: How Judges and Juries Perform*, 33 J. Leg. Study 1 (Jan. 2004); Jeffrey Stempel, *Not-So Peaceful Coexistence: Inherent Tensions in Addressing Tort Reform*, 4 Nev. L. J. 337 (Wntr. 2003/2004); and Joshua Kelner, *The Anatomy of an Image; Unpacking the Case for Tort Reform*, 31 U. Dayton L. Rev. 243 (2006).

4. Kelner, *Anatomy of an Image*, 31 U. Dayton L. Rev. 243, 257 (footnotes omitted).

5. *Id.* at 259–61.

6. Michael Rustad and Thomas Koenig, *Taming the Tort Monster; The American Civil Justice System as a Battleground of Social Theory*, 68 Brook. L. Rev. 1, 50–51 (Fall 2002) (footnotes omitted).

7. *LOTR: Fellowship of the Ring*, movie (New Line Cinema, WingNut Films, 2001).

8. Darryl Weiman, *The McDonald's Coffee Case, Huff Post,* the blog at https://www.huffingtonpost.com/darryl-s-weiman-md-jd/the-mcdonaldscoffee-caseb14002362.html (Jan. 7, 2017, updated Jan. 7, 2018). See also *Liebeck v. McDonald's*

Restaurants, P.T.S., Inc., 1995 WL 360309 (N.M. Dist., Bernalillo Cnty.); and *Hot Coffee, Is Justice Being Served?* Movie (documentary films, 2001).

9. *Id.*

10. Mark Greenlee, *Kramer v. Java World: Images, Issues, and Idols in the Debate Over Tort Reform*, 26 Cap. U.L. Rev. 701, 702–3 (1997) (footnotes omitted).

11. See generally *"Common Sense" Legislation: The Birth of Neoclassical Tort Reform*, 109 Harv. L. Rev. 1765, 1773 (May 1996).

12. James A. Higgins, *Oklahoma's Tort Reform Act: Texas-Style Tort Reform or Texas-Size Compromise?*, 57 Okla. L. Rev. 921, 921 (Wntr. 2004).

13. *Id.* at 921–22 (footnotes omitted). See generally Timothy Howell, *So Long "Sweetheart"—State Farm Fire & Casualty Co. v. Gandy Swings the Pendulum Further to the Right as the Latest in a Line of Setbacks for Texas Plaintiffs*, 29 St. Mary's L. J. 47 (1997); Nancy Costello, *Allocating Fault to the Empty Chair: Tort Reform or Deform?, 79 U. Det. Mercy L. Rev. 571 (Wntr. 1999); and Julie Davies, Reforming the Tort Reform Agenda*, 25 Wash. U. J. L. & Pol'y 119 (2004).

14. *Id.* at 924.

15. Ashley Thompson, *The Unintended Consequence of Tort Reform in Michigan: An Argument for Reinstating Retailer Product Liability*, 42 U. Mich. J. L. Reform 961, 962 (Sum., 2009). See generally Gregory Westfall, *The Nature of this Debate: A Look at the Texas Foreign Corporation Venue Rule and a Method for Analyzing the Premises and Promises of Tort Reform*, 26 Tex. Tech. L. Rev. 903 (1995); Gregory Lensing, *Proportionate Responsibility and Contribution before and after the Tort Reform of 2003*, 35 Tex. Tech L. Rev. 1125 (Sum., 2004); *Part Two: Detailed Analysis of the Civil Justice Reforms*, 36 Tex. Tech L. Rev. 51 (2005); Charles Silver, David Hymen, and Bernard Black, *The Impact of the 2003 Texas Medical Malpractice Damages Cap on Physician Supplied Insurer Payouts: Separating Facts from Rhetoric*, 44 The Advoc. (Texas) 25 (Fall, 2008); Kara Lee Monahan, *State Constitutional Law-Tort Reform-Supreme Court of Ohio Reverses Course and Upholds Limits of Noneconomic and Punitive Damages as Constitutional*, 40 Rutgers L. 1953 (Sum., 2009); Patricia Hatamyar, *The Effect of "Tort Reform" on Tort Case Filing*, 43 Val. U. L. Rev. 559 (Wntr. 2009); Hyman, Silver, Black, and Paik, *Does Tort Reform Affect Physician Supply? Evidence from Texas*, 42 Int'l Rev. L. & Econ. 203 (Jun. 2015); and *Tort Reform, 50 State Statutory Surveys: Civil Laws*, Tort: 0020 Surveys 30 (Thomson Reuters, Apr. 2007).

16. Richard Turkington, *Constitutional Limitations on Tort Reform: Have the State Courts Placed Insurmountable Obstacles in the Path of Legislative Responses to the Perceived Liability Insurance Crisis*, 32 Vill. L. Rev. 1299, 1302–8 (Nov. 1987).

17. Greenlee, *Kramer v. Java World*, 26 Cap. U. L. Rev. 701, 724–925 (footnotes omitted).

18. William C. Smith, *Prying Off Tort Reform Caps. States Striking Down Limits on Liability and Damages, and Statutes of Limitations*, 85 ABA J. 28 (Oct. 1999). See generally Nathaniel Boulton, *The Farmer's Retort to Tort Reform: Why Legislation to Limit or Eliminate Punitive Damages Hurts the Agricultural Sector*, 9 Drake J. Agric. L. 415 (Fall 2004); Linda Mullen, *The Future of Tort Reform: Possible Lessons from the World Trade Center Victim Compensation Fund*, 53 Emory L. J. 1315 (Sum.,

2004); and R. Henry Weaver and Douglas Kysar, *Courting Disaster: Climate Change and the Adjudication of Catastrophe,* 93 Notre Dame L. Rev. 295 (Nov. 2017).

19. See *Liebeck v. McDonalds Restaurants, P.T.S., Inc.,* No. CV-93–02419, 1995 WL 360309 (D. N.M. Aug. 18, 1994); see also Michael McCann et al., *Java Jive: Genealogy of a Judicial Icon,* 56 U. Miami L. Rev. 113 (2001). See generally Shari Seidman Diamond, *Truth, Justice, and the Jury,* 26 Harv. J. L. & Pub. Pol'y 143, 145–46 (2003); Boulton, *Farmer's Retort to Tort Reform,* 9 Drake J. Agric. L. 415, 425–27; and Greenlee, *Kramer v. Java World,* 26 Cap. U. L. Rev. 701, 718–19.

Conclusion

Separating the Wheat from the Chaff

Abraham Lincoln, Mahatma Gandhi, and Nelson Mandela were lawyers. Class actions have effectuated positive change against racism, sexism, and corporate greed. The typical class action involves mass torts, usually in product liability or medical practice, but class actions also can be based on violations of specific statutes, administrative law, and constitutional law. The trick is selecting the wheat from the chaff.

> A federal judge in Philadelphia has awarded $4.6 million to a group of erotic dancers after a jury agreed that the women were cheated out of their wages and tips in a class-action suit in 2013 against the Penthouse Club.[1]

However, the Senate killed regulation that would allow customers to band together to sue banks. Bank customers will still be subject to mandatory arbitration clauses. These clauses are buried in the fine print of nearly every checking account, credit card, payday loan, auto loan, or other financial services contract and require customers to use arbitration to resolve any bank dispute, effectively waiving the customer's right to sue.[2]

RECALL OF BABY FORMULA

The French dairy giant Lactalis sold tainted formula. "Lactalis has offered to compensate victims of the tainted products. Instead, the families say, they will press ahead with their lawsuits."[3]

FORD ACCUSED OF CHEATING ON TEST

At least 500,000 Ford heavy duty trucks were rigged to beat emissions test. These diesel trucks emit as much as 50 times the legal limit for nitrogen oxide pollutants, and were sold from 2011 to 2017 costing $8,400 more than gasoline-fueled trucks. "Ford marketed the trucks as 'the cleanest super diesel ever,' while the lawyer behind the suit said they should have been called Super Dirty."[4]

AIRBAG SETTLEMENT

Auto makers agreed to pay more than $550 million for rupture-prone Takata Corp. air bags, which would explode and spray shrapnel. "The air bags have been linked to 11 deaths and some 180 injuries in the U.S. alone."[5]

VW EMISSIONS FRAUD

Volkswagen paid $2.9 billion to settle emissions fraud charges: Texas share will be doled out by state environment officials. Governor Greg Abbot indicated that the Texas Commission on Environmental Quality will oversee the state's $209.3 million portion of the Environmental Mitigation Trust. The fund was set up after the automaker of Volkswagen, Audi, and Porsche brands settled claims that it cheated U.S. vehicle emissions standards.[6] A top Volkswagen official in the United States was sentenced to seven years in prison for his role in the German automaker's decade long scheme to cheat on diesel emissions tests. The sentencing of Oliver Schmidt, a former Volkswagen manager in Michigan, was the latest turn in a vast scandal that has tarnished the company's reputation and has cost the carmaker more than $20 billion in fines and settlements.[7]

Other ongoing litigation clusters include transvaginal mesh, talcum powder, Marlboro lights, and 3M earplugs.

TRANSVAGINAL MESH

"In recent years, surgeons have begun to use surgical mesh to repair weakened or damaged tissue. Surgical mesh is often used as an alternative to traditional surgical repairs in order to correct pelvic organ prolapse and stress urinary incontinence. Such mesh is commonly referred to as 'transvaginal mesh.' Transvaginal mesh is implanted into the vagina to create what is often referred to as a 'bladder sling,' which is used to help reinforce weakened vaginal walls and reduce the recurrence rate of pelvic organ prolapse or support the urethra when treating urinary incontinence. Transvaginal mesh is made from absorbable biologic material, porous absorbable or nonabsorbable polypropylene, or other synthetic material. Since its introduction, however, many patients have experienced serious complications and adverse effects related to transvaginal mesh. These complications and adverse effects have led to plaintiffs filing hundreds of lawsuits against transvaginal mesh manufacturers claiming that the transvaginal mesh caused complications, including infection, incontinence, and pelvic and vaginal pain. Many of these lawsuits have been filed against large-scale manufacturers of transvaginal mesh, including American Medical Systems, Boston Scientific Corporation, C. R. Bard, and Johnson & Johnson. The cases were consolidated into multidistrict litigation."[8]

TALCUM POWDER

A New Jersey jury awarded $37 million when Stephen Lanzo developed a deadly cancer linked to asbestos as a result of inhaling dust through regular use of Johnson & Johnson's talc powder since 1972. According to his lawyers, J&J officials and IMERYS, its talc supplier, were worried that asbestos tainted talc and other products as early as 1969. The jury awarded Lanzo $30 million and his wife $7 million in compensatory damages. The jury will return for further proceedings to determine whether to award punitive damages. Johnson & Johnson of New Brunswick, New Jersey, has been sued by 6,610 plaintiffs in talc-related lawsuits, largely based on claims that it failed to warn women about the risk of ovarian cancer when talcum powder was used for feminine hygiene.[9]

MARLBORO LIGHTS

The settlement includes all persons who purchased defendant's Marlboro Light or Marlboro Ultra-Light cigarettes in the state of Arkansas for personal consumption from November 1, 1971, through June 22, 2010. Payment will be made to class members who file valid claims and will be calculated as follows: 10 cents per pack for each pack purchased between November 1, 1971, and April 17, 1998; 25 cents per pack for each pack purchased between April 18, 1998, and April 18, 2003; and 10 cents per pack for each pack purchased between April 19, 2003, and June 22, 2010. If the total value of submitted claims exceeds the money available in the settlement fund, each claim payment will be reduced pro rata. If the total value of submitted claims are less than the money available in the settlement fund, each claim payment may be increased pro rata. The *Miner v. Phillip Morris Companies, Inc.* lawsuit resolves claims that Philip Morris advertised, marketed, and sold Marlboro Lights and Marlboro Ultra Lights cigarettes as healthier than regular cigarettes in a way that deceived consumers who purchased Marlboro Lights and Marlboro Ultra Lights in Arkansas. Plaintiffs allege that, during the period in question Philip Morris marketed and sold their cigarettes as "Lights," "Ultra Lights," "lower tar and nicotine," and "low tar and nicotine." The defendants falsely represented that Marlboro Lights and Marlboro Ultra Lights were less harmful and delivered lower tar and nicotine in comparison to regular Marlboro cigarettes. However, the Light cigarettes do not deliver lower tar and nicotine than regular Marlboro cigarettes when smoked. The manufacturer denies the claims but agrees to settle for $45,500,000.[10]

3M EARPLUG LITIGATION

The 3M Earplug litigation involved soldiers who were given faulty Combat Arm earplugs designed, manufactured, and sold by the 3M company. As a result of these defective earplugs, Army combat veteran Scott Rowe and other similarly situated plaintiffs, who used them during training, suffered daily from tinnitus, hearing loss, and other damages. The 3M dual-ended Combat Arm earplugs were too short for proper insertion and would loosen imperceptibly. The company did not disclose this design defect to the military. The Combat Arm earplugs were designed with two options of hearing attenuation: if the earplugs were worn in the closed position, the earplugs block sound similarly as traditional earplugs, but if worn in the open position, they will significantly reduce loud sounds of battlefield explosions while still allowing the wearer to hear quieter sounds such as commands spoken by fellow soldiers and approaching enemy combatants. Plaintiff's claims against 3M included design defect, manufacturing defects, marketing defect, failure to warn, strict liability, negligence, and gross negligence. Plaintiff argues that the Government Contractor Defense is inapplicable since liability for design defects cannot be imposed, pursuant to state law, when the United States approved reasonably precise specifications, the equipment conformed to those specifications, and the supplier warned the United States about the dangers in the use of the equipment that were known to the supplier but not the United States.[11]

In short, defendant 3M Company designed, manufactured, and sold or otherwise placed dual-ended Combat Arm earplugs into the stream of commerce, including transactions with and distribution to the United States military bases and service members located in Texas. 3M always knew during the design, manufacture, and sale of the dual-ended Combat Arm earplugs that the products in question would travel through each state including Texas. These earplugs were specifically manufactured for use by military members in combat or training situations. Because of the design defect that was known to 3M the earplugs would not perform well for certain individuals. There is a higher standard because it was known that the earplugs' users would be in a combat situation.[12]

COLIN KAEPERNICK AND ROGER GOODELL

Two potential class-action lawsuits concern the NFL's response to Colin Kaepernick taking a knee and Commissioner Goodell's personal conduct policy. Both of these potential lawsuits could engender a different type of feeding frenzy. Dallas Cowboys owner Jerry Jones announced that he would bench any player who kneels during the national anthem, which was reciprocated by a filing with the National Labor Relations Board that the players' proposed firing would violate federal labor law. Former San Francisco 49ers quarterback Colin Kaepernick refused to stand to draw attention to issues of systemic racism in society and police brutality. President Trump said that players who protest are "sons of bitches" and called for them to be fired. The comments of Jerry Jones and President Trump could be used as "smoking gun" evidence to support Kaepernick's case that he was improperly exiled because of his protest. In such a suit, Kaepernick will have to prove that NFL owners did not hire him because of his political stance, which is "a right to symbolic speech protected under his First Amendment."[13]

Related to lawsuits based on Colin Kaepernick's symbolic First Amendment protest is NFL Commissioner's Goodell Personal Conduct Policy (PCP) which punishes football players in his role as judge, jury, and executioner.

His PCP gives him free rein to punish players for off-field indiscretions to protect the league's image. Essentially, he's attempting to legislate morality, which never works.

The commissioner's power stems from the Best Interests of Baseball Clause that was a part of the deal for Judge Kennesaw Mountain Landis to agree to be baseball's first commissioner in 1921, with life-time tenure and unlimited power. This power can be classified as an "implied common law administrative accommodation" versus the National Labor Relations Act and the Constitution. Commissioner Goodell *cannot* act unilaterally, without negotiating with the union, if the proposed action affects wages, hours, or conditions of employment.[14]

It appears that class-action lawsuits based on negligence, product liability, employment violations, sexual abuse, constitutional law, the National Labor Relations Act, and consumer laws will continue. Many of these lawsuits create a feeding frenzy generated by lawyer advertisements. Plaintiff's attorneys must be diligent in responding to these insults and differentiating between the wheat and the chaff. Most of these suits, if they get to a jury, are not, by definition, frivolous. It is important that there is no chance for another McDonald's Hot Coffee Case to stagnate and impede beneficial litigation. The Roundup litigation team can easily prove causation. The talcum powder lawsuits have won large jury awards which will facilitate settlements. These suits and transvaginal mesh and 3M earplugs are the next generation of meritorious feeding frenzies with seriously damaged plaintiffs injured as a result of corporate duplicity and greed.

NOTES

1. *Strippers Awarded $4.6 Million,* Houston Chronicle at B3 (Mar. 31, 2008).

2. Ken Sweet, AP, *Wall Street Wins Big in Washington Vote. Senate Effectively Kills Off a Regulation That Would Have Allowed Consumers to Band Together to Sue the Banks,* Houston Chronicle at B5 (Oct. 26, 2017).

3. Liz Alderman, *"My Baby Almost Died": Formula Scandal Sends Shudders Through France,* New York Times at A1 (Feb. 2, 2018).

4. *Lawsuit Accuses Ford of Cheating on Diesel Tests,* Houston Chronicle at B2 (Jan. 11, 2018).

5. Mike Spector, *Car Makers Agree to Air-Bag Settlement,* Wall St. J. at 136 (May 19, 2017).

6. Dug Begley, *TCEQ to Dole Out State's Share of $2.9B Settlement. Volkswagen Emissions Fraud Funds Will Aid Removal of Diesel Vehicles,* Houston Chronicle at A3 (Dec. 5, 2017).

7. Bill Vlasic, New York Times, *VW Official Gets Seven-Years for Emissions Cheating,* Houston Chronicle at B2 (Dec. 17, 2017).

8. C. Gavin Shepherd, *Transvaginal Mesh Litigation: A New Opportunity to Resolve Mass Medical Device Failure Claims,* 80 Tenn. L. Rev. 477, 477-79 (Wntr. 2013) (footnotes omitted).

9. Carmen M. Llona, *Couple Suing Johnson & Johnson over Talcum Powder Wins $37 Million Judgment,* Fox News (April 16, 2018).

10. *Marlboro Lights "Healthier to Smoke" Class Action Settlement (Arkansas Only),* Class Action Rebates at http://www.classactionrebates.com/settlements/marlboro-arkansas/.

11. *Rowe v. 3M Company,* Complaint, 2019 WL 281384 (W.D. Tex.) (Trial Pleading). See also Elizabeth T. Brown, *Earplug Monopolization Suit Against 3M Survives Dismissal Motion;* Moldex-Metric, Inc. v. 3M Co., 22 No. 12 Westlaw Journal Antitrust 8 (Mar. 6, 2015); and Elizabeth T. Brown, *Earplug Maker Gets Partial Win in Monopolization Suit Against 3M,* Moldex Metric, Inc. v. 3M Co., 24 No. Westlaw Journal Antitrust 3 (Jan. 11, 2017).

12. *Id.*

13. Yin Gurrieri, *Three Takeaways from NLRB Charge over Cowboys Protest Policy,* Law 360 at https://www.law360.com/article/973227/print?section=corporate (Oct. 17, 2017).

14. See generally *National Football League Management Council v. National Football League Players Association,* 125 F. Supp. 3d 449, 466 (S. D. N.Y. 2015).

Epilogue

MASH (Mobile Army Surgical Hospital) nurses in Vietnam doused tubs of water on soldiers to remove orange dust. This "dust" was a genotoxic carcinogen that became known as Agent Orange. Although injured, this nurse will never get her day in court. This was just the beginning of a massive cover-up based on obfuscation and lies. Agent Orange litigation was initiated by personal injury lawyers who were met by delays, defenses, and denial.

The system is rigged so that statutes of limitations, mandatory arbitration, fake community groups, tort reform, and caps on damages will eliminate America's constitutional right for jury trials. Torts and civil damages keep our citizens safe. Civil juries are the only mechanism that resolves disputes that involve ordinary people.

The famous spring gun case of *Katko v. Briney* established the principle that it was illegal to set up a spring gun in a vacant house. In this case, tin was nailed over the bedroom window to disguise the danger. Spring gun equals death by surprise, but it also equates to strict liability. A shotgun can kill, but so will opioids or a jet's defective sensor, or defective Pintos, or toxic Agent Orange. In *Katko* there were no warnings of dangerous conditions; instead, there were designs to lure, trap, and give the unsuspecting a false sense of security.

Susan Saladoff's documentary, *Hot Coffee: Is Justice Being Served?* elucidates the real story behind *Liebeck v. McDonald's Restaurants*. The coffee in question was superheated to 190°F, which is only 20 degrees below boiling. There were 700 hot coffee cases filed against the McDonald's Corporation. Stella Liebeck suffered full thickness burns over her inner thighs, perineum, buttocks, and genital and groin area. She was hospitalized for eight days and underwent skin grafting and later debridement treatments. Liebeck alleged that the coffee she purchased was defective because of its excessive heat and inadequate warnings. She only asked McDonald's to pay $90,000 for her medical expenses and pain and suffering. McDonald's countered with a generous offer of $800. At the civil trial, Liebeck also asked for punitive damages since McDonald's acted with deliberate indifference for the safety of its customers.

The jury heard about earlier cases. The evidence against McDonald's was overwhelming. Even with daunting evidence against McDonald's, the organization refused to change its corporate policy and serve its coffee at a safer temperature. At all times, McDonald's displayed corporate indifference and callousness. After seven days of evidence, the jury of twelve citizens unanimously found that McDonald's was guilty of supplying a defective, dangerous product and breach of warranties of merchantability and fitness for a particular purpose.

The jury awarded Ms. Liebeck $200,000 in compensatory damages which were reduced to $40,000 since they found her to be 20 percent at fault. However, the jury also awarded Liebeck $2.7 million in punitive damages, which represented about two days of McDonald's coffee revenues. The case was ultimately settled for an undisclosed amount, less than $600,000, which remains confidential. But big corporations had their tort reform poster child for "frivolous" lawsuits—$2.9 million verdict for hot coffee!!!

Enter Karl Rove, the U.S. Chamber of Commerce, and President George W. Bush. Karl Rove is the corporate Svengali who gained the ear of governor, later President Bush, and used the tort reform banner as a red-herring to misguide the American people on alleged "Weapons of Mass Destruction" as a rationale for the Iraq War. George Bush in his 2003, 2005, and 2006 State of the Union addresses chose "greedy lawyers" as the country's personal hobgoblin. In his 2004 address, he deviated to blame professional athletes who used steroids. He chose lawyers and jocks over 9-11, Al Qaeda, and Osama Bin Laden.

In the movie *Thank You for Smoking*, there was the MOD squad (Merchants of Death), lobbyists for liquor, tobacco, and firearms. Their job was to spin their dangerous addictive products in a sweet-smelling marketing campaign.

Corporate America used a very slick advertising campaign based on the manufactured outrage to the *Liebeck* verdict to decimate the civil justice system. Ralph Nader calls it "Tort Deform." The so-called Tort Reform bill passed the Senate but was vetoed by President Clinton.

The Tort Reform lobbyists then executed Plan B, which was to bring their campaign to the state legislatures. Allegedly spontaneous grass roots groups, derisively called Astroturf groups, like Citizens Against Lawsuit Abuse were formed and empowered by the American Tort Reform Association (ATRA). ATRA was formed in 1986 and consists of 300 major corporations including: big pharma, tobacco, automobile companies, aircraft manufacturers, the insurance industry, municipalities, and associations. The stated goal is to limit the ability of tort plaintiffs to recover against tortfeasors, regardless of their culpability, deception, and venality.

ATRA was carefully orchestrated by Karl Rove through his mouthpiece, George W. Bush. Rove was a consultant for Governor Bush and tobacco giant Phillip Morris. George Bush, as the Tort-Reformer-in-Chief was the direct link between public relations and the ultimate passage of law. The major goal of tort reform is to cap damages, including punitives and noneconomic damages, and to eliminate the civil jury system-which is unconstitutional.

ATRA and the U.S. Chamber of Commerce then turned their sights on judicial elections to control courts and deny jury verdicts. The U.S. Chamber of Commerce is the largest lobbying group for big business. They created front groups, such as Citizens for a Strong Ohio—a probusiness group with the veneer of respectability and spontaneity. Another goal is to force mandatory arbitration clauses in all contractual situations, from employment to health clubs to credit cards to banks to cell phones. This is another way to eliminate the constitutional right of a jury trial, achieved through small print and bullying. It is the overall goal of tort reform to limit the liability of big business regardless of duplicity. It should be "Tort Respect" instead of tort reform. The civil justice system operates to make big business accountable for their mistakes, but the goal of big business is to police themselves. Ironically, tort reform is OK with juries for death penalties, but they do not trust juries to decide corporate liability.

Karl Rove was the former White House Senior Advisor and Deputy Chief of Staff for Policy with President George W. Bush; Rove was the architect of dirty tricks that painted lawyers as Machiavellian criminal masterminds (like Sherlock Holmes' Professor Moriarty). Rove started with a direct mail consulting firm, and then sold the firm for a full-time position with George Bush's presidential campaign.

Mass tort litigation began as a direct response to corporate greed that placed profits over safety. Big business had to be stopped and the civil justice system and trial lawyers were the only defense to rapacious profits. Big business repeatedly displayed their true intentions. The Ford Motor Co.'s Pinto marketing geniuses used a cost-benefit analysis to estimate a life's worth to be $200,000. Over 50 years after the first feeding frenzy on the defective Corvair, made famous by Ralph Nadar's *Unsafe at Any Speed*, big business is still marketing unsafe and dangerous products such as Roundup, opioids, and defective aircraft. The need for attorney advocates to police these atrocities is greater than ever. Big business is now using their "tort reform kit" to spin the opioid crisis.

Index

About the Authors

Walter Champion is a law professor at the Thurgood Marshall School of Law, Texas Southern University, and an adjunct professor at South Texas College of Law Houston. He has written twelve books, including *Sports Law in a Nutshell* and *Gaming Law in a Nutshell.*

Carlos A. Velasquez is the founding partner of VelasquezDolan, PA, Plantation, Florida. He is a nationally-known personal injury lawyer who has successfully litigated airplane and helicopter crash class action law suits.

Printed in the USA
CPSIA information can be obtained
at www.ICGtesting.com
LVHW051333290124
769950LV00016B/14